Preventive Counseling

Preventive Counseling

second edition

Helping people to become
empowered in systems and settings

Robert K. Conyne, Ph.D.

Brunner-Routledge
Taylor & Francis Group
NEW YORK AND HOVE

MT

Cover design: Elise Weinger
Cover illustration: Copyright Images.com/CORBIS

Published in 2004 by
Brunner-Routledge
29 West 35th Street
New York, NY 10001
www.brunner-routledge.com

Published in Great Britain by
Brunner-Routledge
27 Church Road
Hove, East Sussex
BN3 2FA
www.brunner-routledge.co.uk

Brunner-Routledge is an imprint of the Taylor & Francis Group.
Printed in the United States of America on acid-free paper.

Typesetting: Jack Donner, BookType

10 9 8 7 6 5 4 3 2 1

Library of Congress Cataloging-in-Publication Data

Conyne, Robert K.
   Preventive counseling : helping people to become empowered in systems and settings /
Robert K. Conyne.—2nd ed.
        p.   cm.
   Rev. ed. of: Primary preventive counseling. c1987
   Includes bibliographical references and index.
   1. Mental illness—Prevention. 2. Counseling. 3. Preventive health services. I.
Conyne, Robert K. Primary preventive counseling. II. Title.

   RA790.C68176 2004
   158'.3—dc22

                                                  2003024580

11/9/04

Still to Suzanne and Zachary,
who have grown up to be terrific people!

Contents

List of Tables

Preface

The first edition of this book was published in 1987, when prevention was an elusive concept. In fact, as a way to lend definitional clarity, I found it necessary then to indicate by the book's title that it would focus on primary (not secondary or tertiary) prevention for counselors. This clarification, I am pleased to note, is no longer necessary. Contemporary understandings of prevention are sufficient for capturing the directions needed for counselors and other helpers as they try to make a difference in the lives of people in systems and settings. At that time, there seemed to be interest building in prevention for counselors. For instance, I noted in the Preface to that edition (p. vi):

> This gathering movement rides on the swell of primary prevention and goes by various synonyms, including wellness and health promotion. One can scarcely ever pick up the local newspaper or listen to the evening news without being confronted by presentations about the benefits of exercise, the importance of proper nutrition, the deadly hazards of smoking and excessive drinking, ways to manage and reduce stress in our lives, or how important support systems are for good health. People by the legion are learning to take better care of themselves so they can avoid becoming treatable patients.

On the professional front, considerable attention is being accorded prevention. Special issues of journals, some new books, courses being introduced into training curricula, and increased primary preventive practice are appearing. Consider these words about prevention that are drawn from "Counseling Psychology: A Historic Perspective" (Whiteley, *The Counseling Psychologist*, 12, 1984):

A fifth immediate challenge is to regain involvement in the area of prevention. Initiative has shifted to clinical and community psychology for advancing the theoretical and research base for this fundamental role of counseling psychology.... The centrality of prevention to the core role of counseling psychology mandates a fundamental reawakening of interest and activity. (p. 89)

I said at that time that the book *Primary Preventive Counseling: Empowering People and Systems* was intended to be a part of this recent activity. In this work, I have attempted to present an organized picture of how professional counselors and counseling psychologists could become primary prevention agents, and to show how this new approach was rooted in the origins of counseling and counseling psychology.

This interest, however, did not sustain itself sufficiently. Until recently, little scholarly attention was directed at preventive counseling, and virtually no courses emerged in the topic. Moreover, the dominant discourse among counselors and psychologists remained largely focused on treatment and remediation—at the same time as many prevention programs were emerging in the field.

In the first edition of this book, I tended to cast prevention and treatment as antagonists on the battlefield of helping. It seemed to me to be a kind of zero-sum game where the choices were either prevention or remediation. In fact, the language I used was:

The forces of remediation and prevention have struggled like titans throughout the compatible histories of professional counseling and counseling psychology. Is the main goal of counseling to correct deep psychological dysfunction? Or is it to facilitate growth and development? Does psychotherapy rule? Or are short-term counseling and prevention the dominant ways these professionals should help others? Perhaps all of these goals and methods are important and justifiable. However, having offered that, doesn't a kind of "pecking order" exist?

I believe the latter is the case. Remediation and prevention are both consistently endorsed by official statements of the counseling establishment. If anything, maybe prevention has historically been emphasized on paper. For instance, read these words drawn from the American Psychological Association brochure, "What Is a Counseling Psychologist?" (Education and Training Committee of the Division of Counseling Psychology, 1983), which describe how counseling psychologists work:

... These interventions tend to emphasize preventive treatment, health maintenance, short-term or time-limited problem solving, goal-focused counseling, and vocational counseling. Preventive and educative strategies are frequent in the intervention repertoire. . . . Regardless of the setting or evaluation methods, the unique aspects of counseling psychology, in both assessment and treatment, are its identification of impediments to development, appraisal of potential, and focus upon growth. (p. 2)

Yet, in terms of day-to-day practice—for example, how training programs are organized, what third-party payments provide coverage for, the contents of psychologist and counselor-with-endorsement licensing regulations, and how many professionals and doctoral students alike tend to describe themselves to others—clearly reflect a far different reality.

In the real world, remediation, therapy, and long-term counseling hold the upper hand. Thus, the conflict arises between statements about the preeminence of prevention and growth and development, contrasted with the higher practical identification and energies that are given to remediation and long-term therapy.

In this new edition, now some 20 years following the first, conditions have changed for the better. I find it no longer necessary to pitch for remediation against prevention. Each has its own important sector of the span of help-giving. I suggest in this edition that it is now possible to think and act in terms of viewing prevention and treatment along the same helping dimension, viewing them as collaborative partners, not as rivals. This is a far healthier position and is more apt to support both prevention and remediation.

Moreover, it is not necessary to differentiate primary prevention from prevention, in general. Prevention, as currently understood, is a broad umbrella, as the definition I will develop shows:

Prevention is a goal for both everyday life and for service delivery, through which people become empowered to interact effectively and appropriately within varying levels of systems (micro, meso, exo, and macro) and settings (individual, family, school, community, work). Preventive application can yield a reduction in the occurrence of new cases of a problem, in the duration and severity of incipient problems, and it can promote strengths and optimal human functioning.

To elaborate just a moment on that point, this edition draws attention to a new concept: "everyday prevention." Because classic prevention is always understood to be before the fact and based on a large group or population, the first edition of this book emphasized those approaches. As a result, little attention was given to how counselors, psychologists, and social workers in typical practice situations might be able to leverage their ongoing work with clients in preventive directions. I will discuss how counseling practitioners can exercise prevention while remaining largely within their present role and function. Everyday prevention will assist with realizing that goal.

So, the revised title for this second edition of the book reflects the change from *Primary Preventive Counseling* to *Preventive Counseling*, suggesting a broader span of applications. In addition, the book's title reflects a second change in thinking: that empowerment is not done to people, nor does it occur within people and independently within systems. Rather, from an ecological viewpoint, empowerment is accomplished by people in systems. People and systems are not independent but are mutually interactive and dependent. Finally, the addition of "Settings" to the subtitle illustrates the importance for prevention of working within concrete manifestations of settings: families, schools, neighborhoods/communities, and work. These settings provide the arena within which people interact and through which prevention can occur.

A final point I want to make by way of introduction is that much progress has been made in preventive applications over the last 20 years. The first edition was unable to take advantage of these advances, but in this edition I have described in some detail a number of excellent ways that preventive counseling has been delivered. I also describe skill sets that have emerged to support preventive counseling. This material will provide readers with real assistance, helping them learn about successful prevention programs at the family, school, community, and work levels and about how skills can be used to develop these efforts. In addition, readers will become acquainted with several Web-based and more traditional resources to access prevention programs that have been externally evaluated for their effectiveness.

The book is organized as follows:

Section I is titled "Foundations of Preventive Counseling." Chapter 1, "Prevention in Mental Health," traces the historical and contextual development of primary prevention and of prevention in mental health. From it emerges a comprehensive definition of prevention.

Chapter 2, "Everyday Prevention," is entirely new material that focuses on personal and system involvements that people can engage in on a daily basis to enhance their lives and counselors' role in that effort. Chapter 3, "A Conceptual Model," contains an expanded version of my model for preventive counseling, drawing from knowledge and practice that has been produced since 1987. It includes the following definition for preventive counseling:

Preventive counseling is used to help people become empowered in systems and settings. It applies a broad range of counseling methods.

Its application can lead to problem avoidance, reversing the trajectory of new problems, optimal human functioning, and in people becoming their own preventive agents.

Section II, "Describing and Analyzing Prevention Programs That Work," centers on the translation of conceptual understandings of prevention and preventive counseling to implementation and evaluation. Chapter 4, "Program Planning and Evaluation," begins this transition by detailing steps for developing and evaluating preventive counseling programs, and then identifying specific criteria for what constitutes an effective effort. Chapters 5 through 8 each describe in some detail prevention programs in setting levels that have been evaluated as being effective: Chapter 5 addresses family setting programs, Chapter 6 school setting programs, Chapter 7 community setting programs, and Chapter 8 work setting prevention programs.

Section III, "Training and the Future," is concerned with the preparation of future "preventionists" and with trends on the horizon. Chapter 9, "Education, Training, and Skills," examines the preparation of counselors and other helpers for conducting prevention, and it elaborates a skill set that is needed for this work, along with a Self-Check Assessment tool. Chapter 10, "The Future of Preventive Counseling," is used to summarize the book's contents by highlighting major issues and providing directions for future action that will assist preventive counseling in assuming a larger presence in mental health practice.

An appendix is included containing a list of highly recommended supplementary readings, which should assist those interested in pursuing ideas in finer detail. A compiled reference list follows the final chapter.

Who are all of you for whom this book is intended? I envision you as graduate students in professional counseling and counseling psychology, maybe some also in social work, as well as practitioners in the field. This book can be used as a stand-alone text for any course that focuses on prevention, and it should be used as a supplement to existing texts in a number of basic counseling and intervention classes. Although the book speaks most directly to professional counselors and counseling psychologists, those in other helping fields, such as clinical psychology, social work, and community psychology, will find it of considerable interest. In addition, many of you will be counseling practitioners—employed in schools, mental health centers, social service agencies, and corporations—who are intrigued by prevention approaches. Other readers will be the consultants and trainers who sometimes deliver services of various kinds in these settings and, of course, faculty who teach and train all of these people.

Acknowledgments

In the preparation of this book, I remain grateful to all of those whom I thanked during the first edition. In addition, I especially appreciate all the students who have passed through my Preventive Counseling class and have contributed ideas and feedback. To Emily Epstein Loeb (Associate Editor) and George Zimmar (Publishing Director), I owe my appreciation for allowing the book's revision. George, it turns out, also was the editor of my very first book on environmental assessment and design (with Jim Clack). I want to remember with fondness the late Joe Hollis, the publisher of *Accelerated Development*, who took the risk to contract the first edition of this book in 1987, maybe before its time had come. The reviewers of my proposal and of the first book draft deserve special thanks for their insightful suggestions. And, perhaps above all else, I must recognize the consideration and support given me by my family: My life partner, wife, and colleague, Lynn Rapin, and our two children, Suzanne and Zachary. As always, I will be forever in your arms.

Robert K. Conyne
Cincinnati, Ohio
St. Joseph Island, Ontario

Foundations
of Preventive Counseling

This first section of *Preventive Counseling* contains three chapters that provide a needed foundation. These chapters are relatively lengthy because building a foundation is very important. (Subsequent chapters will be more moderate in length.)

Chapter 1, "Prevention in Mental Health," focuses on the history and evolution of prevention in mental health. Clarity about prevention is beginning to emerge, and this chapter traces various sources that have contributed to that clarity. It concludes with a definition of prevention that I intend to be contemporary and comprehensive. Chapter 2, "Everyday Prevention," is an entirely new chapter that contains a range of information supporting attempts by people to become their own preventive agents. Person- and system-centered skills and strategies are discussed, along with suggestions about how counselors and other professional helpers can assist people on an everyday basis to prevent significant problems and promote healthy functioning. Chapter 3, "A Conceptual Model," details the relationship among prevention, preventive strategies, and counseling and presents an integrating conceptual model for preventive counseling. This model is an adaptation of the original model in the first edition of this book (Conyne, 1987), updated to reflect current knowledge and practice.

Now, on to Chapter 1, "Prevention in Mental Health."

CHAPTER **1**

Prevention in Mental Health

Wellness, health promotion, prevention, subjective well-being, positive psychology, quality of life, healthy lifestyles—these terms emerge from the groundswell that is afoot in this country, felt among the general population and professional helpers alike. Every day increasingly larger numbers of people are joining the legions who are committed to leading healthy lives and avoiding sickness and disease.

In 1987, when the first edition of this book was published, it was obvious that the signs of this movement were all around us, and they have only grown in size and stature. A glance at the list of best-selling nonfiction books will typically show, as heading those lists, books on proper nutrition, aerobic exercise methods, stress management, parenting effectiveness, childhood development, self-esteem, organizational excellence, and other topics of interest to people who seem to be almost obsessed with the need for developing and maintaining personal health. Regular television fare, as well as programs beamed by cable or satellite, consistently carry lifestyle programming. A wide range of self-instructional, self-help cassettes is available for home viewing. The Internet has become a primary health-managing source for many. Self-help groups and study circles of all kinds are present in most large communities to help people not only cope better with crises and loss but also to assist them to function even better than they may be presently with such issues as communication, parenting, personal growth, and so forth. The mental health establishment is providing an increasing variety of educational programs in these same general areas that are meant to strengthen the healthy functioning of participants.

Of course, none of this is without cultural and historical precedence. Consideration of common admonitions in our language is enough to illustrate: "An ounce of prevention is worth a pound of cure." "Look before you leap." "Only you can prevent forest fires." "Stop, look, and listen." "Save for a rainy day." "Be prepared." "An apple a day keeps the doctor away." These cultural dicta represent commonsense, everyday notions—passed from generation to generation—with which we are all familiar and accept or reject in different ways as we lead our lives. Their time-honored continuance in our language indicates the strong cultural appeal that minimizing or eliminating danger, misfortune, and emergencies holds for us.

These examples of folk wisdom each represent, at a most basic level of conception, what activities people can perform to help ensure their continued good health. Thus, we can see how people are advised to live intentionally (e.g., "be prepared"), to maintain daily good health practices (e.g., "an apple a day keeps the doctor away"), to avoid danger (e.g., "look before you leap"), and to assist in protecting the larger community (e.g., "only you can prevent forest fires").

As people engage in activities to strengthen their lives and to avoid the excessively noxious slings and arrows that await them in life, they are exercising a form of "everyday prevention," a concept that is becoming an important part of preventive counseling. Everyday prevention will be considered at length in the next chapter.

NEED FOR PREVENTION

George Albee, one of the important shapers of the prevention movement in mental health, told a story that graphically illustrates the need for primary prevention programs and services in mental health (Albee, 1986). Invited to address a group at the Downstate Medical Center, he arrived at its inner-city Bedford-Stuyvesant location. While entering the impressive building, he observed one chauffeur-driven, long black limousine after another arrive through the squalor and chaos of the surrounding inner city and pull up at the medical center. Out of each one, he said, would come an exquisitely dressed woman. Puzzled by this sight, he asked an employee what was going on. To his dismay, he learned that these upper-class women were coming to keep their individual, daily psychoanalytic appointments.

He did not mean for this story to be an indictment of psychoanalysis per se. His point was to emphasize the tragic irony found in that setting. What is this irony? It is the juxtaposition of the "have-nots" in the community with the "haves" from outside it, compounded by the provision of expensive, long-duration individual psychological services to the wealthy amidst an environment of poverty, unemployment, crime, and illness. This anecdote sharply illustrates the need for primary prevention in mental health: Human psychological (and other) needs far outstrip the available supply of professionally trained mental health care providers, such as professional counselors, counseling psychologists, and social workers.

When I introduce the concept of prevention to those who are unfamiliar with it, I often draw from the fable that was reported by Rappaport (1972), who asks us to consider the following (cited in Goodyear, 1976, p. 513):

> Imagine a warm, sunny afternoon. You are in a local park, lounging indolently on a blanket, with a bottle of wine and a good book on the grassy banks of a river below a swimming area. Suddenly you hear thrashing sounds, and a cry for help from the river. Startled you look over to see a person struggling unsuccessfully as the water sweeps him away. You courageously dive in, rescue him, and then return to the serious business of soaking up the sun. There is to be no respite for you, however, for you find yourself repeating this performance with several other drowning people throughout the afternoon. As you are ministering to the final victim, an observer asks a question that is startlingly powerful in its logic and simplicity: "Would it not ultimately be much easier and less dangerous to go to the swimming area and teach those people, collectively, how to swim than to rescue each individually?"

Can we any longer afford the luxury of gearing our helping services around the model of "rescue each individually"? Would it not be more efficacious to take the advice of the observer in the previous anecdote and begin to teach people collectively the competencies they need so that they can successfully cope with the demands of life later? In addition, although the astute observer did not mention this, would it not have been useful for a railing to have been erected at the waterfall to prevent the nonswimmers from falling in and drowning? That is, as a general rule, can we begin designing environmental improvements to protect and enhance human functioning? The teaching of life competencies and the design of environmental improvements, both conducted before the onset of problem formation, represent two ways to correct what can only be described as a need/supply imbalance.

EXAMPLES OF THE NEED/SUPPLY IMBALANCE

Need for Help

A substantial gap exists between people who need helping services and the availability of those services. The imbalance in supply and demand can be found in an array of mental and emotional disorders and with a host of lifestyle and addictive maladies and disorders. To access a comprehensive set of statistics about these and other problem areas, refer to any of several available databases (note: see Romano and Hage, 2000, for a helpful listing, as well as References at the back of this book), such as the Office of the Surgeon General (www.surgeongeneral.gov), FedStats (www.Fedstats.gov), and the National Center for Health Statistics (www.cdc.gov/nchs).

I will present briefly some of the most current data relevant to mental and emotional disorders, then to lifestyle and addictive behaviors, and finally to so-called problems in living. Note that published data typically are two to three years or more behind the present date because of the time needed for their collection, organization, analysis, and publication. As with any of the problem areas discussed briefly in this chapter (and other problems not covered), implementation of comprehensive prevention programs could effectively reduce the incidence, prevalence, disease impact, and economic costs associated with these problems.

Mental and Emotional Disorders

The number of Americans affected with mental and emotional disorders is staggering. An estimated 20% of Americans aged 18 and older, or about 1 in 5 adults, suffer from a diagnosable mental disorder in a given year (NIMH, 1998). As Gullotta & Bloom observed (2003), based on an estimated U.S. population of 288 million, this means that roughly 57,650,000 individuals are in need of help annually. In addition, mental depression, bipolar disorder, schizophrenia, and obsessive-compulsive disorder constitute 4 of the 10 leading causes of disability in the United States and other developed countries. Of course, many people experience multiple types of mental disorder simultaneously, which makes this situation even more complex.

Sadly, the high level of mental disorders is not restricted to adults. Approximately 20% of children and adolescents experience signs and symptoms of a DSM-IV disorder during the period of a year. It is estimated that 25% of American youth engage in multiple health and social risk behavior, while another 25% experiment with some form of risk behavior. The remaining 50% of youth who may not participate in such behavior need assistance to bolster their more positive lifestyle choices (Weissberg, Gullotta, Hampton, Ryan, & Adams, 1997).

The costs associated with the direct treatment of mental disorder, substance abuse, and Alzheimer's disease were $99 billion in 1996, with direct costs for mental disorders alone at $69 billion. Indirect costs (e.g., lost work productivity) amounted to $79 billion in 1990.

Former surgeon general C. Everett Koop put it this way (Koop, 1995):

Diseases are of two types: Those we develop inadvertently and those we bring upon ourselves by failure to practice preventive measures. Preventable illness makes up approximately 70% of the burden of illness in associated costs. (p. 760)

Lifestyle and Addictive Disorder

Diagnosable disorders represent just part of the crushing need for mental health services. Lifestyle and addictive behaviors also account for a huge part. Let us take a snapshot look at just six examples: (1) suicide, (2) alcohol, (3) divorce, (4) cigarette smoking, (5) illiteracy, and (6) school violence.

Suicide

Suicide is a tragic and potentially preventable public health problem. Data from the year 2000 show that there were 29,350 deaths from suicide in the United States (1.2% of all deaths). The death rate was 10.7 per 100,000 population, and suicide ranked eleventh overall as a cause of death in the United States. For ages 20–24 the ranking was of even more concern: third. Older adults also are disproportionately likely to die by suicide. Comprising only 13% of the U.S. population, individuals age 65 and older accounted for 18% of all suicide deaths in 2000. Among the highest rates (when categorized by gender and race) were white men age 85 and older: 59 deaths per 100,000 persons, more than five times the national U.S. rate of 10.6 per 100,000.

Suicide deaths outnumber homicide deaths by five to three. It has been estimated that there may be from 8 to 25 attempted suicides per every 1 suicide death (NIH Publication, April 2003).

Alcohol

Alcohol-related problems remain a severe challenge. In the year 2000, there were 19,358 alcohol-induced deaths in the United States, not including motor vehicle fatalities. Another 13,050 lost their lives through alcohol-related deaths from automobile crashes (29.6% of these deaths occurred in the 16–24 age range and 44.6% in the 25–44 age range). An additional 26,552 deaths occurred from chronic liver disease and cirrhosis, which was the twelfth leading cause of death. In terms of alcohol usage, 62% of Americans age 18 and over drank alcohol in the past year, while 32% percent of current drinkers had five or more drinks on the same occasion at least once in the past year. Numbers show 61% of men 18–24 years and 42% of women in that age group had five or more drinks on the same occasion. Alcohol abuse and alcoholism cost the U.S. society dearly as well—some $117 million (latest computation from 1983).

The National Survey on Drug Use and Health (NSDUH) (SAMHSA, 2002) provided some updated data. The survey included a set of questions asking about the recency and frequency of the consumption of alcoholic beverages, including beer, wine, whiskey, brandy, and mixed drinks.

About half of Americans age 12 or older reported being current drinkers of alcohol in the 2002 survey (51.0%). This translates to an estimated 120 million people. More than one-fifth (22.9%) of persons age 12 or older participated in binge drinking at least once in the 30 days prior to the survey, which translates to about 54 million people. Heavy drinking was reported by 6.7% of the population age 12 or older, or 15.9 million people.

The prevalence of current alcohol use in 2002 increased with increasing age, from 2.0% at age 12 and peaking at 70.9% for persons 21 years old. The highest prevalence of both binge and heavy drinking in 2002 was among young adults age 18 to 25, with the peak rate of both measures occurring at age 21. The rate of binge drinking was 40.9% for young adults and 50.2% at age 21. Heavy alcohol use was reported by 14.9% of persons age 18 to 25 and by 20.1% of persons age 21. Binge and heavy alcohol use rates decreased faster with increasing age than did rates of past month alcohol use. While 58.8% of the population age 45 to 49 in 2002 were current drinkers, 22.5% of persons within this age range were binge drinkers and 7.7% drank heavily. Binge and heavy drinking were relatively rare among people age 65 or older, with reported rates of 7.5 and 1.4%, respectively. Thus, alcohol misuse and abuse continues to be an area of concern, with much potential for preventive action.

Divorce

Marital distress and divorce can negatively affect physical health, mental well-being, and work productivity (Stanley, 2001). In 1998, there were 1,135,000 divorces, or 4.2 per 1000 population. Such divorce statistics suggest that 6 in 10 marriages in the United States will fail, most within the first few years (Howd, 1999). Latest data (2001) show that the rate has decreased some, to 4.0 per 1000 population (National Vital Statistics Report, 2001).

Cigarette Smoking

Cigarette smoking is the leading cause of preventable death in the United States, and it also accounts for significant health-related economic costs (CDC, 2002). During 1995–1999, the Center for Disease Control reported that smoking caused approximately 440,000 premature deaths annually in the United States, while costing approximately $157 billion in annual health-related economic costs. Smoking cigarettes appears to be increasing among women. For example, in 1998, 22% of women smoked cigarettes. In 2000, 29.7% of high school senior girls smoked. Lung cancer is now the leading cause of cancer death among U.S. women.

Illiteracy

Functional illiteracy refers to the inability of an individual to use reading, speaking, writing, and computational skills in everyday life situations. For example, a functionally illiterate adult is unable to complete an employment application, follow written instructions, or read a newspaper. In short, when confronted with printed materials, adults without basic literacy skills cannot function effectively.

In September 1993, the U.S. Department of Education released the most detailed portrait ever available on the condition of illiteracy in this nation. The National Adult Literacy Survey (ALS) evaluated the skills of adults in three areas: prose, document, and quantitative proficiency. The results showed that 23% (40 to 44 million adults) were at Level 1, the lowest of five levels. This group is the functionally illiterate. Another 25 to 28% (50 million adults) were at the second lowest level, meaning that their literacy repertoire is quite limited. The literary proficiencies of young adults were found to be somewhat lower, on average, than the proficiencies of young adults who participated in a 1985 study (the National Assessment of Educational Progress). The statistics make it clear: illiteracy is on the increase in the United States, and less than 10% of the population is being reached. Moreover, when absolute figures are considered, the number of illiterate people in the United States (10 million) exceeds the number in Iraq (4,848,000), Afghanistan (8,160,000), and Mexico (6,246,000), to cite just three underdeveloped countries for comparison (UNESCO, 1995).

Studies indicate that illiteracy has a significant impact on the economy. An estimated 15 million adults holding jobs today are functionally illiterate. A Literacy at Work study done by the Northeast Midwest Institute and the Center for Regional Policy found that business losses attributed to basic skill deficiencies run into the hundreds of millions of dollars because of low productivity, errors, and accidents. The Department of Education estimates that 60% of the unemployed lack the basic skills necessary to be trained for high-tech jobs.

School Violence

School violence has become a focus of national concern, heightened by the tragedies that have occurred in several schools across the nation in recent years. According to a survey of the National School Board Association that was conducted before these tragedies (1993), schools had been reporting an increase in the number of students bringing weapons to school and in drive-by shootings. Weapons and shooting are not the only forms that school violence takes, however. Among kindergarten and elementary-age children, 10 to 20% are reportedly teased, threatened, or attacked by their peers. In addition, 42% of children from kindergarten to grade 5 reported witnessing gang activity in the last two weeks at their school, and many third graders admitted to being involved with gangs (Leff, Power, Manz, Costigan, & Nabors, 2001). The costs of school crime and violence have been estimated at $200 million per year.

Problems in Living

A whole additional category not covered through diagnosable diseases, lifestyle, or addictive behaviors can be subsumed under the general category of "problems in living." Interestingly, approximately one-third of all those who are receiving help from a mental health professional are free from any diagnostic classification. Such individuals bring so-called problems of living concerns to their helpers: adjustment and situational problems and disorders, such as marital and family concerns, identity diffusion, career choice, anger management, loneliness, change quandries, and the like.

These are the "normal neurotics" all around us, including you and me (assuming we are not included in the categories considered previously). Maybe these are the kind of people to whom Shaw (1986) was referring when he wrote:

> Who are these ineffective people? They are your friends and mine. They are your relatives and mine. They are people we all know. Their suffering may not be apparent because most of them do not have obvious problems. They are unhappy or miserable people who live in constant psychological pain while attempting to live their everyday lives. They are people whose productive lives and social interactions may be highly ineffective. They are that large group of people whom Thoreau was describing when he wrote, "The mass of men live lives of quiet desperation." (pp. 624–625)

This range of problems—from severe mental and emotional disorder, through lifestyle and addictive behaviors, to problems in living—pose serious personal and societal consequences. The resources available to address them, however, are inadequate, especially if a traditional, individual, remedial helping model is exclusively employed.

The Supply of Helpers

The United States Surgeon General's Report on Mental Health (1999) documented evidence intended to improve understanding of mental health, mental illness, and treatment, and as such was of monumental import. It indicated that the overall annual prevalence rate of mental disorders in the United States is about 21% of adults and children, and that this prevalence rate is similar for both whites and racial and ethnic minorities. It outlined treatments that work. The report contained the following recommendation for all Americans:

> Seek help if you have a mental health problem or think you have symptoms of a mental disorder.

Followed by the supplement *Mental Health: Culture, Race, and Ethnicity* (2001), the two documents contributed strongly to an understanding of the central place of mental health in the overall health and productivity of the nation. These documents also demonstrated that access to mental health care in the United States is limited. Only 10% of children and adults who need mental health services receive them from mental health specialists or general medical providers in any given year.

This disconnect between the need for mental health services and their delivery is a national failure. In addition, and even worse, access to mental health services is more limited for ethnic and racial minority members. In fact, striking disparities exist between access to mental health services for whites and for minorities.

The supplemental report of the Surgeon General identified four specific disparities that impact mental health care for racial and ethnic minorities, compared with whites: (1) minorities have less access to and availability of mental health services; (2) minorities are less likely to receive the mental health services they need; (3) minorities often receive poorer quality treatment; and (4) minorities are underrepresented in mental health research.

Although all of these disparities are alarming, the first two are most immediately pertinent with regard to prevention. The high need for mental service is not matched with its provision or with access to it.

There are many barriers to obtaining mental health services. It is costly. Services are too often fragmented. Many Americans do not have health insurance and, if they do, the mental health coverage may be inadequate or cumbersome to arrange and maintain. Services may not be located within reach for many who need them. For many, a stigma is attached to being involved with mental health services and so they avoid using these services. In sum, the overall supply of mental health professionals is not sufficient to meet the overall demand, especially if mental health services are delivered remedially to one individual at a time.

Implications of the Need/Supply Imbalance

Millions of people in our society are simply not receiving the kind of help they so keenly need. These are the casualties of life, those who have been unable to adequately negotiate this complex, often impersonal, and uncaring society. Furthermore, the negative consequences of this unfortunate situation are apparently felt not only by the individuals affected but also by their families and the nation as a whole. Just as these people face a future that may be described as ranging from uncertain at best to desperate at worst, so, by extension, does the country face such a future. As is well known, the continued health of the nation (and of the world, for that matter) is dependent on the productive functioning of effective persons.

Reliance on Traditional Services Is a No-Win Situation

Attempting to correct the millions of psychological and educational ills before us by relying mainly on the traditional method of individual, remedial services is a no-win proposition. It is no-win because, as we have seen, the need/supply imbalance is simply staggering. It is no-win because remedial services, such as psychotherapy, are after-the-fact approaches that can do nothing to stem the tide of new cases. It is no-win because the access to traditional clinical services is becoming increasingly more difficult and expensive as cost containment and efforts to monopolize the health-care industry become commonplace. It has always been a no-win situation for the typically underserved—or nonserved—in our society, and it is becoming even more so, given the above trends. Thus, the poor, the unemployed, the culturally different, the homeless, and untold others who are most in need are least able to get help. And it is a no-win situation because professional counseling, counseling psychology, and other helping professions, in their laudable attempts to ensure that providers are trained well and consistent with accreditation, licensing, and certification standards, unintentionally restrict the number of helpers who are available.

That exclusive or main reliance on individual, remedial services affords "no wins" does not mean that they are "losing" approaches. The case is quite the contrary. Individual, group, and family counseling and psychotherapy are critically important helping modes for people who have already developed evidence of debilitation. Moreover, in cases of early problem onset, it remains possible for counselors to exert a preventive effect. Using individual, group, or family counseling, they can help clients avoid a full-blown emotional and mental disorder by positively altering the trajectory of the problem.

Yet, individual, group, and family counseling and psychotherapy are essentially *treatment* approaches that cannot reduce the incidence of problems. The concept of incidence refers to the number of *new* cases of any psychological or educational problem that occurs, or the rate of development of such new cases. Incidence is unaffected by treating problems that are currently being experienced by clients or patients. Said in everyday language, treatment can repair the casualties or the damages already present. Although problem correction is an enviable and important goal for professional counselors, counseling psychologists, social workers, and other helpers, all the efforts of all the helpers in the world who are providing reparative services alone will not prevent the appearance of new sufferers. Indeed, this was the message contained in the "drowning person" story presented earlier.

Therefore, for those who are concerned about stemming the tide of new problem cases, the traditional palliative approaches must be supplemented by other methods that seek to lower incidence; that is, they are offered to avert the occurrence of problems in the first place. These programs and services are subsumed under the rubric of prevention in mental health.

PREVENTION

Various Conceptions and Streams of Influence

Prevention is still defined in various ways today. Its Latin meaning is "to come before," which still rings true for prevention in counseling. However, as prevention is applied, no one model or definition enjoys universal acceptance and usage. Besides being untidy and bothersome to some, the lack of agreement also contributes to imprecision and a high degree of variance in the way prevention may be approached. At the same time, a range of vantage points can foster a kind of creativity that might not otherwise be possible.

In the next section, I will briefly review some of the important sources for understanding prevention and then will move toward interlacing them in a way that might be helpful for counselors, counseling psychologists, and social workers. Prevention can be envisioned as a large river with many feeder streams, not unlike the Mississippi River being fed by the Ohio or the Missouri. These prevention "streams" are discussed next.

Public Health Perspective

The basic public health understanding of prevention (Leavell & Clark, 1953), which has been applied with astounding success in the prevention of many physical illnesses that spread by infection, is concerned with an identifiable linkage among environmental source-carrying agent–hosts. For example, in the case of malaria, the environmental source (swamps) gives rise to infectious agents (mosquitoes) that then infect the host (persons), leading to the development of the disease. Malaria can be prevented through interventions within each and all of the pivotal partners in the causal chain. The swamps (environmental source) can be drained, mosquitoes (agent) can be killed, and people (host) can be strengthened through vaccination.

In similar fashion, if a causal link can be established (and this is the challenge), this public health approach can be extended to the mental health arena. Theoretically, a problem such as academic failure could be prevented in this way. However, what is the precise causal pathway that leads to academic failure? What is the environmental source? school? home? relationships? genetics? public policy? What is the agent? peers? limited classroom resources? lack of social support? inadequate teaching? How can the host be strengthened? skills? mentoring? medication? study groups? Educational and mental health problems result from a complex interplay of many factors, and it is difficult to isolate precise causal relationships. However, the environment–agent–host public health perspective contributes importantly to our understanding of prevention and to prevention practice.

The public health perspective has also contributed the concepts of primary, secondary, and tertiary prevention, and the related terms of incidence and prevalence. Primary prevention involves efforts to reduce the incidence of a disorder (such as diagnosed depression), that is, the number or the rate of development of new cases of that disorder. Secondary prevention is concerned with reducing the prevalence of a disorder, that is, new cases and the duration and severity of existing cases. Tertiary prevention is concerned with rehabilitation, that is, returning those affected by a disorder for a substantial period of time to community functioning.

Preventive Psychiatry

Caplan (1964) linked prevention of mental illness with community and with population, consistent with a public health perspective. In this classic view of mental health prevention, the critical goal is to lower the rate of new cases of mental disorder in an entire population over a certain period by counteracting harmful circumstances before they have a chance to produce illness. In this viewpoint, prevention does not seek to prevent a specific person from becoming sick. Instead, it seeks to reduce the risk for a whole population so that, although some may become ill, their overall number will be reduced. It thus contrasts with individual-oriented psychiatry, which focuses on a single person and deals with general influences only insofar as they are combined in a person's unique experience

Blended Model of Prevention

The blended model for viewing prevention originates from public health, where the term *prevention* was an overarching one, incorporating a full range of health services. The blended model assigns help-giving to primary, secondary, *and* tertiary categories, each being an outgrowth of the temporal sequence through which the onset of dysfunction can occur. Thus, within the blended model, primary prevention was intended to reduce the incidence of new cases of disorder; secondary prevention was directed at early intervention and reducing the intensity, severity, and duration of an existing disorder; and tertiary prevention focused on those already suffering the disorder. The blended model has been praised for incorporating under one umbrella all forms of intervention, while criticized for being tied too exclusively to a linear, sequential view of the onset of dysfunction and to a system that may tend to blur distinctions among different forms of intervention, thus leading to confusion and improper use (Felner, Felner, & Silverman, 2000).

Unique Model of Prevention

The unique model of prevention provides a different perspective on prevention, seeking to disregard continued usage of the public health terminology of primary, secondary, and tertiary prevention in favor of: (a) prevention, (b) early intervention (formerly, secondary prevention), and (c) treatment (formerly, tertiary prevention). This step would assign a unique status to prevention.

Within this framework, prevention is defined as incorporating four features that are not tied solely to conditions of onset (Felner et al., 2000). These four features are:

1. "Before-the-Fact" onset, so that the number of new cases of a disorder can be reduced
2. Mass or population level of analysis, with interventions being directed universally to all persons in a population, or to selected persons who are at risk or find themselves in risky situations (Gordon, 1983; Mrazek & Haggerty, 1994)
3. "Developmental pathways" being a focus of change efforts so that evolving processes are targeted that are hazardous to health and that are protective and enhance competencies and strengths
4. Health promotion and wellness (Cowen, 2000) focused efforts aimed at strengthening people against future at-risk conditions

Inclusive Model of Prevention

Romano and Hage (2000), in their major contribution in *The Counseling Psychologist* on "prevention in counseling psychology," posited a conception of prevention that seeks to be inclusive of some major strands. Some critics might view these strands as competing, but Romano and Hage offer them as encompassing "the multiple ways in which prevention can be implemented" (p. 855). From this perspective, prevention would possess one or more of these dimensions: (a) stopping a problem from occurring (primary prevention); (b) delaying the onset of a problem (secondary prevention); (c) reducing the impact of a current problem behavior (tertiary prevention);

(d) promoting emotional and physical well-being (risk reduction through strength-building); and (e) supporting policies (of institutions, community, government) that promote well-being (risk reduction through indirect means). This broad conception of prevention holds appeal for counselors, counseling psychologists, social workers, and other practitioners because it spans a range of applications they find familiar and usable, all under the prevention umbrella.

Science of Prevention Model

The main objective of a "science of prevention" approach (Coie et al. 1993) is to prevent or moderate serious and major human psychological disorder. Those conducting a preventive intervention program would intervene in the chain of events between risk and prospective disorder by (a) identifying the serious dysfunction that is to be prevented; (b) analyzing risk and protective factors associated with the disorder; (c) conducting pilot projects and evaluating their efficacy; (d) expanding pilots that were effective in larger prevention projects; and (e) promoting community-wide adoption. This system is very logical and sequential, and resonates with the public health model discussed earlier (source–agent–host). However, it fails to account for the various pathways through which risk and disorder may be associated and the reality that the same set of risk conditions may lead to a wide variety of dysfunction, not just the anticipated one, or to none at all. It also is constrained by its exclusive focus on the prevention of serious mental and emotional disorder.

Institute of Medicine Model

The Institute of Medicine (IOM, 1994) identified definitional problems associated with prevention and then offered an influential recommendation that encompassed three approaches. Basically, the three approaches were defined as:

1. *Prevention*, which refers to services aimed universally (to an entire population), selectively (to those who may be at risk), and to indicated populations (to those in early stages but not yet diagnosable) to ward off the initial onset of a mental disorder.
2. *Treatment*, which refers to identifying cases and providing standard remediation to individuals with mental disorders, including interventions to reduce the likelihood of future co-occurring disorders.
3. *Maintenance*, which refers to interventions intended to reduce relapse and recurrence, and to provide compliance with both long-term treatment and rehabilitation.

One effect of this IOM recommendation is that it moves away from use of the public health terminology of primary, secondary, and tertiary prevention. In addition, the definition of prevention is restricted to reducing the onset of serious mental disorders. By doing so, the IOM definition omits both mental health promotion and the omnipresent and powerful "problems in living" aspects of prevention.

Disorder Reduction (DR) vs. Health Promotion (HP) Approaches

Diebold (1998) commented on two large independent reviews of the prevention literature (by Mrazek & Haggerty, 1994, and by Durlak & Wells, 1997). Both reviews found that prevention was efficacious, but the reviewers tended to define prevention differently. Mrazek and Haggerty focused on the reduction of new cases of disease (Disorder Reduction: DR), while Durlak and Wells emphasized the reduction of incidence of adjustment problems and included the promotion of mental health functioning (Health Promotion: HP). The DR approach to prevention operationalizes the science of prevention approach, discussed earlier. It is a positivistic-hypothetico-deductive model framed by linking risk factors to specific clinical disorders. The HP approach tends to be prospective and targeted more broadly, including skill development, social pathology, and the concept that risk factors and disorders are not clearly linked.

At-Risk Perspective

A continuum of "at-riskness" proposed by McWhirter et al. (1995) offers a useful way to conceive of prevention. They suggested that being at risk is not a discrete, black or white situation, but needs to be understood as existing along a continuum. They hold that a category of "no risk" does not exist, that everyone is susceptible to some form of vulnerability. The series of steps along the at-risk continuum begins with the lowest level of minimal risk and then proceeds incrementally to include remote risk, high risk, and imminent risk, finally reaching the at-risk category. McWhirter et al. suggest that prevention can be launched anywhere along the at-risk continuum. For instance, they maintain that treatment provided to a dysfunctional family system can simultaneously provide a preventive effect for the children, potentially derailing their progression toward one or more of the at-risk categories contained in the continuum.

Routes to Psychological Wellness Perspective

The late Emory Cowen developed a conception of prevention that became focused on psychological wellness, and he offered it as an alternative to a risk detection-disorder approach to prevention. He pointed out that the current mental health system is reactive, not proactive. Cowen drew from Antonovsky's (1979) observation that pathogenesis (how disease processes emerge) was a well-established concept in mental health but that there was no accepted terminology for how health processes develop (the term *salutogenesis* was suggested). Cowen maintained that sound early-wellness interventions may provide the best "inoculation" against a host of adverse situations and that all people, not just those at risk, can benefit from wellness-enhancement activities. He identified (1994, 2000) five wellness-enhancement strategies to advance wellness applications within prevention: (1) promote wholesome caregiver–child attachment relationships, (2) help children to develop early competencies that are stage appropriate; (3) fashion wellness-enhancing environments within which people can interact; (4) bolster people's capacity to cope with and manage stress; and (5) enhance the sense of empowerment people feel in their lives.

"Nikki Principle"

Seligman (2002a) and others (see the *Handbook of Positive Psychology* edited by Snyder & Lopez 2002) have been developing the concept of positive psychology, and have been amassing an accompanying research and litera-ture base. Positive psychology is highly consistent not only with Cowen's psychological wellness emphasis but also with mainstream counseling and counseling psychology. It is focused on developing strengths and resources rather than on avoiding deficits and deficiencies—the latter representing the essential focus of psychology practice to date, according to Seligman.

Within positive psychology, Seligman has discussed "positive prevention." He maintains that major strides in prevention over the last 50 years have occurred where the focus has been on systematically developing competen-cies and not on correcting weakness. He suggests that these wellness competencies provide a set of buffers—what he calls "positive human traits"—that can work against psychopathology. And he maintains that most of the work being done by practitioners in their offices and in the commu-nity can be based on developing strengths rather than on ameliorating deficits. Seligman calls this attention to strengths as a way of doing effective prevention the "Nikki Principle," named in honor of a major life lesson his young daughter, Nikki, taught him. Here is one way that Seligman put it: "Much of the task of prevention in this new century will be to create a science of human strength whose mission will be to understand and learn how to foster these virtues in young people" (p. 5).

Ecological Models and Levels

An ecological perspective holds that human behavior needs to be under-stood in context (Bronfenbrenner, 1979) and that behavior emerges from a transaction (Felner et al. 2000) occurring between people and the environment (Lewin, 1951). Conyne and Cook (2004) have devoted an edited text exploring how counselors can apply ecological approaches in their work at various levels of intervention. In that text, Chronister, McWhirter, and Kerewsky (2004) specifically address prevention from an ecological perspective. They suggest that such a perspective on prevention allows counselors to systematically examine contextual influences and power dynamics, leading to preventive interventions that can empower people to effect change across multiple levels of systems.

As Felner et al. (2000) observed, an ecological framework for prevention permits a comprehensive and integrative approach, including "interactions between the various parts of total ecological and psychological systems, rather than only between individuals and their proximal environments" (p. 23). That is, an ecological approach sanctions giving attention not only to direct influences (such as a child's experiences in school) but also to those that arise more indirectly (such as impending war), and it signals the importance of considering the influences of multiple systems on human development and functioning. In practice, the nexus of prevention and ecology leads practitioners to work with participants in prevention programs to create an empowered concordance with the systems of their lives (Conyne, 2000), where their life contexts are experienced as being more satisfying, effective, and appropriate.

Social Justice/Social Experience Perspective

George Albee champions the "social justice" approach to prevention (see, for example, Albee, 1986, 2000). In his view, as mentioned earlier in this chapter, treating one person at a time will provide no substantive, systemic redress of the major social problems faced by millions today. He is less than sanguine, too, about prevention approaches that rely on wellness and competency-enhancement efforts, however well constructed and delivered. Over the decades he has called all who are compelled toward prevention to anchor their efforts to seek social justice, because "economic and social class variables are most important in perpetuating stress, social injustice, and exploitation" (Albee, 2000, p. 850). More recently, Wyche (2003 in Dittmann) has expressed some worry: "I am concerned that many of our colleagues are not interested in social class factors, nor in poverty and how it influences the outcomes of people's lives" (p. 36).

Because the poor and exploited among us suffer the most (Albee draws from Mirowski and Ross, 1989, who have documented that 85% of all stress occurs among the poor), prevention needs to be directed at the basic social, economic, and political conditions that serve to maintain economic disparity. Albee calls on preventionists to help produce a "just society" (1986) in which sexism, racism, consumerism, ageism, patriarchy, and homophobia are all reduced or eliminated, thus allowing systems to develop more humanely, with positive effects on people.

Empowerment Perspective

Empowerment is defined in several ways but nonetheless has a strong relationship with prevention. It is understood generally as increasing self-efficacy, control over situations, and the sharing of power. Rappaport (1971, 1981), Rappaport, Swift, and Hess (1984), and several contributions by Albee (e.g., 1986) contended that empowerment involves the redistribution of power and influence in society and that social justice can remove many of the causes of psychopathology.

E.H. McWhirter (1994) defined an empowerment approach to counseling as assisting people, groups, or organizations that are presently powerless or marginalized to gain strength in certain ways. She said that people become more empowered through increased awareness of: (a) how power dynamics affect their lives, (b) how they can gain increased control over their lives without infringing on others, and (c) how they can exercise empowerment in such as way as to actively support the empowerment of others in the community.

This notion of empowerment being connected to strengthening the environment and community is echoed by others. Empowerment can focus energy to create an environment in which people can develop character, competence, and synergy (Covey, Merrill, & Merrill, 1994; Terry, 1993), while the ultimate outcome of empowerment is a community that can produce the best possible results for all. The goal of empowering people and systems is naturally consistent with prevention.

Proactive and Reactive Perspectives

Macroenvironmental change as an empowerment strategy was articulated classically by Catalano (1979) and Catalano and Dooley (1980). They stressed the importance of macroeconomic factors in producing psychological maladjustment. In examining this issue, these authors differentiated between what they saw as two major forms of primary prevention: proactive and reactive.

Proactive approaches to primary prevention are used to eliminate noxious stressors present in the macroenvironment, as evidenced in the large systems of our society—for example, excessive political power, discrimination, restrictive child-care policies, unequal wealth distribution, health-care inequities, inadequate social security benefits and procedures, and so on. The idea behind the proactive approach is that removal of these kinds of stress sources will serve to strengthen the psychological health of the populace.

Reactive attempts at primary prevention aim to increase the ability of individuals to cope more adequately with existing pathogenic environmental stressors. For instance, employees in an organization participate in a stress management program conducted in the workplace. This effort is intended to help these employees to adapt more satisfactorily to stressors already present, that is, to the present working conditions. Alternatively, a proactive approach would seek to eliminate the undesirable work stressors themselves.

System-Centered and Person-Centered Strategies

From this perspective (Cowen, 1985), prevention in mental health can be sought through two main strategies: system change and person-centered change strategies.

System-centered change strategies in prevention involve eradicating, reducing, or positively changing environmental sources of stress. They are directed at macrolevel change in such conditions as poverty and the ending of various forms of discrimination.

Poverty, as you have read, is a pervasively powerful promoter of discord and dysfunction that cries out for system-centered change in prevention. Living in poverty can lead to a host of substantial problems, including low self-efficacy, helplessness, hopelessness, limited access to health care and medical insurance, and depression, among other factors (Dittmann, 2003).

In the United States, a family of two with a household income of less than $12,120 per year falls below the poverty line. The poverty rate in the United States for 2002 was 12.1%, up from 11.7% in 2001. This percentage included 34.6 million citizens, 1.7 million more than in 2001. The condition of poverty varies by race and ethnicity, including 8% of non-Hispanic Whites, 10% of Asians, 22% of Hispanics, and 24% of Blacks (U.S. Department of Labor, 2003). These percentages remain alarmingly high.

System-centered approaches to prevention afford substantial potential for promoting health and eliminating dysfunction among individuals. This is so because the elimination of the underlying conditions that serve to dehumanize and disenfranchise people from participation in the full range of possible options in this society would release human potential rather than squash it, with accompanying positive physical and psychological benefits. At least this is the (perhaps Utopian) vision that undergirds the system-centered approach. Working toward improving the major subsystems of society, such as job opportunities, justice, education, housing, and health care, needs to be continued, if not intensified, by counselors and other helpers.

Person-centered change strategies in prevention arguably are the most well suited to counselors and counseling psychologists because they are directly connected with helping people—something that counselors know a whole lot about. These strategies can involve: (a) altering how high-risk transitions and developmental situations will be faced (e.g., divorce, high school graduation), and (b) enhancing competencies in people at various levels. The enhancement of competencies can be approached through improving high-risk settings (microsocial units) that people engage with directly (e.g., work, school), through undergoing specific training and education in wellness skills, or through engaging in competency-facilitating experiences where one can receive and benefit through giving (e.g., the tutor whose self-esteem is elevated).

Definitions of Primary Prevention

Many streams of influence flow into the prevention river, including how primary prevention has been defined. Some samples of primary prevention definitions follow.

Going back to 1963, Bower (1963) identified the overall objectives of primary prevention as being twofold: (1) to reduce the incidence of new instances of emotional distress or disturbance, and (2) to promote emotional robustness (cited in Klein & Goldston, 1977, p. 27).

Goldston (1977), who served as director of the National Institutes of Mental Health Office of Prevention from 1981 to 1985, provided this definition of primary prevention:

> Primary prevention encompasses those activities directed to specifically identified vulnerable high-risk groups within the community who have not been labeled as psychiatrically ill and for whom measures can be undertaken to avoid the onset of emotional disturbance and/or to enhance their level of positive mental health. Programs for the promotion of mental health are primarily educational rather than clinical in conception and operation with their ultimate goal being to increase people's capacities for dealing with crises and for taking steps to improve their own lives. (p. 27)

Cowen (1983) suggested that to be considered a primary prevention program, it must be before-the-fact; it must be mass- or group-oriented and not targeted to individuals; it must be directed to presently "well" people who are unaffected, or to those who are expected or known (epidemiologically) to be at risk for disturbance; and the program must be intentional.

Prior to that, Cowen (1980) described primary prevention as follows:

> Programs that engineer structures, processes, situations and events that maximally benefit in scope and temporal stability, the psychological adjustment, effectiveness, happiness and coping skills of many (as yet unaffected) individuals (p. 264).

Albee (1985) and Albee and Gullotta (1997) emphasized that incidence reduction is the key to primary prevention. Albee presented an equation that has been frequently cited to seek the primary prevention of problem incidence, involving reducing the strength of factors contained in the numerator while strengthening factors within the equation's denominator, as follows:

$$\text{Incidence} = \frac{\text{Organic Factors + Stressors + Exploitation}}{\text{Coping Skills + Self-Esteem + Support Groups}}$$

Others (e.g., Dusenbury & Botvin, 1992; Elias & Branden, 1988) have presented adaptations of this equation to emphasize various aspects of the equation.

Martin Bloom (1996), writing from a social work perspective, defined primary prevention as follows:

> Coordinated actions seeking to prevent predictable problems, to protect states of health and healthy functioning, and to promote desired potentialities in individuals and groups in their physical and socioculutral settings over time. (p. 2)

Bloom then offered his own adaptation of Albee's equation, through what he has termed a "configural analysis." This version incorporates ecological considerations, arguing that parts should not be considered separately and that the factors are interrelated and reciprocal.

Conyne (1983, 1994, 1997) defined primary prevention in this way:

> Primary prevention is (1) proactive and (2) population-based. It includes (3) anticipating potential disorder for a (4) population at risk and introducing (5) before-the-fact interventions that are delivered (6) directly or (7) indirectly. These interventions are intended to (8) reduce the incidence of the disorder by (9) counteracting harmful circumstances that contribute to it by (10) promoting emotional robustness in the population at risk so that population members are both (11) protected and (12) becomes more fully competent. (p. 332)

In 2000, Conyne provided the following understanding of primary prevention:

1. It is intended to decrease incidence; that is, the development or rate of development of new cases of any disorder(s).

2. It occurs through intentionally and collaboratively planned programs.
3. Groups of healthy people or with people at risk participate in primary prevention programs within their own ecological settings.
4. It is conducted to reduce risk factors such as stressors and exploitation while building protective capacities.
5. It results in an empowered concordance between people and systems.

TOWARD MERGING THE STREAMS OF INFLUENCE: TWO INTEGRATED DEFINITIONS OF PREVENTION

The various and often meandering streams of influence upon prevention are many, as you can see. This variability has led not only to a richness of input but also to confusion as to what prevention really is. Current understandings of prevention tend to coalesce around the points that it includes interventions that occur prior to onset of a disorder and that prevention is located on a continuum that includes treatment and maintenance.

When considering the role and function of counselors, the restriction of prevention to disorder prevention delimits the helping potential. Counselors are concerned not only with treating and preventing disorders but also with promoting healthy functioning and healthy settings and processes. Counselors understand that health needs to be understood as much more than the absence of illness and that the promotion of health in persons (first-order change) and of healthy settings and processes (second-order change) can both serve as powerful preventive strategies.

Therefore, there is a need for a broader understanding of prevention that is more compatible with the ethos, role, and function of counselors today. This more comprehensive definition needs to be "true" to prevention (that is, to reduce incidence and early prevalence), to embrace an expanded scope of intervention, and to emerge from the various streams of influence that we have examined up to this point.

In the *Encyclopedia of Primary Prevention and Health Promotion* (Gullotta & Bloom, 2003), the editors constructed a definition of primary prevention that they intended to be comprehensive and directed at "what practitioners need now and in the near future" (Gullotta & Bloom, 2003, p. 13):

Primary prevention is the promotion of health and the prevention of illness that involves actions that help participants (or to facilitate participants helping themselves) (1) to prevent predictable and interrelated problems, (2) to protect existing states of health and healthy functioning, (3) and to promote psychosocial wellness for identified populations of people. These consist of: (a) whole populations in which everyone requires certain basic utilities of life; (b) selected groups of people at risk with potential; (c) indicated subgroups at very high risk. Primary prevention may be facilitated by increasing individual, group, organizational, societal, cultural, and physical environmental strengths and resources, while simultaneously reducing the limitations and pressures from these same factors.

This definition embraces many important facets of primary prevention, including protection, prevention, and promotion; the aspects of prevention contained in the Institute of Medicine definition (universal, selective, indicated); and multiple strategies for implementing primary prevention.

WHAT IS PREVENTION IN COUNSELING AND MENTAL HEALTH?

It may no longer be useful or necessary, however, to try distinguishing between primary prevention and prevention. The definition of "primary" prevention that concluded the preceding section (Gullotta & Bloom, 2003), in fact, aptly describes "prevention." Consistent with other viewpoints, it is important to emphasize that contemporary understandings of prevention adequately encompass the domain for practical involvement by counselors, psychologists, social workers, and others interested in reducing incidence, reversing trajectories toward more positive directions, and optimizing healthy functioning.

In light of the extensive foregoing discussion of prevention, therefore, I offer the following definition of prevention:

Prevention is a goal for both everyday life and for service delivery, through which people become empowered to interact effectively and appropriately within varying levels of systems (micro, meso, exo, and macro) and in settings (individual, family, school, community, work). Preventive application can yield a reduction in the occurrence of new cases of a problem, in the duration and severity of incipient problems, and it can promote strengths and optimal human functioning.

As you can see, this definition represents a departure from some other definitions and from my own previous work. Here, I am reflecting an understanding of prevention that is broader in many dimensions.

This new definition is quite compacted. It is structured around seven key concepts that have been distilled from other existing definitions. Let's unpack it by examining these seven key concepts. Four concepts have also been indicated that represent "departures" from previous definitions offered:

1. *Prevention is a goal.* Prevention means to stop new cases of problems from developing, to reduce the number or the rate of development of new problem cases or situations, to shorten the duration or the severity of new cases that have only recently occurred, or to promote optimal human functioning. It is a goal for counseling, not a method or a process (Morrill, Oetting, & Hurst, 1974), just as remediation and development are goals. Moreover, Departure 1 from previous work indicates that prevention is a goal not only for service delivery but also for everyday life. (The concept of "everyday prevention" will be examined more fully in Chapter 2.)

2. *Through which people become empowered:* Helping people to identify and/or build strengths and competencies is a chief function of counselors and counseling psychologists, as well as of other helping professionals. Prevention is best served by enhancing wellness (Cowen, 2000; Seligman, 2000) rather than reducing deficits, and by helping people to develop greater efficacy and control in their lives, without infringing on others.

3. *To interact effectively and appropriately:* The ecological, interactive processes of people within systems are critically important for preventive interventions (Bronfenbrenner, 1979; Felner et al. 2000). Developmental pathways (conditions, settings, and processes) need to both challenge and support people who move through them, and people can learn how to interact in ways that meet their goals and do not infringe on others.

4. *In levels of systems:* This concept qualifies as Departure 2 from earlier definitions. The classic public health understanding of prevention is that it is targeted at a population level. This focus works very well for the prevention of certain diseases for which there is a known etiology, route of progression, and means for intervention (e.g., malaria or smallpox). For counselors, who must deal frequently with less certain circumstances and conditions, it is important to orient prevention at all levels in order to promote positive human functioning. Microsystems, mesosystems, exosystems, and macrosystems themselves may be at risk, just as people can be, and they are amenable to improvement. A route to systems is through settings, such as the family, school, community, and

work (Bronfenbrenner, 1979; Conyne, 1987; Conyne & Cook, 2004; Romano & Hage, 2000).

5. *Preventive application can reduce new cases of a problem from occurring:* The classic understanding of prevention is that it is intended to reduce the onset of new cases (Albee, 1985). Prevention is first of all concerned with stopping a bad thing (e.g., academic failure) from occurring in the first place or with reducing the rate at which these bad things develop. This is the public health concept of "incidence." Use of the term *problem* qualifies as Departure 3 from earlier definitions. The generic word "problem" is used intentionally, rather than the terms *dysfunction* or *disturbance*, or *disease*. It is important for counselors to understand that prevention services can be undertaken to address not only diagnosed mental disturbance but also the full range of human problems, including lifestyle, addictions, and problems in living, such as loneliness, sadness, and anger (Romano & Hage, 2000).

6. *Preventive application can reduce the duration and severity of incipient problems:* This qualifies as Departure 4 from earlier definitions. Prevention extends beyond incidence to include reversing the trajectory of problems that are newly formed, not yet entrenched, and not yet diagnosable. Crisis intervention and counseling (not therapy) services are good examples of how prevention of this kind can occur (see Romano & Hage, 2000).

7. *Preventive application can promote optimal human functioning:* Prevention is concerned not only with problems (avoidance or reversing direction of early stage problems) but also with promoting healthy processes and outcomes, a concept that is a centerpiece of "positive psychology" (Seligman, 2002) and one that has historically been at the heart of counseling and counseling psychology.

CONCLUSION

Prevention in mental health is a foundation for preventive counseling. It undergirds efforts taken by counseling practitioners and other helpers to enhance health and diminish disturbance. These efforts, you will come to know, are to be described as preventive counseling.

The intention of this chapter was to underscore the need for prevention in mental health, to explore many of the meandering "streams of influence" that have shaped the development of prevention, and to provide a contemporary and comprehensive definition of prevention.

In terms of need, the demands for service far outstrip the availability of helpers, especially if one-to-one direct remedial service remains the core means of delivery. Prevention provides an important and unique complement to an overall service delivery approach, as it seeks to reach people and systems before—or very early—in problem development.

Like explorers, we took brief excursions in 17 various streams of influence as they feed into the broader waters of prevention. To recap, these streams are: (1) public health perspective, (2) preventive psychiatry, (3) blended model of prevention, (4) unique model of prevention, (5) inclusive model of prevention, (6) science of prevention model, (7) Institute of Medicine model, (8) disease reduction (DR) vs. health promotion (HP) approaches, (9) at-risk perspective, (10) routes to psychological wellness perspective, (11) "Nikki Principle," (12) ecological model, (13) social justice/social experience perspective, (14) empowerment perspective, (15) proactive and reactive perspectives, (16) system-centered and person-centered strategies, and (17) various important definitions of primary prevention.

The intermingling of these streams of influence form the mighty, and sometimes still somewhat muddy, waters of prevention. This chapter moves toward conclusion by presenting and discussing the comprehensive prevention definition offered by Gullotta and Bloom (2003) in the *Encyclopedia of Primary Prevention and Health Promotion*. This definition contains an emphasis on prevention, promotion, and protection, as well as other factors. Finally, I provide a definition of prevention that is premised on seven key concepts that have been culled from previous work and that contain some important departures: (1) prevention is a goal not only for service delivery but also for everyday life, (2) prevention is applied at the population level and at all other levels, (3) in addition to diagnosable dysfunctions, a broad range of life problems can be prevented, and (4) prevention includes incidence reduction but also effect on the duration and severity of incipient problems.

As you have seen in this chapter, counseling psychologists, professional counselors, social workers, and other helpers need to include prevention within their helping repertoire. Failing to do so may have grave consequences for this society as human needs far outstrip the available helping resources.

How practitioners can integrate this perspective with their own established legacies becomes the ongoing topic for this book. Effective integration can greatly multiply their power as health stimulators in this society. Preventive counseling offers one organized method for accomplishing this worthy goal.

ISSUES FOR REFLECTION AND DISCUSSION

1. Why is the concept "rescue each individually" a "no-win" situation, incompatible with the present need/supply balance in mental health? Give some examples.

2. References were made to the primary prevention concept of "incidence." Define it and indicate why it is so important for prevention in mental health.

3. Suppose you were asked to give a short speech to the Rotary Club in your community on mental health. You decide to focus on underscoring the importance of prevention in mental health. Develop an outline for a 15-minute talk that contains key points you would like to make.

4. Join up with a partner. Take a look at the 17 "streams of influence" discussed in this chapter that have served to shape a contemporary understanding of prevention. Which three streams seem most important to each of you? Why?

5. Catalano and Dooley have differentiated reactive and proactive primary prevention. What do they see as the difference? Give an example of each type.

6. System-centered prevention holds much prevention potential but is difficult to undertake. Explain both aspects of this statement, identifying some ways that professional counselors and psychologists can try to effect system change.

7. Focus on the seven concepts that are central to the definition of prevention provided at the chapter's end. What do you agree with most? With which do you disagree? Discuss in a small group.

8. The rest of the book will focus on how counselors can draw from prevention to guide their work. What early ideas might you have about this topic, even before you have read other chapters? Jot down some ideas. Keep track of them as you read on. See what is confirmed, what you might not have thought of yet, what ideas might change, and then—note what may be missing that is important!

CHAPTER 2

Everyday Prevention

A young man went to the famous Sage and asked: "What can I do to be useful and happy?" He said he had tried everything: yoga, running, meditation, fasting, religion, psychotherapy, hard work, falling in and out of love, world traveling, deep discussions, psychedelic drugs, groups of all kinds, tantric sex . . . nothing had worked; he said he was still miserable and unproductive. The Sage listened carefully throughout. When the young man had finished, the Sage looked at him all-knowingly and whispered this advice: "Try optimism."

INTRODUCTION

This chapter focuses on the concept of "everyday prevention." It is connected to optimism and other aspects of positive psychology, as well as to a number of other person- and system-centered approaches that will be summarized here. The role of counselors and other professional helpers in everyday prevention also will be considered.

Research is beginning to accumulate around the concept of positive psychology, or moving away from a focus on psychopathology to one of building positive qualities. The popular song of several years ago, "Don't Worry, Be Happy," expressed in a nutshell a key concept in positive psychology: As the Sage suggested above, to develop a sense of optimism. Optimism and other human strengths, such as courage, interpersonal skill, future mindedness, faith, hope, work ethic, perseverance, honesty, and the capacity to achieve flow and insight, can act as buffers against malaise, dysfunction, and mental illness. Human strengths such as optimism are not enough, of course. A positive psychology seems to depend also on cultivating positive experiences that are associated with happiness and subjective well-being, on the capacity to adapt and organize to successfully meet changing conditions, and to interactions that occur within positive social contexts (Seligman & Csikszentmihalyi, 2000).Positive psychology is understood as "the scientific study of ordinary human strengths and virtues" (Sheldon & King, 2001, p. 216). Note the adjective *ordinary*.

Resilience, a very important skill, illustrates (among other things) the importance of the ordinary. For instance, Masten (2001), in discussing resilience in children, emphasized "the power of the ordinary" (p. 235). Based on a review of resilience studies involving children, Masten observed:

> Resilience does not come from rare and special qualities, but from the everyday magic of ordinary, normative human resources in the minds, brains, and bodies of children, in their families and relationships, and in their communities. (Masten, 2001, p. 235)

In another look at resilience in terms of its ordinary nature, the American Psychological Association's Practice Directorate developed a public education campaign following the September 11, 2001, attacks. Called the Road to Resilience, the campaign set out the following principles: (a) resilience is a set of learned behaviors that are not automatic, (b) it is a personal journey that is involved with others, (c) it is an ordinary, not an extraordinary, experience, and (d) it demands that improvement be accomplished through small, persistent steps (Murray, 2003).

This perspective of positive psychology that focuses on ordinary and everyday circumstances leads us to think in terms of a kind of "everyday prevention" that is within the reach of people and that counselors and other practitioners can intentionally bring to their work with clients and client systems. Everyday prevention should infuse and guide the work of all preventionists.

Everyday prevention is a concept that did not find its way into the 1987 book edition, and it is made possible now through recent advances associated with such forces as positive psychology, health promotion, managed care, and integrative medicine approaches. Today, for example, many of the deadliest diseases of the last century are routinely cured or managed. However, as exciting as curing disease is, it is far better never to get sick at all, and there is considerable scientific work underway to prevent disease in the first place.

In addition, the American population has moved beyond being passive recipients of expert-provided care to assume a much more personal responsibility for their own health and mental healthcare needs. People, including children, are viewed as active decision makers, selecting from available choices and preferences and shaping their environment, with the possibility of masterful and efficacious living. Many have begun to assume greater initiative and responsibility for the direction of education and schools; the rise in home schooling, the spread of e-educational programs, and the charter school movement are just three examples. This active involvement in health care and education will become a dominant theme for the twenty-first century.

Professionals and professional training programs are beginning to respond to this significant change in personal orientation and responsibility. For instance, training programs in integrative medicine are developing (e.g., at Duke University and University of Arizona), where the primary goal is to assist people to experience optimal vitality and wellness, integrating mind, body, and spirit as well as allopathic, alternative, and complementary medical approaches. Counseling and counseling psychology programs are beginning to address prevention more directly (albeit still slowly; see Chapter 9) through coursework and training experiences. Healthcare plans are being created that are comprehensive and dynamic, geared to promoting optimal well-being.

But, of course, millions of Americans are not waiting for the healthcare and education establishments to alter themselves in the direction of increased integration and variety. Instead, many are experimenting with their own choices. They research, read, surf the Internet, learn from one another, and test out various combinations of exercise, diet, herbs and vitamins, spiritual practice, social support, and alternative treatments to find what works for them. Much of this experimentation is proceeding without external expert monitoring and may be risky to health, in some degree. Conversely, countless millions are organizing for themselves what they view as healthy practices that seem to be yielding improved vitality and more satisfying lifestyles.

All of this activity is a virtual wellspring of prevention, occurring at all ecological levels in our society. Our "cultural blueprint" is being rewritten at the macro level and is being put into practice by individuals and groups to say, in effect: "We are empowered." Organizations are slower to adapt because they have traditions, regulations, policies, revenue streams, and other forces and elements that require longer to turn around—sort of like turning around the *Titanic*. But organizations are beginning to revise and reinvent themselves, too; witness the increasing number of programs and initiatives that take a health-promoting orientation.

Where does the professional practice of prevention by counselors and other helpers fit with this paradigm shift toward a more autonomous and experiencing style of health care and education? Right now a gap exists, as prevention is still tied closely to disorder-reduction, population-based models under the control of "preventionists" who work conscientiously, and often effectively, to help avert dysfunction. While I may be overdrawing this situation, the tilt of prevention is not yet toward including an "everyday prevention" prominently in its armamentarium.

WHAT IS "EVERYDAY PREVENTION"?

Yet, everyday prevention does not stand apart from prevention. It is defined as follows:

> Everyday prevention refers to people enacting daily life best practices in context to optimize functioning and avert significant problems.

A chief role for counselors and other professional helpers is to help people incorporate everyday prevention within their lives on a daily basis. This role can be carried out in three ways: (1) by brokering proven everyday prevention practices to people, (2) by creating and delivering good everyday prevention practices, and (3) by infusing everyday prevention within all aspects of preventive counseling.

Everyday prevention is a strand within the fabric of autonomous and experiencing health care and education. It is a means for personal empowerment, based on the view that people can take fuller charge of their lives in context. Everyday prevention is a day-by-day process of implementing personal best practices. As Craik (1991) observed, "Lives are lived day by day, one day at a time, from day to day, day after day, day in and day out. Lives as we experience them are inherently quotidian" (p. 1). This daily regimen of personal best practices can provide people with opportunities to empower themselves in systems, leading to optimal functioning and the avoidance of predictable problems.

The "Ruby and Oren Principle"

Ruby and Oren were neighbors who were in their mid-80s when my wife (Lynn Rapin) and I (early 30s) lived next door to them in Bloomington, Illinois, during the mid-1970s. We learned a lot from them. I've elevated one of these items learned to the status of a "principle," similar to Seligman's "Nikki Principle" (see Chapter 1).

Ruby and Oren told us one day that they had perhaps missed their Saturday card game with friends only three times over the last 35 years—two of those misses were due to funerals and one to a huge ice storm when the roads were not passable. I was surprised, especially for someone who can find absolutely no value in playing cards! How could this possibly be?

Of course, it turns out that playing cards had very little to do with it. Ruby and Oren said that card playing provided a chance for them to get together with lifelong friends at least once a week to spend time, catch up, gripe and moan, celebrate successes, and tell stories. Now I could understand—it was their consistent way of giving and getting social support, what we know as a critically important factor in promoting health and preventing isolation and decline. Thus, the "Ruby and Oren Principle."

It should be the ultimate goal of every counselor for individual clients, groups, families, organizations, communities, and the population as a whole to find the equivalents of their own "Ruby and Oren Principles." Let's take a look at some person-centered and system-centered possibilities.

PERSON-CENTERED AREAS THAT EVERYDAY PREVENTION CAN ADDRESS

The "Good Life"

Within the context of positive psychology, Seligman (1999) and others wonder about the following question: "What is the 'good life'?" He is quick to indicate that what he means by the good life is not a "Porsche, champagne, and a suntan."

Seligman suggests that what positive psychology needs is a taxonomy for the good life, the main purpose of which would be to guide the formulation and building of the "good life." He observes that psychological science has been able to produce an exhaustive (and exhausting) compendium to describe and diagnose human dysfunction and psychopathology (the *Diagnostic and Statistical Manual* (*DSM-IV*) and its editions), but that there is no companion product to describe and prescribe human health and positive functioning. There is a concerted effort under way to develop a taxonomy of the "good life."

The positive psychology perspective is based on a particular assumption of what is the best way to promote mental health, a way that is 180 degrees different from that which has been in effect within psychology and psychiatry (Maddux, 2000; Maddux, Snyder, & Feldman, 2003). This previous way is to correct dysfunction and to prevent any of the hundreds of clinical syndromes contained in the *DSM*. Instead, positive psychology alters the focus from the reduction and prevention of human psychological disabilities and disturbances to the enhancement of human strengths and abilities. This focus centers on authentic happiness (Seligman, 2002) from the eudaemonic approach—that is, happiness that is centered on meaning and self-realization (Ryan & Deci, 2001), as well as the choices people make about their lives and how they construe what occurs (Maddux et al. 2003).

For example, authentic happiness (Seligman, 2002) is an area within positive psychology that is being intensely studied and that is addressing issues surrounding the "good life." Visit the Web site (http://www.authentichappiness.org) to peruse some of this work that, among other things, includes a variety of questionnaires and assessments (e.g., Fordyce Emotions Questionnaire, PANAS Questionnaire, General Happiness Scale, Satisfaction with Life Scale, and VIA Signature Strengths Survey). Interestingly, with regard to the concept of "everyday prevention," the work related to positive psychology—and authentic happiness—appears frequently in the popular press as well as in professional/scientific outlets; "The Happiest Guy" (McCafferty, 2003), an article on Seligman's authentic happiness, in the *USA Weekend* Sunday newspaper insert, is a case in point. This work is becoming part of mainstream America, increasingly available to people on an everyday basis.

Of course, authentic happiness is not the same as "A little song, a little dance, a little seltzer down your pants" (the theme of Chuckles the Clown from episode #500, October 25, 1975 of the old Mary Tyler Moore television situation comedy), although it could be said that both glee and fun are relevant. In his book on authentic happiness (Seligman, 2002), Seligman presents a "happiness formula:" $H = S + C + V$. That is, an enduring level of Happiness (H) is a function of one's biological Set (S) range, plus Circumstances (C) to which people are subjected (both generally positive in relation to enduring happiness, such as marriage and sociability, and those that are generally negatively related, such as money and race), plus Voluntary control (V), the choices one makes in life, such as a range of positive emotions like optimism, hope, faith, trust, and confidence. Although a large component of authentic, enduring happiness seems to be set by biology, it is the voluntary choices over which people can exert control that serves as the bellwether test of positive psychology. People can learn how to enhance their capacity to make positive choices on a daily basis.

The VIA (Values in Action) Signature Strengths seeks to assess twenty-four "signature strengths" that are associated with authentic happiness. The VIA Questionnaire was developed by the Values-In-Action (VIA) Institute, which is directed by Peterson and Seligman, and funded by the Mayerson Foundation. It is copyrighted by VIA. The questionnaire is obtainable on the Web site (http://www.authentichappiness.org/)

The twenty-four signature strengths are organized within the broader categories of:

1. *Wisdom and Knowledge*—five cognitive strengths involving the acquisition and use of knowledge. These strengths include creativity, curiosity, open-mindedness, love of learning, and perspective taking.

2. *Courage*—four emotional strengths involving the will toward goal accomplishment even when there is internal or external opposition. These strengths include bravery, industry/perseverance, authenticity, and zest.
3. *Love*—three interpersonal strengths that include supporting and caring for others. These strengths include intimacy, kindness, and social intelligence.
4. *Justice*—three strengths that undergird healthy communities. These strengths include citizenship/teamwork, fairness, and leadership.
5. *Temperance*—four strengths that moderate and protect against excessiveness. These strengths include forgiveness/mercy, modesty/ humility, prudence, and self-control/self-regulation.
6. *Transcendence*—five strengths that help to connect with the universe and provide meaning. These strengths include awe/appreciation of beauty and excellence, gratitude, hope, playfulness, and spirituality.

Seligman (2002) indicates that everyone possesses many signature strengths. He suggests that individuals complete and score the VIA, examine their top strengths, and apply a set of nine criteria to each one of the top strengths. As examples, three of these nine criteria are as follows: a strength engenders a sense of ownership and authenticity, a feeling of excitement while displaying it, and a rapid learning curve as it is first practiced. If a strength is matched by one or more of these criteria, he suggests that it is a signature strength and should be used frequently and across many settings and situations. Seligman provides examples in the areas of work, love, raising children, and finding general meaning and purpose in life. In sum, he (2002) holds the following with regard to the good life:

> Use your signature strengths every day in the main realms of your life to bring about abundant gratification and authentic happiness. (p. 161)

Long before work began in positive psychology to examine the good life, Socrates (born 470 B.C.E.) had given it some thought! Gross (2002) reviewed Socrates' seven principles, which are often thought to be associated with the good life, and how they can be used on a daily basis. These are:

1. *Know Thyself.* This one, we hear most frequently. To know thyself means to be self-aware, to review and reflect on actions, and to develop and revise plans to fit personal values within the community context.

2. *Ask Great Questions.* Be inquisitive. Seek to actively learn all the time, everywhere, from everyone.
3. *Think for Yourself.* Monitor what you say and what you do. Ask if these actions are reflective of you and your values and thoughts. Make up your own mind after weighing evidence.
4. *Challenge Conventional Wisdom.* Resist getting caught up in the currents running around you. Don't blindly do what everyone else does. Develop the capacity to act consistent with personal conviction.
5. *Grow with Friends.* Connect with others and seek appropriately to interact at genuine and deep levels.
6. *Speak the Truth.* Avoid lying, shading the truth, or faking it. Spot these behaviors around you, and those where truthful behaviors occur, and allow both to guide you.
7. *Strengthen Your Soul.* Build into each day opportunities and experiences that are restful, bring joy, and are kind.

Socrates provided a good start on defining the good life. A fuller description of the good life might provide some functional guideposts for what everyday prevention efforts ought to address. Work being conducted in the areas of subjective well-being, wellness, and life skills training can provide some direction for our consideration.

Subjective Well-Being (SWB)

Subjective Well-Being (SWB) is a condition that reflects a "preponderance of positive thoughts and feelings about one's life" (Myers & Diener, 1995, p. 11). It is defined by three distinct factors that are also correlated: (a) relative presence of positive affect, (b) absence of negative affect, and (c) life satisfaction.

Associating happiness with SWB, Myers and Diener have pondered the question: Who is happy? They and others (e.g., Little, 2000; Willi, 1999) have found that happy and effective people (i.e., those with high SWB) tend to:

1. Possess particular inner fixed or natural traits: self-esteem and acceptance, personal control/autonomy, optimism, and extraversion
2. Exhibit free, or adaptive, traits that are culturally scripted patterns enacted within one's goals and projects, and are independent of fixed traits
3. Have warm, positive, trusting, and satisfying interpersonal relationships

4. Find "flow" in work and in leisure (Csikszentmihalyi, 1990), where engagement in mindful challenge, with adequate support, is realizable
5. Possess a religious or spiritual faith
6. Adapt positively to change and show environmental mastery
7. Find or create personal niches that enrich their lives
8. Live within a cultural worldview that is generally positive
9. Have a purpose and find meaning in life
10. Have personal goals that guide personal growth

Thus, happiness can be thought of as a side effect of other main effects and their interaction. Happiness can also be viewed as the dessert and not the main course.

Science of Mental Health

In moving toward conceptualizing a science of mental health, Keyes and Lopez (2002) described complete mental health as combining high levels of symptoms of psychological well-being, social well-being, and the absence of recent mental illness. The authors enumerated dimensions of psychological well-being and social well-being as part of this conception. Psychological well-being represents dimensions of well-being that are primarily private and personal.

Psychological Well-Being dimensions are:

- *Self-acceptance,* or holding a positive attitude about oneself, both present and past.
- *Personal growth,* or being open to new experience and continued development.
- *Purpose in life,* or possessing goals and direction for guiding one's life.
- *Environmental mastery,* or feeling competent and capable of managing complexity and choosing or creating environmental contexts that are meaningful.
- *Autonomy,* or being independent and self-determining, consistent with internal guidance.
- *Positive relations with others,* or developing and maintaining warm and trusting relationships that include empathy, intimacy, support, and altruism. An expression of the value of personal relationships can be found in a quote attributed to Thomas Fuller, "Friendships multiply joys and divide griefs."

Keyes (1998) suggested that social well-being is a complement to psychological well-being. Social well-being contains dimensions that are public and less personal.

Social Well-Being dimensions are:

- *Social acceptance,* or holding positive attitudes about others and generally accepting them
- *Social actualization,* or believing that society is basically positive and can continue to improve
- *Social contribution,* or believing that people can give something valuable to society and that their daily activities are valued
- *Social coherence,* or viewing the social world as being largely predictable and understandable
- *Social integration,* or feeling that one belongs, is supported, and shares much in common with the community

Both the psychological and the social well-being dimensions are validated and reliable (Ryff, 1989) and have been confirmed in the MacArthur Foundation's Successful Midlife in the U.S. (MIDUS) study (Ryff & Keyes, 1995). Taken together, they represent one conception to guide everyday prevention efforts.

Flow

People can find enjoyment through their everyday activities. Flow (Csikszentmihalyi, 1990) is a psychology of optimal human experience that is based on the importance of becoming absorbed in experience rather than focused on desired end states, such as happiness. In fact, Csikszentmihalyi suggests that the key element of the optimal human experience is that it is an end in and of itself.

Flow is a theory derived from over two decades of studying human experience around the world using the Experience Sampling Method (ESM). People would be beeped electronically at random moments about eight times a day for a week to record what they were doing and how they were feeling at the time. Over 100,000 cross sections of human experience were gathered and analyzed in this way, leading to the theory of Flow.

These studies have indicated that the phenomenology of flow includes eight elements, as follows:

1. Experience occurs where one is confronted with challenges that can be met with available skills (where one is neither over- or undertaxed).

2. Concentration is applied to the experience.
3. and 4. Concentration is facilitated when the task undertaken has clear goals and can generate immediate feedback.
5. Deep but effortless participation occurs that is free from everyday anxiety.
6. A sense of control is exercised over actions.
7. Focus on self vanishes, while a stronger sense of self emerges following the flow experience.
8. The sense of time is altered, so that it may seem like time has stretched out or passed quickly.

Worldwide research (Csikszentmihalyi, 1990) conducted on flow using the ESM suggests quite clearly that people can translate potentially entropic experience into flow by applying these key steps: Set goals; become immersed in the activity; pay attention to what is occurring; get feedback; learn to enjoy immediate experiences; derive meaning from these experiences. Flow provides another route to what we are calling "everyday prevention."

Wellness

Lifestyles matter. For example, lifestyle factors account for as much as 80% of the incidence of cardiovascular disease (CVD). For many, therefore, CVD can be preventable, yet 950,000 Americans die of this disease every year, incurring $352 billion in medical costs. Such specific lifestyle behaviors as cigarette smoking, obesity, high cholesterol, unbuffered stress, untreated diabetes, and weakened social supports contribute to the onset of cardiovascular disease.

Wellness is a health-promoting perspective rooted in positive lifestyle choices that are made on a daily basis. Making healthy lifestyle choices each day is important to what I mean by everyday prevention. Wellness reflects a concern with optimum human functioning, and it draws from holistic, developmental, and preventive sources (Myers, 1992). Wellness is not the absence of illness but a lifestyle, a way of being that reflects positive choices aimed at enhancing daily living and serving to prevent disease and illness.

There are different ways to conceptualize what comprises wellness. As Greenberg (1985) described it, wellness involves the integration of the major components of health: physical, social, mental, emotional, and spiritual, with "high-level wellness" resulting when these integrated components are also in balance. Hettler (1991) extended the conception of wellness, focused largely on the university student population, to include the domains of occupational and of intellectual wellness. Witmer and Sweeney (1992) developed a holistic, life-span model for wellness that is based on Adlerian counseling theory. They identified five life tasks that represent the characteristics of healthy individuals. These life tasks may take on different aspects for people at different phases of human development. A retiree has different issues surrounding these life tasks than an elementary school student, for example. The life tasks are: spirituality, self-regulation, work, friendship, and love. Witmer and Sweeney indicated that these life tasks interact continuously with life forces: family, community, religion, education, government, media, and business/industry, as well as being influenced by global events such as wars and pollution.

Myers (1992, 2003) outlined several ways that counselors can assist others in wellness pursuits. Because wellness is generally understood as a process that is based on daily lifestyle choices made by individuals, counselors can further wellness through education and through assistance with making choices.

The work of Prochaska and Norcross (2003) on a transtheoretical therapy model based on processes and stages of change is important in relation to wellness education. This model suggests that what to change (levels) depends on doing the right things (processes) at the right time (stages). For instance, education about the need to open up with others (a form of Hettler's emotional wellness) can assist with those who are at early stages of change readiness, while helping with making choices about self-disclosing with a loved one can occur most effectively at a later stage of change readiness.

Wellness initiatives that are directed at individuals or through programs to groups and populations can address any of the dimensions that have been touched on above. For example, based on Hettler's (1991) six dimensions of wellness, these initiatives can target the following (Myers, 1992).

Social Wellness

Wellness education and choice-making assistance addresses improving relationships, support networks, connections with the community, and general involvement with others. Applications might entail becoming involved in a support group or serving in a soup kitchen, among many others.

Connecting with others activates the therapeutic factor of altruism (Yalom, 1995), and it is socially supportive (Pearson, 1990). It can aid one's development in multiple ways. The "helping connection" is discovered when volunteers engage in regular, helping, face-to-face contact with a variety of people they do not know for at least one hour per week. These activities may include tutoring, cleaning up the environment, delivering toys or food to needy families, raking leaves for senior citizens, raising money for needed surgery, and countless other projects. (For an especially dense concentration of such involvements, note the "Make a Difference Day" events that occur during National Volunteer Week in April). Luks (2001) documented the value of altruism by asking 3000 volunteers at 20 different organizations how they felt when they did something kind. He found that medical and scientific documentation of the responses of those who help others revealed the following common experiences:

A more optimistic and happier outlook on life
A heightened sense of well-being
A sense of exhilaration and euphoria
An increase in energy
A feeling of being healthy
A decrease in feelings of loneliness, depression, and helplessness
A sense of connectedness with others
A greater sense of calmness and relaxation
Better weight control
An improvement in insomnia
A stronger immune system
A reduction in pain
An increase in body warmth
A healthier cardiovascular system
Speedier recovery from surgery

Many described physical sensations akin to those experienced by people who exercise vigorously, when the body releases endorphins, a natural painkiller. That feeling was typically followed by a longer-lasting period of calm, a phenomenon dubbed the "helper's high."

Physical Wellness

Physical activity is one of 10 leading health indicators. It is central to the health objectives set out for the United States, captured by the initiative "Healthy People 2010" (Office of Disease Prevention and Health Promotion, 2002). Physical wellness includes, but exceeds, physical activity. Physical wellness involves making healthy lifestyle choices in physical activity, nutrition, physical safety (e.g., using seat belts), and preventive medical care, as well as avoiding drug use. People can be educated and learn to make positive daily choices in such areas as losing weight, stopping smoking, and exercising daily. Implementing such physical wellness measures clearly affects psychological and emotional health. For instance, I am training for a running marathon (26.2 miles). This daily and demanding regimen (e.g., I ran 19 miles in the snow last Saturday, and "paid for it" on Sunday and Monday!) affects many other aspects of my life. I eat more but don't gain weight, have lost fatty tissue, have lowered my cholesterol level and pulse rate, and think that I manage stress more easily. But I am also much consumed by getting ready for this event, and it takes a lot of time to train, both of which serve to lessen my availability to others.

Occupational Wellness

This dimension of wellness involves deriving satisfaction and personal enrichment from one's work or career. The place of leisure in one's life also may be related to occupational wellness. Occupational values and interests, life experience and roles, aptitude, contextual supports and constraints, and other career development variables are important to consider in relation to this dimension (Super & Sverko, 1995; Wicker & August, 2000). I fall victim, as do many of my colleagues, to complaining about how hard we work (of course, working hard also is a "badge of honor" for too many). There is not nearly enough time. We say we are doing way too much, isn't there any relief? In fact, we may be out of balance in this domain. Examining why this may be is important. For instance, if one reason is choice—that is, I choose rather than am told to take on responsibilities—then perhaps something can be done to reduce the stress being experienced.

Spiritual Wellness

This wellness dimension centers on seeking and finding meaning in daily life and discovering meaning and purpose in one's overall existence (Reker & Chamberlain, 2000). This exploration may be driven by spiritual and/or religious motivation (e.g., Burke & Miranti, 1995), or it may be secular (Frankl, 1962); considerable scholarly work is under way today exploring both approaches.

Counseling from an existential theoretical base has always illuminated issues of meaning with clients. Other approaches may include those from an Eastern perspective, such as meditation and yoga. Still others may be focused on values clarification and choice-making through workshops and groups. Connections between religious practice may be explored with clients by counselors who are comfortable with this domain, referrals can be made to pastoral counselors or to clerics, and program collaboration between counselors and religious organizations (i.e., churches, synagogues, mosques, temples) are occurring with increased frequency.

Intellectual Wellness

This domain of wellness focuses on gaining knowledge, on enhancing one's mental acuity, and on appraising events in an accurate and healthy manner (e.g., Beck, 1991; Neimeyer, 1993). Mental stimulation and growth can be accomplished through active involvement with tasks, such as doing crossword puzzles, reading books, surfing the Internet, tutoring others, and generally being active with challenging problems.

Intellectual wellness also can be enhanced through being socially engaged, that is, getting together with friends and family, and sharing private thoughts and concerns. Ybarra studied the relationship between social engagement and cognitive functioning in both the United States and Middle Eastern countries. The author's conclusions demonstrated a positive correlation between higher levels of social engagement and lower levels of impaired cognitive functioning.

Remaining intellectually engaged is important at all ages and is uniquely significant as one matures into "senior status." Although much emphasis is placed on important lifestyle practices such as exercise and diet in "staying younger," intellectual activity seems to get relatively short shrift. A significant marker for long life and the prevention of Alzheimer's disease is found in mental involvement. Studies with people who have dementia, for example, have found that those who engaged regularly in mind-stimulation activities (watching television, playing cards and other games, visiting museums) realized a decreased incidence of Alzheimer's disease, compared with those in a control group situation.

Emotional Wellness

Both emotional awareness and emotional management are aspects of this wellness domain. To function well, people need to be aware of their thoughts and feelings, and how to monitor and manage them effectively and appropriately. This domain has received the most attention from counselors and other helpers, especially in terms of remediation (e.g., see counseling theory texts) but also with skill-building programs for those functioning without major dysfunction (e.g., see Lewis, Lewis, Daniels, & D'Andrea, 2003). Moreover, counselor educators and counseling psychologists have developed effective skill-training programs to help trainees in their work with clients (e.g., Cormier & Nurius, 2003; Ivey & Ivey, 2003). Counselors can draw from a vast reservoir of activities to assist people to develop an enhanced emotional wellness (e.g., Kraus, 2003). Stress management, communication skills, guided imagery, psychoeducation groups, and other vehicles for personal growth are frequently used.

Mutual Interaction of the Wellness Dimensions

These six dimensions of wellness are not independent, even though each is described as if it were. That is more a matter of communication convenience. In reality, these dimensions mutually interact.

Humans are not compartmentalized into separate domains where the mind exists separate from the body. Wellness enhancements to develop mental functioning can benefit physical functioning, and the reverse. Becoming more physically fit can elevate mood, for instance. Enhancements in the social domain very well may affect the spiritual domain, and vice versa.

Becoming more connected with others may evolve a deeper sense of connection with nature. So, it is proper to think in terms of the "human system," where people incorporate interactive combinations of these and other domains, and in relation to larger systems, such as family, school, work, and community, in which they are embedded.

Optimum human development is the goal of wellness initiatives, whatever the domains of interest. This goal is completely consistent with "everyday prevention." Helping people at any of multiple levels of intervention (e.g., individual to population) to become all that they can be in as many wellness domains as possible—each and every day—is a worthy goal for all counselors.

Essential Qualities of Highly Healthy People

The popular press is replete with products that address healthy functioning. Larimore (2003) has developed a set of strategies derived from his medical practice in sports and family medicine and a survey he conducted of more than 3000 doctors all over the world. He reduced the survey data into what he terms the 10 "essentials" of highly healthy people. These essential characteristics are:

1. Balancing physical, emotional-mental, social, and spiritual domains, which is the essential key to maintaining a state of high healthiness
2. Self-care, with people becoming their own "health-care quarterback," which contributes to medicine becoming increasingly more patient-centered than doctor-centered
3. Forgiveness of self and others, which frees up energy for positive growth
4. Reducing stress, depression, and anxiety, through learning skills and techniques and engaging in behaviors to buffer or reduce these problem areas
5. Relationships, or socially connecting with others in a deep and meaningful way
6. Spirituality, or developing a faith in a power higher than oneself
7. Positive self-image, or accepting and feeling good about oneself
8. Aspirations, or setting life goals that motivate and guide energy
9. Personal responsibility and empowerment, or taking charge of one's life through choices and actions that are self-propelling and do not intentionally affect others negatively
10. Teamwork, the capacity to work effectively with other people to accomplish goals

Larimore emphasizes the role of balance in maintaining health. To illustrate this point, he uses the metaphor of health being a four-wheeled vehicle, with each wheel representing one of the following domains: physical, emotional and mental, social or relationships, and spiritual. If any of these wheels gets out of balance, then the vehicle provides a bumpy ride or might eventually break down. Larimore emphasizes that it is very important to keep the four wheels operating effectively and efficiently as a balanced system.

Life Skills

Life skills are organized, specific tools that people can learn and apply in everyday prevention. The United Nations International Children's Emergency Fund (UNICEF), the World Health Organization (WHO), and several training programs have focused on a related construct: life skills. Each source begun to identify sets of life skills that seem generally important in boosting children and adolescents' self-confidence, self-esteem, self-control, and autonomy, as well as being better able to resist or avoid potential problems, such as substance abuse.

UNICEF (1997) has recognized three major categories of life skills:

1. Basic psychological and social skills that are strongly shaped by cultural and social values
2. Situation-specific skills, such as negotiation, assertiveness, and resolving conflicts
3. Applied life skills, including refusing drugs and challenging gender roles

The WHO has developed a set of life skills to be included within school-based programs. These life skills are intended to help young people to make healthy lifestyle choices and to reach optimal physical, social, and psychological well-being. WHO (1993) considers the following set of life skills to be most generally essential abilities and skills, but each is dependent on cultural influences. These are the ability to:

Make decisions
Solve problems
Think creatively
Think critically
Communicate effectively
Establish and maintain interpersonal relations
Develop knowledge of self

Feel empathy
Manage emotions
Handle tension and stress

Botvin and Tortu (1988), Botvin and Kantor (2000), and Botvin, Griffin, Paul, and Macaulay (2003) have developed a life skills training curriculum for preventing substance abuse for middle or junior high school students (see Chapter 6 for elaboration). The program has demonstrated effectiveness not only with White students but also with Hispanic and African-American populations, with behavioral effects on smoking, alcohol, marijuana use, and multiple substances and illicit drugs. It is designed to impact substance abuse knowledge, attitudes, skills, and norms. A foundation for the program is that social skills are key vehicles that people need to function effectively, and that their mastery improves the quality of life and can prevent a host of both specific and general negative consequences.

The program is based on a group-based approach to teaching life skills (but also uses other methods) aimed at resisting social influences that may encourage drug use and to promoting the development of self-management and interpersonal skills. The life skill components that are taught follow a cognitive-behavioral approach and involve episodes of instruction, demonstration, behavioral rehearsal, feedback, social reinforcement, and focused practice that includes homework assignments and booster sessions.

The Life Skills Training program includes three major parts: (1) general self-management skills, (2) social skills, and (3) information and skills specifically related to drug use. Each part contains a number of 45-minute sessions that can be delivered as an intensive mini-course or once a week. Skills are taught in a psychoeducation group format using strategies of instruction, demonstration, feedback, reinforcement, and practice.

There is considerable agreement across life skills "systems" about what the life skills are and how they can be beneficial. Life skills represent a particularly strong potential for everyday prevention due to their highly teachable nature.

Positive Youth Development (PYD)

Positive Youth Development (PYD) is an approach to prevention that emphasizes the development of youth in context rather than attempting to prevent separate problems faced by youths (Pittman & Fleming, 1991). Many youth outcomes are affected by the same protective and risk factors, making interventions that address several personal-social and setting domains important.

A set of PYD constructs has been developed in an effort to operationally define positive youth development. These constructs are relevant to our discussion of everyday prevention. Positive Youth Development programs and strategies seek generally to achieve one or more of the following objectives (Catalano, Berglund, Ryan, Lonczak, & Hawkins, 2002):

1. *Promote bonding:* developing a child's relationship with a healthy adult, positive peers, school, community, or culture
2. *Foster resilience:* developing adaptive coping strategies to stress and change, and enhancing flexibility and overall capacity
3. *Promote social competence:* developing appropriate interpersonal skills in such areas as communication and conflict resolution
4. *Promote emotional competence:* developing skills in identifying and managing feelings and emotional reactions, such as in empathy and frustration tolerance
5. *Promote cognitive competence:* developing ability to use logic, analytic thinking, abstract reasoning, problem solving, goal setting, and related skills
6. *Promote behavioral competence:* developing skills in nonverbal and verbal communication and in taking prosocial action
7. *Promote moral competence:* developing empathy, a sense of right and wrong, what is moral and just, and a respect for rules and standards
8. *Foster self-determination:* developing the ability to think for one-self, to take action that matches the thought, to be autonomous, and to be able to chart one's own course
9. *Foster spirituality:* developing a belief in a higher power, a belief system, or a sense of spiritual identity/meaning/practice
10. *Foster self-efficacy:* developing a sense that one can accomplish goals through one's own action, involving personal goal setting, mastery skills, and ways to reverse self-defeating thoughts
11. *Foster clear and positive identity:* developing a coherent sense of self, including positive identification with a supportive social or cultural subgroup
12. *Foster belief in the future:* developing a belief about the future that is based on optimism about possibilities
13. *Provide recognition for positive behavior:* developing ways to reward positive behaviors
14. *Provide opportunities for pro-social involvement:* developing strategies for becoming actively involved in pro-social activities, making a contribution, and experiencing healthy interactions with others
15. *Foster pro-social norms:* developing understanding of accurate normative behavior (e.g., the number of contemporaries who

actually use drugs), mentoring to assist others (and oneself) with forward movement, creating clear expectations for minimizing health risks, and enhancing social support (pp. 15–22)

These 15 PYD objectives provide a robust direction not only for professionals to pursue but also for everyday prevention efforts. Relatedly, Lopez and McKnight (2002) discussed what they termed "light-handed interventions" in PYD. Light-handed interventions are everyday occurrences that can make a difference in peoples' lives (also known as experiences that enhance competency). These authors proposed that an efficient approach to PYD might be facilitated by what they termed "everyday luxuries" in which all youth do not have opportunities to indulge, such as attending a sporting event or a musical, relaxing, playing, and writing about life events.

Personal Health Care

Personal health care is very much on the leading edge of everyday prevention, as mentioned earlier in this chapter. According to national survey results conducted in 2002 by the Stanford Center for Research in Disease Prevention, nearly 70% of Americans use alternative heathcare and therapy approaches for personal health care. This percentage has escalated from 47% in 1998. It is estimated that $27 billion per year is spent on these approaches in the United States (Owens Scott, 2003).

The source from which this last item was extracted, *Spirituality & Health: The Soul/Body Connection* (Web site: www.SpiritualityHealth.com), is an appropriate example of media participation in the personal health-care movement. Another example includes *Psychology Today* (Web site: www.psychologytoday.com), which has addressed mental health issues for the public for decades. Another long-standing popular publication that translates scientific information to the consumer is the magazine, *Prevention* (Web site: www.prevention.com). The following "Message to Readers" appears in each issue of that magazine: "Every month *Prevention* brings you up-to-date health information that's thoroughly researched and factchecked. Our aim is not to replace your medical caregiver but to help you achieve a healthy lifestyle." My aim is not to promote these three magazines or Web sites as superior to others, but to present them as illustrations of how good, personal healthcare information is available to the average consumer today.

Perhaps located at a step between the popular press and professional scientific journals are reputable newsletters on health and wellness. Three of these are the University of California-Berkeley *Wellness Letter* (Web site: www.berkeleywellness.com), the *Harvard Health Letter* (Web site: www.health.harvard/edu), and the *Johns Hopkins Health after 50 Newsletter* (Web site: www.hopkinsafter50.com). These sources, through hard copy or via the Internet, provide consumers with regular, direct, and salient, scientifically valid information about a range of wellness and lifestyle issues.

Complementary and Alternative Medicine (CAM) and Integrative Medicine

The federal government also has formally recognized the wide attention to and participation in personal healthcare practices. The venerable National Institutes of Health has established and funded its National Center for Complementary and Alternative Medicine (NCCAM). NCCAM defines Complementary and Alternative Medicine (CAM) as a group of medical and healthcare systems, practices, and products that are not currently included within conventional medicine. Complementary medicine is used together with conventional medicine, whereas alternative medicine is used in place of conventional medicine.

Major types of CAM include:

1. *Alternative medical systems.* Examples are traditional Chinese medicine and homeopathic medicine
2. *Mind-body interventions.* Examples include prayer, meditation, and therapies using the creative arts
3. *Biologically based therapies.* Examples include naturally occurring substances, such as herbs, foods, and vitamins
4. *Manipulative and body-based methods.* Examples include chiropractic and osteopathic manipulation, and therapeutic massage
5. *Energy therapies.* These include biofield therapies (e.g., qi gong, Reiki therapeutic touch) and bioelectromagnetic-based therapies (e.g., magnetic fields, alternating current, or direct current fields) (http://nccam.nih.gov)

Integrative medicine combines mainstream medical approaches with those CAM therapies that hold scientific evidence of safety and effectiveness. Dr. Dean Ornish (1990) developed an integrative medicine program for reversing heart disease without drugs or surgery. The program, called the "Opening Your Heart" program, is designed to change the relationship between lifestyle and health. Ornish claims that those who followed the program most fully accomplished the greatest reversal in their coronary artery blockages. The program consists of several interlocking everyday prevention general components:

Techniques for increasing self awareness
Techniques for increasing intimacy with others
Techniques for connecting to a higher power
Techniques for managing stress more effectively

> A diet very low in fat and cholesterol
> A system to stop smoking and remove other addictions
> A program of moderate exercise

Many of these program components are familiar to counselors. Let us take a closer look at one such familiar component: increasing intimacy with others. This program goal is approached through working on improving: (a) communication skills, (b) altruism, compassion, and forgiveness, and (c) group support and sharing secrets.

With regard to group support and sharing secrets, the Opening Heart program asserts what counselors have long known:

> But if you never have any place that you feel safe enough to show who you really are, anyone with whom you can really be yourself, then . . . it's ultimately stressful and isolating (p. 225)

Participants in the study met twice a week in a small group to discuss their progress and any problems. As these groups evolved, it became obvious that they provided a means to achieve a deeper level of sharing and a greater source of both intimacy and altruism. Members valued the closeness, the opportunity to connect and to reveal parts of themselves to others that had long been kept hidden. The sense of community that emerged seemed to become a very important part of the overall program.

The Opening Heart program for reversing heart disease is directed at those who have a diagnosed heart disease. All of the program components were closely monitored. Positive results were found.

Ornish suggests that this program has the potential to be far more than a treatment program for those already suffering. He offers it as a comprehensive personal system to help heal not only the heart but also the soul. He suggests that people from all walks of life (after securing any needed physician review) try it out. He puts it this way:

> Try it and see. In only seven days, see how much better you feel, whether or not you have a heart problem. In four weeks your cholesterol level will be significantly lower. After a few months, I hope you'll recognize even more profound and rewarding changes in how you look and feel. Experience the difference for yourself. (p. 6)

Person-Centered Areas in Summary

All the approaches discussed in this chapter are central to promoting "everyday prevention." Their components have much in common. The key is to find a good plan and to follow it persistently. Everyday prevention requires people to incorporate these ways into their ongoing lifestyle on a daily basis, by choosing to enact a set of personal "best practices"—just as we have best practices for psychotherapy, group work, and other professional service modes of delivery. Everyday prevention can occur when people institute personal best practices each and every day within their life contexts. It can improve one's life and prevent many problems through ordinary, normal, everyday best practice, such as connecting with and helping others regularly, developing positive emotions such as hope and optimism about the future, seeking happiness that is linked with a deep investment in meaningful activity, opening up to and providing support for others, exercising physically each day, and finding ways to relax and revitalize. The challenge for counselors and other helpers is to develop strategies for promoting everyday prevention in their ongoing work.

SYSTEM-CENTERED AREAS THAT EVERYDAY PREVENTION CAN ADDRESS

A Way to Conceptualize Systems as Settings and Levels

As powerful as person-centered approaches are, everyday prevention cannot be fully accomplished exclusively through implementing person-centered best practices. The person-centered perspective must be balanced with a system-centered one. People live their lives in context and in systems, and each is mutually influencing (Walsh, Craik, & Price, 2000). This is an ecological perspective (Conyne & Cook, 2004), and it is central to prevention in general.

Involvement in organizations provides one example of the person-environment context. Based on organizational ecology, Becker and Steele (1995) have envisioned five key criteria for organizational health that can illustrate everyday prevention from a system-centered perspective. These organizational health criteria are as follows:

A sense of personal and work identity is fostered
Reality testing is provided so that members can get feedback
Task accomplishment is realized
Problem solving and adaptability are supported
Energy flow is fostered from members connecting, collaborating, and generating together

Another example of this ecological perspective is captured by the notion, "habitats of the heart" (Little, 2000). That is, people link with environments and tend to value those special places and personal niches (Willi, 1999) where they can be themselves, pursue fundamentally important projects, communicate deeply, and realize interpersonal effectiveness. Incidentally, just as the "good life" mentioned earlier lacks a taxonomy, please also note that there is no existing taxonomy of situations or environments that promotes human functioning (Hogan & Roberts, 2000) either, although Insel and Moos (1974) and Eccles and Gootman (2001) have made useful contributions. This deficit also needs correcting so that prevention can proceed more clearly: taxonomies for the "good life" and situations that foster human growth both are awaiting development.

Perhaps we can make a start by identifying some important ways in which everyday prevention can occur within major systems of our lives. I draw from an adaptation of Maton (2000) to Bronfenbrenner's classic conception of ecosystem levels (i.e., microsystem, mesosystem, exosystem, and macrosystem).

Maton envisioned a person interacting within and across settings (family, neighborhood, workplace, school). These settings, in turn, are embedded within an ever-enlarging set of mutually influencing levels (community, society, world). This model provides a way to conceptualize people within environments using concepts (e.g., settings and levels) that are common to our experience. It shows how people interact within and across settings that are embedded within increasingly complex levels, explicating one way to view everyday prevention from a system-centered perspective. People will not become successful preventive agents in their own lives by seeking person change only. These efforts must be contextualized.

Felner and Adan (1988) instituted an outstanding example of a successful contextualized prevention program in their Ecological–Transactional School Program (see Chapter 6 for a more extensive discussion). In this effort, middle school students who were to transition developmentally upon graduation to the bigger and less structured high school environment were assisted in that move through restructuring the high school situation in such a way as to reduce the ongoing flux. For instance, the redesigned high school environment allowed students to operate from a homeroom with a consistent set of fellow students and a homeroom teacher, and to take classes in adjacent rooms.

The program illustrates clearly how system change can be beneficial. Yet in this case prevention planners, not the students, designed and implemented the system changes. Compared with the work that has been done and is ongoing in developing person-centered skills and strategies (see above), much less work has been done to date on how people can directly and intentionally affect the systems of their lives and on what kinds of competencies would be appropriate. The list of 10 strategies below represents a start.

TEN SYSTEM-CENTERED STRATEGIES FOR EVERYDAY PREVENTION

Needed is a set of system-centered actions or best practices, comparable to the various sets of person-centered best practices that you read about earlier in this chapter. (Note that this section on system-centered best practices is considerably shorter than the one devoted to person-centered best practices, reflecting the relative amount of development in each area.) The operable question is: "What can people do within settings and systems to improve their own health and that of others?" Some useful directions can be found in the counselor social advocacy literature (e.g., Lee & Walz, 1998; Lewis, Arnold, House, & Toporek, 2002), but little exists in relation to how people can become "everyday preventionists" through system-centered involvement.

The following 10 suggestions are guided by Maton's setting-level analysis (1999) and others cited here:

1. Develop relationships and support (Insel & Moos, 1974) within and across settings (Maton, 2000) because it is through human relationships that people feel validated and supported.

2. Connect with the natural environment (Capra, 1996) because people and societies are embedded in and dependent on the cyclical processes of nature.

3. View oneself as an active participant in and across settings— family, work, school, neighborhood/community (Maton, 2000)— because passive acceptance or ignorance of events and conditions fosters dysfunction, while active participation can empower change. The value of volunteering ("helping connection") to help others is a powerful means.

4. Collaborate with others on responsible change efforts in and across settings (Maton, 2000; Moos, 1973), as collaboration with others provides the best means of effecting social improvement.

5. Empower oneself and others toward greater opportunity, mastery, and collective efficacy (Bandura, 1997; McWhirter, 1994). Empowerment in context becomes the guiding frame of reference to building genuine mastery.

6. Work with others to create positive settings (Eccles & Gootman, 2001; Insel & Moos, 1974) that are characterized by being physically and psychologically safe; appropriately structured, flexible, and orderly; supportive and challenging; providing opportunities to belong; possess positive social norms; furnish support for efficacy and mattering; generate opportunites for autonomy and skill building; and integrate efforts across family, school, work, and community.

7. Become more aware of how distal forces (e.g., world economic, political, and educational policies; media and advertising messages) affect the self and others (Bronfenbrenner, 1979; Maton, 2000). Our everyday life experience is influenced by local forces as well as by distant ones. Finding a University of Cincinnati

Bearcats basketball hat for sale on a remote outer Chinese island was a surprise to me, but it also tangibly illustrates how we are all part of one globe and how interdependence predominates.

8. Develop resilience (Masten & Reed, 2002), or the capacity for good adaptation under extenuating circumstances. This is a powerful resource. People cannot control events and experiences, but they can learn how to cope well in response to surprises and challenges.

9. Develop social well-being (Keyes & Lopez, 2002), including social acceptance, social actualization, social contribution, social coherence, and social integration (see earlier discussion in this chapter about social well-being).

10. Develop environmental competence (Steele, 1973) and ecological concordance (Conyne & Cook, 2004), or the ability to be aware of one's environment and its impact—and of one's impact on the environment—and to use or change it to provide a more optimal fit.

ROLE OF THE COUNSELOR IN EVERYDAY PREVENTION

Everyday prevention is conceptualized as a continuous program of involvements that people engage in directly within their life contexts. These involvements might be consistent with any of the broad array of person- and system-centered domains discussed in this chapter.

A chief characteristic of everyday prevention, therefore, is the locus of change. Everyday prevention is not something that counselors do but what people do. Counselors, however, as well as other healthcare providers and educators, can be of great assistance in helping people to exercise everyday prevention within their ongoing life contexts.

The counselor role in everyday prevention is to serve as an "honest broker," linking and spreading knowledge, skills, and strategies with individual clients, groups, in organizations, communities, and across a designated population through:

1. Prevention programs that have demonstrated effectiveness (such as the Opening Heart program, but many others, as well: see Chapters 5 through 8 on Prevention Programs in Family, School, Community, and Work Settings)

2. Sets of person-centered skills (such as in the Life Skills program, but many others as well: see Chapter 9)

3. Sets of system-centered skills (these need further development, but an example might be how to develop support in a setting)

4. To develop and/or to adapt effective prevention programs to be spread broadly through new applications (see Chapter 4)
5. To infuse everyday prevention within all aspects of their work, that is, seeking toempower people and systems to become more fully functioning on a daily basis

Everyday prevention is undertaken by people within their ordinary lives. These people are the change agents, the decision makers, the enacters of prevention in their own lives. Counselors can assist people in reaching that goal. Indeed, that is the premise underlying the subtitle of this book on preventive counseling: "Helping People to Become Empowered in Systems and Settings."

CONCLUSION

Everyday prevention is a new goal for prevention. Indeed, prevention remains a main goal for service delivery and needs to be used more in this way. However, in addition, prevention needs to be understood as a way of life. Lifestyles and choices within lifestyles are strong influencers of health and dysfunction. They represent avenues through which people can exert some personal control, at least within reason. In addition, developmental pathways (settings, contexts, processes) exert an everyday influence on peoples' lives, and this influence often can be enhanced or modified through intentional action. Although everyday prevention is not the exclusive property of helping professionals but is available to everyone, practitioners can assist its broader-scale adoption through their work. The key is to intentionally empower people in systems to become their own everyday preventionists, thus enhancing their lives, those of others around them, and the systems in which they function.

ISSUES FOR REFLECTION AND DISCUSSION

1. You are a seventh grade teacher who has just attended a continuing education workshop on "everyday prevention." You want to communicate this concept to your 25 students through some type of interesting and involving 30-minute class exercise. Sketch out some ideas and then pair up with another person to jointly create two learning exercises.
2. Take a few minutes to survey your life. What are you doing that is consonant with everyday prevention? What seems contradictory? How might you strengthen the current "successes" and how might you change the discrepancies? Be specific.

3. Everyday prevention can be used to improve systems, settings, contexts, and so on. Choose a concrete example of a system, setting, or context of which you are a part (e.g., your family, a religious institution, an academic program, a neighborhood, your work, etc.). How might everyday prevention be applied in that setting?

4. Positive psychology was discussed at some length in this chapter. How does positive psychology connect with helping professions today? What is its relationship to your own discipline or profession (e.g., counseling, counseling psychology, social work)?

5. How can you integrate everyday prevention in your counseling practice? What would you do the same or differently? What skills would you draw from especially? How could you tell if you were being effective?

CHAPTER 3

A Conceptual Model

FIVE GENERAL STRATEGIES OF PREVENTION

Let us now move to examine strategies in prevention, building from the realization that "everyday prevention" (see Chapter 2) is a goal that should infuse every strategy. The most thorough review of prevention strategies has been accomplished in the volume edited by Gullotta and Bloom (2003). This study identified five strategies, observing that they are not exclusive and often blend, and that the most effective prevention efforts usually employ some combination of them.

This chapter on a model for preventive counseling will begin with a review of these general prevention strategies. Then, we will explore how these strategies can be incorporated within a model of counselor interventions (the Counselor Functioning Cube of Morrill, Oetting, & Hurst, 1974). This integration will yield a model for preventive counseling, which will be the focus of the remainder of the chapter.

Education is the most frequently used prevention strategy. However, by itself, education generally cannot produce lasting, sustainable change because attitudes, behavior, and conditions surrounding the learner are not usually affected (Gullotta & Bloom, 2003). Despite that deficiency, education is an important preventive strategy. Gullotta and Bloom point out that education takes three forms: (1) public information, in the form of messages (e.g., warnings on alcohol bottles); (2) anticipatory guidance, in the form of teaching or training about an event prior to its occurrence (e.g., pre-retirement programs); and (3) self-instruction, where people learn how to manage their own thoughts, emotions, or behavior (e.g., cognitive-behavioral self-talk).

The five general prevention strategies are:

1. Education Strategy in Prevention

2. General Prevention Strategies (Gullotta & Bloom, 2003)

3. Education

4. Social Competency Facilitation

5. Natural Caregiving

6. Community Organizing and Systems Intervention (COSI)

7. Redesign of the Physical Environment

An instructional strategy I am experimenting with at the University of Cincinnati is called Problem-Based Learning (PBL). In PBL, students are organized into small groups and are given a predeveloped problem that is intended to be real world in nature, fuzzily phrased, and complex—the last two criteria requiring the participation of all in the group to "solve" the problem. PBL is a form of active, experientially based learning that leads with a problem, not with a lecture. Students need to determine what they know, what they don't know but need to learn, and how to do that. They need to form and work in an effective team to accomplish their tasks. Assessment indicates that content learning is no better or worse in PBL classes than in other educational strategies, but that additional objectives can be realized in PBL: improved skills in team functioning, problem solving, and communication skills. PBL can serve as a preventive educational strategy by helping students to gain or enhance life skills that will enable them to function more effectively and be more satisfied in the "real world." Moreover, PBL may represent an educational strategy that contradicts the consistent evidence that educational strategies cannot produce broader or durable change.

Social Competency-Facilitation Strategy in Prevention

Social competency involves connecting people to groups and communities in viable ways through which they both make contributions and receive benefits simultaneously. Belonging, being of value, feeling satisfied, enjoying a sense of mastery and self-efficacy, and possessing a positive self-esteem are all associated with social competency. Social competency can be fostered through such means as volunteering at a soup kitchen, reading to a blind person, or mentoring an adolescent from an impoverished environment. As was pointed out in Chapter 2, the "helping connection" is a major contributor to benefits in our society, both for those helped and for those providing the voluntary assistance.

My son Zachary (age 17) served as a teacher in a local Summerbridge program last summer. The purpose of the program is to help middle school students from low SES situations to better "bridge" into the next level of schooling for them and to more broadly affect their level of aspiration. Zack wound up working long hours and being energized by the role demands he was facing. He got to really participate in the role of teacher and saw kids become challenged, supported, and progress. He would be the first to acknowledge that he learned and benefited as much as, and maybe more, than the middle school students who were enrolled in the program.

Natural Caregiving Strategy in Prevention

This strategy refers to people in their natural environment being of help and service to others, without the direct involvement of counselors or other helping professionals. Gullotta (1987) identified three forms of natural caregiving: (1) the mutual self-help group, where people of like minds and needs come together to share, support, and help each other through life demands; (2) the indigenous trained caregivers, those who are trained in a profession (but not in mental health) and to whom people often turn for assistance, support, advice, and comfort (e.g., clergy, teachers, and police); and (3) indigenous caregiving, people who have no particular training related to helping but are instinctively sought out by others for help, including friends, family, barbers, and bartenders.

Prevention can be well served by finding ways to support the naturally occurring sources of caring that operate daily within our families, neighborhoods, schools, workplaces, and places of formal and informal service delivery. Chapter 2 mentioned the "Ruby and Oren Principle," where natural support was obtained and provided through more than 35 years of weekly card playing. Many other examples of such indigenous support can be identified, such as the role of the beauty parlor or the barbershop in African-American culture—not just related to caring for the hair, but also to caring of the person, the easy and helpful exchange of relevant information, and the sustenance of meaningful connections.

Community Organizing and Systems Intervention (COSI) Strategy in Prevention

Gullotta and Bloom indicate that the COSI prevention strategy is the most powerful. This strategy is concerned with how a community provides opportunities and support for involving people in community activities and processes, particularly as these relate to governance and quality of life. There are four types of COSI: (1) community development, where people participate to express their concerns and develop solutions related to important aspects of community life (e.g., crime, recreation, politics, race relations); (2) systems intervention, where existing institutions and organizations are led to examine their practices, policies, and procedures to correct dysfunction and make them more effective (e.g., adding a local school decision-making committee to increase parent involvement in the school); and (3) legislative change and judicial action, where preventive initiatives are pursued through advocating with lawmakers and judges to provide for broad, sweeping change (*note*: not everyone may approve or even benefit from such legislation).

The city of Cincinnati, where I live, has experienced race-related disturbances in its inner-city core, called "Over-the-Rhine," so-named by the German immigrants who saw a resemblance of the area to the old country they had left behind. My Preventive Counseling class was set to hold its first class meeting of the spring quarter in an Over-the-Rhine community service agency when, the night before, a riot broke out, closing down the whole area for a few days. Originally contracted to provide consultation for developing a preventive program on family education, we had to reconfigure our purposes to fit more appropriately within the changing community dynamics—as well as to reevaluate whether the conditions were suited to this kind of work at that time. This whole series of events provided a superb opportunity to examine community dynamics, race relations, and the role of an "outside" group entering a community system to "do good." We did finally conduct our work within the agency, but it took on a different aspect: much more the listener than the doer, much more the collaborator than the intervener. Context is important in all change efforts, and, within the community, it simply cannot be ignored.

Redesign of the Physical Environment Strategy in Prevention

This strategy, as discussed by Gullotta and Bloom, refers to how built and natural environments can coexist in such a way as to promote an ecologically sustainable future. Lewin's conception that behavior is a function of people interacting with environments ($B = P \times E$) is a venerable one in the helping fields. This ecological perspective is beginning to receive renewed attention (e.g., see Conyne & Cook, 2004). Within this perspective, the issue of sustainability is critically important. Fast, expensive, or intrusive solutions to problems may not be the most ecologically appropriate or hold the most promise for health and continuation (Conoley & Haynes, 1992). When considering the redesign of physical environments as a prevention strategy, Geller's (2003) imperative of increasing Environmental Responsible Behaviors (ERB), while decreasing environmentally destructive ones, represents an important goal for creating a world sustained by harmony and equilibrium among all species.

An Additional Strategy: Developmental Pathways

These five strategies are not necessarily inclusive of all important prevention strategies. One significant strategy Felner, Felner, & Silverman, 2000 omitted is enhancing, disrupting, or modifying the developmental pathways (processes, settings, and conditions) that lead either to increased well-being or to serious dysfunction or social problems. This change approach involves elements of risk reduction and of protection enhancement, focused on contexts such as institutions, policies, and settings, rather than on individuals.

Because prevention strategies are frequently intended to be before the fact, they cannot be applied to prevent dysfunctions that have already occurred and are entrenched within a person, a population, or a setting. Thus, in the developmental pathways strategy, what are targeted are the *unfolding* processes, conditions, and settings that may give rise to the emergence of either wellness or dysfunction. Cowen (2000), as was discussed in Chapter 1, had much to say about the unfolding processes that seem to be associated with wellness; he identified the following productive pathways: (a) promote healthy caregiver–child attachment relationships, (b) assist children to build early, stage-appropriate life competencies, (c) socially engineer environments that are wellness-enhancing (e.g., healthy schools), and (d) enhance the sense of empowerment and personal control people experience in their lives. At the same time those unfolding processes, conditions, and settings that may give rise to dysfunction need to be identified, disrupted, and modified to become more positive pathways. Examples include disorganized and uncaring schools, families, and workplaces.

DIMENSIONS OF COUNSELOR FUNCTIONING

When the Dimensions of Counselor Functioning Cube of Morrill, Oetting, and Hurst was published in 1974 (prior to the birth date of many readers, one can be certain), my professional life was forever changed. What I had pretty strongly suspected, and had been practicing to some extent in my work as a counseling center counseling psychologist at that time, was validated by the contents of the Cube: counseling was not restricted to a remedial process occurring between a skilled professional counselor or psychologist and one other person needing help. Instead, counseling was a kind of "multisplendored thing," capable of being employed in a variety of ways, for different reasons, and with a range of recipients.

Certainly, counseling included one-to-one remedial activity, but, according to the Cube, it also legitimately embraced such other activities as community consultation, training and supervising of paraprofessional helpers, and use of a variety of media (e.g., newspapers, television, computers) to reach a targeted audience with a preventive message.

The Cube model served to organize counseling in a way that invited innovation, thus greatly expanding potential counseling applications. This model virtually exploded conceptions of what counseling was and what it could do. This is so because 36 counseling interventions are generated by the Cube, not just the one intervention of individual, remedial, direct service (i.e., the traditional understanding of counseling). Moreover, the place of prevention in counseling was ratified because it stood alongside remediation and development as a full partner.

Defining the Cube's Dimensions

Because the preventive counseling model emerges from the Cube, one needs to be knowledgeable about the dimensions of the Cube first. Therefore, a brief look at these dimensions is provided to set the stage properly.

Morrill, Oetting, and Hurst (1974) pictured counseling interventions as consisting of three main dimensions: their targets, purposes, and methods. As they wrote, counseling interventions are comprised of the following:

The Target of the Intervention

Interventions may be aimed at (a) the individual, (b) the individual's primary groups, (c) the individual's associational groups, or (d) the institutions or communities that influence the individual's behavior.

The Purpose of the Intervention

The purpose may be (a) remediation, (b) prevention, or (c) development.

The Method of Intervention

The target population may be reached through (a) direct service, which involves direct professional involvement with the target; (b) consultation with and training of other helping professionals or paraprofessionals; or (c) indirect interventions utilizing media; that is, computers, programmed exercises, books, television, and other media.

Any intervention has these three dimensions: who or what the intervention is aimed at, why the intervention is attempted, and how the intervention is made (pp. 355–356). The authors added a postscript to their discussion of these dimensions—that is, the counselor functions of assessment and evaluation override all three dimensions. They rightly observed that all decisions relating to the proper selection of purpose, method, and target are based on the use of effective assessment procedures. Similarly, whatever counseling intervention is attempted must be subjected to appropriate evaluation procedures to determine program effects. Realistically, the considerable promise of the Cube is dependent on a thorough grounding in assessment and evaluation procedures, just as is any other counseling model.

The Cube model for counselor functioning not only provided a conceptual mechanism for organizing and understanding alternative modes of intervention. It also served the important function of stimulating counselors to consider the interrelationship of intervention targets, methods, and purposes in order to select and use the combination carrying the highest probability for counseling success. Use of this model spurred on creative thinking about differential counseling approaches as well as the intentional evaluation of what was done.

PREVENTIVE APPLICATIONS OF THE COUNSELING CUBE MODEL

Since the Cube has four levels of intervention target, three levels of intervention purpose, and three levels of intervention methods, 36 possible counseling interventions ($4 \times 3 \times 3 = 36$) are produced from all interactions of target with purpose and with method. With regard to the preventive domain in particular, which is the focus of our attention, the Cube model allows for the possibility of 12 preventive interventions. Table 3.1 depicts these general possibilities for prevention, which emerge from the 12 combinations of target and method.

To illustrate use of Table 3.1, two theoretical examples will be provided. The first entry of the table suggests the possibility of a direct service method being delivered to an individual target in order to meet preventive goals. This could occur when a professional counselor meets with a university faculty member who is going up for tenure consideration in the next six months. The counselor helps the individual to create an appealing alternative career plan that stands a good chance of successful implementation, in case the tenure quest fails.

The last entry of Table 3.1 suggests that media can be used in a community or an institution to reach some specified preventive ends. Such a situation can arise when a professional counselor, in combination with a public education television station, creates and delivers a 10-week television program on community development skills for formal and informal community leaders. As an integral part of this community–media intervention, these leaders meet in small groups to discuss how they could apply the televised material to increase the participation of senior citizens in community life. Achieving this preventive goal is based on the idea that active community involvement can serve as a general antidote to psychological and physical deterioration and a promoter of health and well-being.

Table 3.1 Twelve Preventive Intervention Directions Based on the Cube Model

Target Dimensions	Method Dimensions
Individual	Direct Services
	Consultation & Training
	Media
Primary Group (e.g., family)	Direct Services
	Consultation & Training
	Media
Associational Group (e.g., club)	Direct Services
	Consultation & Training
	Media
Institution or Community	Direct Services
	Consultation & Training
	Media

TOWARD A PREVENTIVE COUNSELING MODEL

Earlier Discussions of Preventive Counseling

The Cube model provides the conceptual framework for designing and conducting preventive applications. In a sense, it elaborates the three roles that Jordaan, Myers, Layton, and Morgan (1968) suggested long ago for counseling psychologists—remedial, developmental, and preventive.

Since these contributions, others have mentioned and briefly defined preventive counseling itself. For instance, Pietrofesa, Hoffman, and Splete (1984) identified four counseling types: crisis, facilitative, preventive, and developmental. They saw preventive counseling as being programmatic, focused on a particular time span, and related to a specific concern, such as drug awareness, retirement options, or the sex education of elementary school children. In terms of the counselor's role, they stated:

> In preventive counseling, the counselor may present information to a group or refer individuals to relevant programs. The counselor may also continue to work individually with clients—either on a group or a one-to-one basis. Thus, in the area of preventive counseling, we often find the counselor's work with individual clients being complemented by clients' involvement in other relevant programs. (p. 12)

Belkin (1984) provided another early example of how preventive counseling was described. He viewed preventive counseling as one of the several ways in which health counseling is being conducted.

To help better understand his position, Belkin viewed health counseling as one of nine major counseling applications. The other eight applications he identified are counseling over the life span, family counseling, group counseling, crisis intervention counseling, rehabilitation counseling, counseling in the schools, career counseling, and cross-cultural counseling. Within health counseling, in addition to preventive counseling, Belkin saw the other important topics as medical-surgical health counseling, nutritional counseling, health and stress control, fertility counseling, problem pregnancy counseling, and alcohol abuse counseling.

Belkin viewed preventive counseling within health counseling as representing the "holistic perspective." In his words:

> Preventive counseling brings together individual counseling actions as well as public education and group counseling approaches. Its rationale is that "an ounce of prevention is worth a pound of cure." The holistic emphasis on health as "positive wellness" takes into account all aspects of the person's environmental, physical, and spiritual-interpersonal reality. (p. 395)

Belkin went further to indicate that two general types of preventive counseling approaches, the individual and the public, are present. In working with an individual, preventive counseling is used to find the areas where the person needs information; the presupposition is that the individual is willing to learn how to avoid future problems but does not currently possess adequate knowledge. He gave this example:

> Susan, age thirteen, was having sexual relations but not using contraception. She was under the belief that if she confined her sexual relations to the week after her period, she could not become pregnant. Her counselor explained the vicissitudes of fertility and ovulation, and informed Susan about the different kinds of contraception available. The counselor then referred Susan to Planned Parenthood. (p. 401)

In the public approach to preventive counseling, Belkin suggested that the task is to identify the needs of the audience to which a large-scale information effort will be directed. He illustrated this approach through efforts of a health counselor attempting to inform the public through advertising, brochures, publications in local newspapers, and other media about the range of health resources available to them so that they would be better able to remain healthy.

These brief definitions of preventive counseling contain similarities and differences. Authors of each definition agreed that preventive counseling is a new type of counseling, although Pietrofesa et al. emphasized its generic aspects, while Belkin viewed it as a subsidiary of health counseling. According to both definitions, preventive counseling is employed not only with the individual but also much more extensively. It is used frequently with groups and large collections of people. Furthermore, the consensus is that preventive counseling often involves bringing information to people so that they can cope more effectively in any number of ways (Pietrofesa et al.) or remain healthy (Belkin). Finally, the planned nature of a preventive counseling intervention seems to be part of each definition.

Neither definition reviewed accords a prominent place to system change or to the microsocial component of competency enhancement that were cited by Cowen (1985) and others as being critically important to primary prevention efforts. Nor does either one include the variety of preventive intervention modes that were made conceivable in the counseling Cube of Morrill et al. that we examined earlier in this chapter. In fact, the Pietrofesa et al. and Belkin definitions of preventive counseling seemed to identify only information-giving and referral as the means of conducting preventive counseling. A final observation is that none of these treatments of either preventive intervention or preventive counseling stressed such critical concepts of "at-risk," universal application, systems intervention, or of "before-the-fact" work.

Perhaps the most important point to be made, however, is that definitions of prevention and of preventive counseling, however brief and incomplete, had begun to appear in the *Introduction to Counseling* textbook literature during the 1980s. By the 1990s this recognition largely had faded within that particular market, one notable exception being Gibson and Mitchell's text (1995), which devoted a chapter to prevention and wellness.

Other more specialized texts (e.g., Lewis, Lewis, Daniels, & D'Andrea, 2003), however, devoted expansive coverage to prevention and to preventive activities conducted by counselors in the community, and Romano and Hage's (2000) special section in *The Counseling Psychologist* revived an interest within counseling psychology toward prevention. Other illustrations of renewed interest in prevention can be noted through Division 17 (Counseling Psychology) of the American Psychological Association having formally approved and established a Prevention Section and the APA conventions having presented a series of focused prevention programs over the last few years (including a four-hour Continuing Education workshop at the 2003 APA convention on "Teaching Prevention"). In addition, primary prevention and health promotion have developed to such an extent as to warrant an impressive encyclopedia (Gullotta & Bloom, 2003). These kinds of activities provide a valid index of prevention's growing status in the field of counseling, counseling psychology, and social work.

Preventive Counseling Defined

Preventive counseling, as its name implies, is a type of counseling. In that sense, I wholeheartedly agree with the general perspective of Pietrofesa et al. (1984) who, as you have read, divide counseling into four types: crisis, facilitative (frequently called remedial), preventive, and developmental (life span). I certainly agree with their statement, "One would hope that, in the future, professionals will be able to expend as much time and effort in developmental and preventive counseling as they do now in the crisis and facilitative areas" (Pietrofesa et al., 1984, p. 14).

In addition to being a type of counseling, preventive counseling repre sents a marriage between two heretofore separate fields of knowledge and practice: prevention and counseling. This is why so much material has been presented in early chapters about primary prevention and prevention (Chapter 1). Preventive counseling emerges from an integration of prevention, preventive strategies, and counseling interventions. Yielded is a proactive, group-based approach that is applied appropriately across any of several levels of system and in a range of settings, and its practitioners are more concerned with building and broadening health than in alleviating dysfunction (Fredrickson, 2000).

An integration of prevention and counseling is based on at least three assumptions: (1) that the application of prevention concepts can stand to benefit greatly through incorporation of counseling methods, (2) that counseling can profit, perhaps even more so, through incorporating prevention concepts, thereby reinvigorating its original preventive thrust, and (3) that, most significantly, the successful integration and application of prevention and counseling will multiply the positive effects on people who are served.

This "marriage" of prevention and counseling can work only if its two partners are conceptualized as being broad and flexible. The narrow scope of traditional counseling is inadequate to this task. The counseling Cube of Morrill et al. (1974), which was summarized earlier in this chapter, is one model that sufficiently meets the necessary criteria. Its salient points are as follows:

Counseling Interventions Defined

Counseling interventions provide for a variety of targets (from the individual to the community) and a range of methods (from direct to indirect)—all capable of being used for preventive purposes.

In turn, the conception of prevention needs to be comprehensive, embracing traditional understandings and newer ones, associated with positive psychology and with everyday prevention. Furthermore, it needs to be attuned to counseling applications. The prevention definition described in Chapter 1 meets these criteria:

Prevention Definition
Prevention is a goal for both everyday life and for service delivery, through which people become empowered to interact effectively and appropriately within varying levels of systems (micro, meso, exo, and macro) and settings (individual, family, school, community, work). Preventive application can yield a reduction in the occurrence of new cases of a problem, in the duration and severity of incipient problems, and it can promote strengths and optimal human functioning.

Preventive Counseling: A Contemporary Definition

Preventive counseling integrates these understandings of prevention and counseling to yield the following definition:

Preventive counseling is used to help people become empowered in systems and settings. It applies a broad range of counseling methods. Its application can lead to problem avoidance, reversing the trajectory of new problems, optimal human functioning, and in people becoming their own preventive agents.

A CONCEPTUAL MODEL FOR PREVENTIVE COUNSELING

A model for preventive counseling will be helpful for advancing the use of this type of counseling. Not unsurprisingly, the model presented in the remainder of this chapter draws from primary prevention, particularly the work of Cowen on competency-enhancement approaches to person change, and from counseling, especially the counseling Cube of Morrill et al.

Generally, preventive counseling can be regarded in terms of the three dimensions of the Cube: purposive strategies, methods, and targets (Conyne, 1987). That is, what are the intentional plans that preventive counseling draws to reach its goals (its purposive strategies)? In what ways can these purposive strategies be employed (its methods)? And what level of system and setting will be addressed by preventive counseling? Table 3.2 displays preventive counseling in relation to the dimensions of purposive strategies, methods, and systems and settings, and is followed by a descriptive narrative.

Table 3.2 Preventive Counseling Model

Dimensions	Types
Purposive Strategies	**System-Centered Approach** Reducing poverty, illiteracy, unemployment, poor nutrition, and oppression through political, economic, cultural, environmental, and policy change
	Person-Centered Approach *Situational/Transitional:* Natural transition; Stressful life situation
	Competency Enhancement: Skill training; Microsocial change
	Everyday Prevention: Ecological skills; Eudeamonic; Happiness; Optimism
Methods	**Direct Services** *Education:* Anticipatory guidance; Self-instruction; Training; Counseling (Individual, Group, Family)
	Organization: Group facilitation and leadership; Community Organization and Systems Intervention (COSI); Developmental pathways
	Indirect Services *Consultation:* Media; Assisting with natural caregivers; Social competency-facilitation; Advocacy; Supporting physical environment changes
Systems & Settings	**Microsystem** Individual
	Mesosystem Micro-Exosystem linkages
	Exosystem Family; Work; School; Neighborhood/Community
	Macrosystem Cultural blueprint; Media messages; Global influences; International events; Climate, Total ecology

Purposive Strategies in Preventive Counseling

The main purpose of preventive counseling is that of prevention itself: to build and broaden strengths and capacities in people and in systems, and to reduce the incidence of dysfunction in a designated collection of people. Stated very simply, preventive counseling is used to lower the probability of human suffering and to increase the opportunities for optimal human productivity, health, and satisfaction. A second purpose is to reverse the trajectory of early-stage problems so that these do not proceed toward entrenchment. Finally, preventive counseling is intended to mobilize peoples' own everyday efforts at prevention.

But these words are too lofty; they need to be made more operational in this model. To do that, three forms of purposive strategies are discussed; that is, the major plans that are designed to guide preventive counseling activities.

System-Centered Change

System-centered change is sought to remove societal impediments to leading a full life. In Chapter 1, you may remember, such barriers as poverty, illiteracy, unemployment, and malnutrition were cited as prominent examples, along with attempting to lessen the effects of an array of system infections, the "isms" of oppression (e.g., racism, sexism, ageism). These forms of oppression can be accomplished through political, economic, cultural, environmental, and policy-level change attempts, often implemented at the macrolevel. System-level change is the paramount strategy for the attainment of preventive counseling goals. Yet it is the most complex, demanding, and frustrating to attempt. It is the furthest removed from existing methods and roles and from the training of counseling psychologists and professional counselors. These reasons have prevented system-level change from being frequently attempted.

Person-Centered Change

Person-centered change is the second class of purposive strategies. As described by Cowen (1985, 2000) and summarized in Chapter 1, person change is attempted in two major ways. The first, called a situational or transitional focus, seeks to aid people faced with a stressful life event (such as divorce) or with a natural developmental transition point (such as graduation from high school) to more adequately cope with it. In that sense, the situational focus is said to be reactive (Cowen, 1985). The second major focus is called competency enhancement. It is used to proactively develop assets and strengths in people (skill training) or to modify social environments that are inhibiting healthy functioning (microsocial change).

The situational-focused approach to person change has many advantages. The research evidence is building impressively to show it to be a most promising avenue. Yet, at present the competency enhancement mode of person change appears to be most amenable to preventive counseling. Its proactive emphases on skill development and on microsocial change are particularly consistent with the ethos and training of the vast majority of counseling psychologists and professional counselors. Here counseling practitioners can make their most immediate impact on preventive counselors. For this pragmatic reason (and that of space) subsequent discussions of person-change methods will be limited to the competency-enhancement approach.

Everyday Prevention

Everyday prevention, the subject of Chapter 2, is the third purposive strategy in preventive counseling. Everyday prevention addresses the goal of people empowering themselves to become their own preventive agents on a daily basis and across systems and settings. They can move in this positive direction by developing ecological skills that aid in flexibly mastering movement within levels of human systems and settings, by developing an optimistic and hopeful attitude about one's capacity to achieve and about the future, and by learning a eudaemonic approach to life that views happiness as evolving naturally from a deep involvement in the process of positive goal accomplishment. This purposive strategy should inform all the ongoing work of preventive counselors, regardless of method used and across every involvement. In a very real sense, helping people to achieve prevention in their lives and in the systems in which they interact on a daily basis is the ultimate goal of preventive counseling.

Methods in Preventive Counseling

Two major classes of methods are used to carry out the purposive strategies of system change and person change. These are called direct and indirect services. Direct services place the professional counselor in personal contact with the target. With indirect services, however, the counselor works through other people or through systems to reach the target. A brief overview of these methods is supplied in this chapter.

Assigning methods to a direct or to an indirect classification, although generally descriptive, is somewhat arbitrary and does not always apply. Counselors typically will use combinations of direct and indirect interventions in their work, and so the categories may blend, or sometimes an intervention may be used indirectly while at other times it may be used directly. In preventive counseling, it is good practice to include multimethod, multilevel interventions within programmatic efforts and, by definition, a blending of methods (and levels) may result.

You will note later in this book that descriptions of successful applications of prevention that are amenable to counselor functioning will not be organized by method used, because the best programs include multiple methods. (This is a significant departure from the first edition of this book.) Because the number of successful applications has grown considerably since 1987, it makes more sense now to organize applications by some system other than the method used previously. Although any such system that is selected is arbitrary, nonetheless applications will be organized by four dominant settings in American life (Maton, 2000): (1) family, (2) school, (3) work, and (4) neighborhood/community. These are not the only important settings in which people interact (e.g., religious settings are not specified), but they are important in and of themselves and as proxies for other salient settings.

Now, let's return to the discussion of methods in preventive counseling. A good example of how an intervention might be considered direct or indirect can be found in systems intervention. Counselors can intervene directly within systems to improve the system (e.g., educational change within a school). Yet, this intervention might be viewed as indirect in relation to the goal of providing students with an improved curriculum.

While recognizing this fuzziness, the overview to follow connects direct and indirect preventive counseling methods with the five categories of general strategies for primary prevention identified by Gullotta and Bloom (2003), which were discussed earlier in this chapter. All of the direct service interventions will be discussed here because they have been so influential within the history of counseling, and our focus will be on three of the indirect ones: consultation, media, and advocacy.

Direct Services

Education. The direct services of education have been available to the counselor for generations. They provide the greatest counselor control in the helping endeavor, and they allow the professional person to exert the most personal influence (Gullotta & Bloom, 2003; Ketterer, 1981; Ketterer, Bader, & Levy, 1980). Individual, group, and family counseling are the "bread-and-butter" of the counseling practitioner. When these familiar counseling methods are used for prevention, however, they are focused on helping clients to reverse the course of their present direction and to forestall the emergence of related negative conditions. For example, a counselor may work with a recently unemployed client to assist with plans for becoming re-employed but also to avoid the development of depression. Myers (2003) has shown how family counselors can use a wellness-oriented, strengths-based approach to help caregivers cope with stress.

Although education is the most frequently used prevention strategy, as mentioned before both experience and an extensive research base suggest that education alone cannot prevent dysfunction and promote healthy functioning (Gullotta & Bloom, 2003). Education can increase knowledge and sometimes can change attitudes, but very seldom can education alone change behavior (see my earlier comments about problem-based learning, however). It takes a combination of strategies to change behavior and to change it in any lasting way—education plus social competency, plus natural caregiving, for example, all organized and delivered in an intentional and appropriate way.

Anticipatory guidance and training are related and important educational services in preventive counseling. They are often delivered in group formats, frequently to those who are assessed to be free of the problem to be prevented. For example, anticipatory guidance is provided to prospective retirees to help them to gain information, skills, and tools to ease their functioning in their future retirement, or to high school seniors regarding expectations for college life. Training is used to equip those who will deliver helping services to do so more effectively and appropriately—volunteers, for example, who may work in the schools to provide tutoring to elementary school students. People can teach themselves (through videotapes, meditation, reading, the Internet) about any number of life skills, such as relaxation, problem solving, and forming friendships. Traditional, remedial application of counseling also can exert an intended preventive effect, even on a one-to-one basis. A client can unlearn negative ways of being and doing, and the preventive counselor can assist the client to develop a plan on how to apply positive learning to new situations.

Organization. Organizing, the second category of direct services, involves the counseling practitioner in a number of activities with the intent of mobilizing target members to take action for improving their situation. Because organizing interventions almost always involve working with groups or with systems, they are the most directly synchronized with preventive counseling.

Group facilitation represents one important instance of organizing. Group facilitation in preventive counseling includes helping-oriented groups, such as psychoeducation groups (Brown, 1997; Conyne & Horne, 2001), prevention groups (Conyne, 2004), and task groups (Conyne, 1989, 1999; Conyne, Rapin, & Rand, 1997).

Psychoeducation groups are an outstanding example of a helping-oriented group in preventive counseling. They are designed to convey needed information, provide training in important skill development, and to intentionally harness group resources to support the acquisition and application of both information and skills. Task groups are ubiquitous in our society (e.g., meetings, committees, task forces, educational classes, and many organization development activities), and they often are ingredients of larger change programs in schools and communities. Therefore, providing group facilitation and training others to become good group facilitators are central aspects of preventive counseling.

Gullotta and Bloom termed another form of the Organizing intervention, "Community Organization and Systems Intervention (COSI)," the most powerful in prevention. Direct delivery forms of these services include community development and systems intervention. In community development, members of a community are assisted to develop programs and projects that serve to strengthen the fabric of the community and provide challenge and support for community members. Helping to create and implement a community- or school-wide substance abuse program, or a new park, are examples. Systems interventions are used to correct community conditions that presently impede members' health and functioning. Preventive counselors might become involved in helping to form a neighborhood watch association, created in response to safety concerns in the area, or to design an evaluation study for a community commission focused on high unemployment.

Felner et al. (2000) highlighted the importance of focusing on developmental pathways through prevention programs aimed at reducing risk and enhancing protective factors in settings, such as family, school, work, and neighborhood. Here, attempts are initiated to positively alter or strengthen the environmental settings and circumstances through which people move in their lives, rather than focusing on person change.

The impact of settings can range from positive to negative. In terms of positive features, settings provide physical and psychological safety, are structured appropriately, offer supportive relationships, afford opportunities to belong, are characterized by affirmative social norms, contribute to efficacy and mattering, and offer opportunities for skill building (Eccles & Gootman, 2001). Of course, the opposite also can occur in settings that negatively affect development.

Indirect Services

Indirect services are much newer on the counseling scene. Therefore, more will be said about them here. Many counseling practitioners intuitively dislike these services because they place the counselor once or twice removed from target members. For the most part, counselors have been attracted to the field because they enjoyed and were effective at working directly with people in a helping way. Yet, as you read in Chapter 1, the imbalance in supply and demand for counseling has led many professional counselors and counseling psychologists to experiment with new ways to extend their reach. Therefore, indirect services have emerged to assist in expanding the impact that any one counselor could be expected to exert. The idea is that by working in a one-to-one situation, any single counselor is limited to only a few client contacts per work day. When working through others or when using informational systems to reach designated targets, the same counselor's impact—at least theoretically—is multiplied. Several forms of indirect services are available for use in preventive counseling. These are (1) consultation, (2) education, in the variety of public media that are available, (3) assistance with natural caregivers, (4) promotion of social competency, (5) COSI, in the form of legislative and judicial action (i.e., advocacy), and (6) support of physical environment changes. Three of these indirect preventive counseling methods are consultation, media, and advocacy (see also the earlier discussion of prevention strategies).

Consultation. In consultation, the professional counselor typically is involved in a triadic effort (Conyne & O'Neil, 1992; Dougherty, 2000; Gallessich, 1982, 1985; Kurpius & Brubaker, 1976). The consultant (Point "A") works through others (Point "B") to benefit a third party (Point "C"). This demonstrates the indirectness of the triadic process of consultation.

This triadic orientation is frequently implemented when a counseling psychologist consults with the "manager" of a situation or organization (e.g., the teacher of a classroom, the director of a corporation, or a guidance counselor working with a particular student) to enable that manager to improve his or her effectiveness in working with the situation or organization. The consultant's focus is on improving the work of the consultee (the manager). Through consulting with the manager the third party benefits.

Therefore, in addition to a triadic orientation to helping, consultation is also characterized by its primary focus on professional or work problems (Bardon, 1985). This work emphasis serves to further delineate consultation from other modes of helping, especially clarifying it from the personal orientation of psychotherapy.

Media. One of the fastest-growing methods since the first edition of this book in 1987 is mass media, which includes any delivery of a planned message to a targeted audience (Fogel, 2003). This is an indirect educational method, used in preventive counseling to persuade audience members to do something different, something in a more healthy way; for example, to stop smoking (Flynn et al., 1994), prevent HIV/AIDS (Stephenson et al., 1999), or reduce cardiovascular disease (Farquhar et al., 1994). In the latter study (the Stanford Three-Community Study), mass media interventions were used in combination with social competency promotion and natural caregiving to produce positive results in cardiovascular health in such indicators as reduced cholesterol and blood pressure. This interlacing of methods, where media is one of several important parts, can increase the potential preventive yield.

The variety of media available today is impressive, including radio, television, video, computer, the Internet, pamphlets, books, articles, bumper stickers, messages on products (such as cereal boxes, or warnings on liquor bottles or cigarettes), newspapers, and more. Their successful use depends on many factors, including pegging what kind of message is needed for people at what stage of readiness for change (Prochaska, Norcross, & DiClemente, 1994), with what form of media, in combination with what other methods.

The use of media by professional counselors is an untapped resource, although one that is certainly not without potential harm. Klonoff (1983) observed that the scope and efficiency of the media as a mass communication vehicle make it a natural for conducting public education that has as its goal the prevention of human problems. Use of the media to reach a target population is clearly indirect; the counseling practitioner works through a communication channel of some kind and should always consider incorporating media with other methods. Use of media offers cost efficiency, because whole masses of people can theoretically be reached. Yet media nearly completely remove the counselor from personal contact with members of the target population, and its use must be carefully safeguarded through giving special attention to ethical considerations (Klonoff, 1983). As a multiplier of counselor impact, however, the mediated approach is unsurpassed.

Advocacy. Advocacy is primarily an indirect intervention that is of increasing importance for all counselors and certainly for preventive counselors. For example, both American Counseling Association (ACA) and American Psychological Association (APA) have public policy and legislation advocacy programs that are intended to benefit the profession, professionals, and clients. As part of these programs, counselors and psychologists can receive training in public policy advocacy as a means of improving their effectiveness as advocates. Advocacy competencies for counselors (Lewis, Arnold, House, & Toporek, 2002) were approved by the American Counseling Association in March 2003. Advocacy is commonly understood as a systems intervention, but the authors indicate that it also includes the implementation of empowerment strategies in direct counseling with individuals, families, and groups.

Advocacy competencies involve counselors acting with and on behalf of clients and members of school and communities to reach goals. As an illustration, a counselor can serve a preventive effect by confronting oppressive policies and procedures within an institution, thus intending to benefit large numbers of people, "clients" and nonclients alike. That same counselor can help empower others to serve as their own advocate in seeking redress of grievances or in promoting positive work environments (Lewis, Lewis, Daniels, & D'Andrea, 2003). A key consideration is the following: "When counselors become aware of external factors that act as barriers to an individual's development, they may choose to respond through advocacy" (Lewis et al., 2002).

Systems and Settings in Preventive Counseling

As you will recall from Chapter 1, the targeting of settings, or situations, was recommended for preventive intervention (e.g., Price, 1974). In particular, Price suggested that "high-risk situations" become the focus for such attention. Of course, such an approach is entirely consistent with an ecological perspective, which argues for viewing people in the contexts of their lives (Conyne & Cook, 2004).

Settings, and the systems that contain them, show high promise for preventive counseling because they are powerful shapers of human behavior, and they provide access points for the potential delivery of preventive counseling interventions. So, in response to my new acquaintance (and others who wonder about this question), I talk of how counselors can help to prevent human problems through involvement in the major settings of human life in this society. These settings are major enculturators in American life. They are where most of us spend most of our lives, and, as has been noted, they contribute greatly to personal satisfaction or lack of the same.

Family, Work, School, and Neighborhood/Community. The literature identifies major settings in different ways. For instance, the edited book by Price, Ketterer, Bader, and Monahan (1980) proposed the settings of schools (see Jason, 1980), diversion programs, such as juvenile justice (see Vandenbos & Miller, 1980), industry (see Foote & Erfurt, 1980), and social networks (see Gottlieb & Hall, 1980). Remer et al. (1984) suggested what they called a "meta-system" for the delivery of primary preventive interventions. This meta-system includes the delivery vehicles of the family, church, and school. Of course, the counseling Cube (Table 3.1) identifies as targets the individual, primary group, associational group, and the community or institution. Finally, Pearson (1985) stressed the importance of including the individual and small group as viable primary preventive targets. He maintained that because many standard definitions of (primary) prevention exclude the individual and small group from consideration (i.e., most of them emphasize populations or, less frequently, settings), many counselors miss the opportunity to turn individual and small-group counseling in the direction of prevention. The systems and settings included in the model for preventive counseling presented in this chapter draw from the previously listed contributions, as well as other sources (e.g., Maton, 2000). The individual and small group, the family, school, work, neighborhood and community, churches and others all contain fertile social environments in which preventive counseling efforts can be launched (Vincent & Trickett, 1983).

Micro-, Meso-, Exo-, and Macrolevels of Systems. Bronfenbrenner (1979) conceptualized ever-widening levels of systems (which include settings) in his ecological understanding of how human development occurs. These system levels, which are all mutually influencing (Conyne & Cook, 2004) were labeled: (a) microsystem (the individual or family unit of analysis; (b) mesosystem (a "connector" system interlacing micro- and exosystem levels; (c) exosystem, containing proximal settings in which interaction and involvement occurs, such as family, school, work, and neighborhood/community; and (d) macrosystem, a larger, more distal level containing broad cultural, political, and economic "blueprints" that are influential. Others (such as Kasambira & Edwards, 2000) have expanded these system levels to include an ultimate distal level, global, capturing the "world as a village" phenomenon.

Both systems and settings need to be considered in preventive counseling. Settings are situated within exosystems. In the preventive counseling model, settings are identified as including family, work, school, and neighborhood/community (cf. Maton, 2000). These are the places and spaces in which most of us spend most of our time and through which we are both challenged and supported. These settings, of course, can be for good or ill. They represent not only the fulcrums of our daily lives but also the primary entry points and contexts for delivering preventive counseling.

How to deliver preventive counseling is an important issue. Too often, well-planned programs are not attended, which brings to mind the phrase: "Have you ever given a party and no one shows?" Therefore, one of the critical strategic problems facing the delivery of preventive counseling is, simply, how to do it (Conyne, 1983). When I explained to a new acquaintance the other day that counselors can work in ways to prevent the occurrence of dysfunction in peoples' lives, she thought that was a wonderful idea but quickly asked the inevitable question: "How do counselors get involved with people before they have problems?" (I have heard this very good question more times than I can remember!) Indeed, as Remer, Niguette, Anderson, and Terrell (1984) observed about this issue: preventive interventions must have an effective, efficient delivery system. In the past, even with cogently compelling interventions (e.g., fluoridation), implementation has met stiff resistance. An effective delivery vehicle is a sine qua non in the mental health area, where values conflicts are rife and the necessity for a particular intervention is not nearly so clear cut (p. 30).

CONCLUSION

Chapter 3 contains the basic ingredients for defining preventive counseling and for conducting it. "Preventive counseling is used to help people become empowered in systems. It applies a broad range of counseling methods. Its application can lead to problem avoidance, reversing the trajectory of new problems; optimal human functioning; and people's ability to become their own preventive agents." It is hoped that both this definition and the preventive counseling model will contribute to a better understanding of what this type of counseling is and will provide a useful kind of road map in guiding future action.

All new models are built on the shoulders of previous thinking. So the situation is with this model, which integrated various concepts from primary prevention with those from professional counseling, counseling psychology, and community psychology. Of particular importance were the works of Cowen on competency enhancement in person change, of Morrill et al. on the counseling Cube, and of Maton on social transformation across ecological levels. The chapter also highlighted other important conceptions of preventive counseling.

The product of this integration, the preventive counseling model, contains the dimensions of (1) purposive strategies, (2) methods, and (3) systems and settings. The text described each of these dimensions, and Table 3.2 presented an outline of the model.

Having a conceptual understanding of preventive counseling is very important because it is an emerging practice. Understanding it can be helpful for applying it in situations. The next chapter, focused on program planning and evaluation, will provide criteria for how to design good preventive counseling efforts and how to determine if good designs actually work.

ISSUES FOR REFLECTION AND DISCUSSION

1. What are some of the major ideas from primary prevention and from counseling that have contributed to preventive counseling?
2. What is meant by purposive strategies? What are they in this model?
3. What is the main difference between direct and indirect methods of intervention in preventive counseling? Give an illustration of each. Identify the direct and indirect interventions that are part of preventive counseling.
4. The "target" in preventive counseling is sometimes defined with reference to systems and settings. What are systems and settings, and why are they important?

5. You are the new director of Mental Health Services—Core, a community agency that has served the inner-city population for 25 years. You were brought in to provide a "new look," especially through a focus on preventive strategies. The staff is not quite sure what is meant by preventive strategies, and you decide that you need to embark on a professional development program with them. Drawing from the "general strategies of prevention," discussed in the beginning of this chapter, develop a 15-minute oral presentation that would clearly communicate these strategies to your staff. Give this presentation to your partner and get feedback.

6. Turn to a partner and discuss the preventive counseling model found in Table 3.2. Alternate responsibilities for each section, as follows: **Person A,** take: Purposive Strategies, **Person B,** take: Methods, and then both of you take the Systems and Settings. Work together on explaining and answering questions. Take 45 minutes to do this, trying to improve each of your understandings of this model.

7. What features of this model attract you? About what aspects of it are you uncertain? What might you be able to do well? What would you need more education and training to do?

8. How do you think this model fits with the world of education and mental health? What seems a particularly good fit? What seems a particularly poor fit? What would need to change, if anything, to make this model work best?

SECTION II
Describing and Analyzing Prevention Programs That Work

How is prevention actually done? What works? Why do these things work? This section is motivated by such questions. Each prevention program, then, will be described using the following format:

- What is it?
- How is it done?
- What works?
- Why does it work?
- Implications for counselors and other helpers
- Conclusion
- Issues for Reflection and Discussion

As I wrote the first edition of this book in 1987, there were few examples of excellent prevention programs in mental health and virtually no organized access sources. Over the intervening years, both situations have markedly changed for the better.

For instance, in 1988 Price et al. published their work through the American Psychological Association, *14 Ounces of Prevention: A Casebook for Practitioners*. This outstanding resource described in detail 14 prevention programs that had been reviewed and selected as being "excellent" from over 900 programs that had been submitted to the review committee. These excellent programs ranged across a developmental spectrum: early childhood, children and youth, and adults and the elderly. In 1992, an educational video (*An Ounce of Prevention*) was made available as part of a series of videos on

Abnormal Psychology. This video, again with Richard Price centrally involved, presented in detail programs across the age span.

A highly recommended Web source was organized in 1996 by the Center for the Study and Prevention of Violence (CSPV) at the University of Colorado (http://www.colorado.edu/cspv/blueprints/). The project is called Blueprints for Violence Prevention (Sharon Mihalic, Director) and provides informational and technical assistance resources. The Web site contains a wealth of useful information not only about violence prevention programs but also about programs cutting across the wide range of prevention areas. From over 600 programs reviewed, 11 have been identified that meet a strict standard of program effectiveness, with another 21 programs identified as being promising. A matrix of program evaluation criteria is accessible, as is an effective program selection interactive search function. Using this function, one can search the Center's database using these categories: (a) risk factor (e.g., school, community); (b) target age (e.g., infant, late adolescence); (c) audience (e.g., all youth, parents); (d) program type (e.g., mentoring, home visitation); and (e) blueprint type (e.g., model and/or promising programs). In another matrix provided through the Blueprints project, one can discover how various other agencies engaging in the evaluation of prevention programs have scored those programs also evaluated by the Blueprints project in terms of effectiveness. These other agencies include: American Youth Policy Forum, Center for Mental Health Services, Center for Substance Abuse Prevention (CSAP), Department of Education—Safe Schools, Communities That Care—Developmental and Research Programs, National Institute of Drug Abuse (NIDA), Strengthening America's Families, the Surgeon General's Report of 2001, and Title V (OJJDP).

The Web site organized by the Substance Abuse and Mental Health Administration (SAMHSA) (http://modelprograms.samhsa.gov/matrix_all.cfm) provides a similarly wonderful opportunity to identify and follow up on numbers of prevention programs that have been carefully evaluated as being excellent, promising, and/or model programs. These kinds of resources epitomize the growth in and quality of prevention activity and the increasing sophistication in the capacity to access prevention activity. Effective models of prevention programs are now available for consideration and adaptation by the everyday preventionist.

This section of the book contains four chapters, each focused on a particular setting for prevention: Chapter 5 on Family; Chapter 6 on School; Chapter 7 on Work; and Chapter 8 on Neighborhood/Community. Each chapter will describe in some detail three prevention programs that have been evaluated by external sources as being excellent. We will then draw from the "Criteria for Evaluating Preventive Counseling Programs" discussed in Chapter 4 to tease out factors that seem to account for program success.

It is important to note that examining prevention programs within independent settings, such as family, school, work, and neighborhood/community, is an arbitrary approach selected because it allows more easily for discussion; it frequently does not capture what is best prevention practice. (As a contrast, the first edition of this book was organized by method, not setting.) In any case, prevention programs in the "real world" need to be comprehensive. This often means that they will be implemented across settings (and methods), with strands occurring not only in the family but also in school and maybe in the neighborhood, too. Nonetheless, this process of description and evaluation of successful prevention programs will provide readers with a concrete sense of what model prevention efforts consist of and also of how to develop these kinds of efforts.

In 2003, the SARS (Severe Acute Respiratory Syndrome) virus was spreading from an area around stall 17 of the Dongyuan market south of Guangzhou, China, through pockets of the Far East to Toronto, Canada, and beyond. The public health hunt is on in full force to eliminate the sources of the infection, to quarantine and disable its transmission, and to discover a vaccine to inoculate populations at risk for acquiring the virus. This public health model, so impressive in thwarting past instances of diseases such as cholera and malaria, is made for situations such as this one where there is a direct linkage among source, transmission, and infection of people. However, in mental health and education, these linkages are usually complex, distal, and multifactorial. Thus, programs that are of interest in preventive counseling also need to reflect these characteristics.

In what is known as the greatest and clearest triumph of public health, in 1854 John Snow removed the handle from the Broad Street pump in the Golden Square area of London, thus preventing access to polluted water-borne cholera. Snow was able to map the distribution of cholera cases, resulting in a pattern configured around the Broad Street water pump, which was available to the general public as a water source. He then counted the number of cholera cases occurring subsequent to the removal of the pump handle, with results showing that the number of new cases dropped dramatically. This was a kind of naturalistic experiment. Preventing the water-borne cholera from being consumed eliminated the cholera. This was a brilliant deduction and a preventive act with remarkable, life-saving consequences.

We shall not see such direct and simple examples of prevention as we examine the prevention programs to follow. However, they are "state of the art" for our complex field, and they hold many lessons.

WEB SITE RESOURCES

These two sites are representative of the wealth of resources on prevention that are available to assist in searches.

http://www.colorado.edu/cspv/blueprints/
http://modelprograms.samhsa.gov/matrix_all.cfm

CHAPTER 4

Program Planning and Evaluation

CONTEXT

Many programs and services being offered today are said to be "preventive." Fully satisfying the criteria for determining whether prevention goals are actually being met by any one program is difficult. It is highly likely, therefore, that a large number of offerings currently wrapped in the banner of prevention may not truly qualify. For instance, a target group may not be at risk, an intervention may not be offered before the fact, or nothing may have been prevented by the effort.

These critical comments are offered not to discourage explorations in the area of preventive counseling. Rather, let them serve to introduce the importance of assuring quality throughout every phase of effort that is undertaken. This kind of quality can best be achieved by being certain that sound program planning and evaluation processes are in place for any preventive counseling activity.

Proper program planning, for instance, allows one to develop a credible conceptual base, to accurately identify community needs, to determine at-risk groups, to establish attainable preventive goals, and to design an intervention program that is valid both conceptually and practically. Program evaluation allows one to determine if the intervention is being delivered according to plan, if modifications are required along the way, and if the program goals were met. Program planning and evaluation are fundamental processes to help ensure that the program is designed with reference to prevention criteria and is being implemented accordingly. If these are done, then the program will have its best opportunity to demonstrate desired primary preventive effects.

Over 15 years ago, the APA Task Force on Promotion, Prevention, and Intervention Alternatives in Psychology announced 14 "showcase" primary prevention programs that were selected from 900 nominees (Bales, 1987). (Several of these programs are mentioned in this book.) One of the critical criteria these programs had to meet successfully was to show program evaluation effectiveness. "We wanted to identify programs that worked and had documented evidence of their effectiveness," said Richard Price, the task force chair (Bales, 1987, p. 18). This intention cuts directly to the heart of the program planning and evaluation process.

Thus, program planning and evaluation are essential to the assurance of quality in primary preventive counseling. The material contained in this chapter will be helpful for anticipating planning and evaluation issues and for effectively working with them.

IF YOU DON'T KNOW WHERE YOU'RE GOING, HOW WILL YOU KNOW IF YOU GOT THERE?

Planning—whether for a long trip, a financial future, or a primary prevention program—helps to ensure the directed use of resources to reach stated goals. Although planning cannot guarantee anything, it does increase the odds for success.

Planning increases in value in direct proportion to the complexity of an intended activity. A personal note here may be illustrative. I love to "hang-loose," to do things spontaneously, whenever possible. This orientation was challenged for several years with the birth of our two children. My wife (a practicing psychologist) and I found that we had to plan, plan, and plan some more in order to accomplish even the most mundane of activities, such as shopping. Our living situation had become more complex, requiring us to become very organized and to plan in trying to lead as balanced a life as possible. (Looking back, it is very clear that it was well worth it!)

Conducting prevention programs is an involved and complex endeavor (Heller, Price, & Sher, 1980). A key ingredient to success in this effort is to include a thorough planning process. As Craig (1978) wrote on the fly-page of her excellent planning and evaluation manual, "The more you know about where you're going, the closer you are to being there."

GETTING THERE IS ONE THING, BUT IS IT THE RIGHT PLACE TO BE?

This question is illustrated by the story of the prisoners who developed an elaborate escape plan that involved digging a one-half mile tunnel under the prison with spoons and other pointed objects they had managed to pilfer. After three years of dangerous and exhausting work, they broke through the ground at their planned target site, only to find themselves still well inside the prison yard! Demoralized and dejected, their jig was up.

What had happened? The plan itself was accurate and detailed. Had it been faithfully followed, the prisoners would have exited outside the prison grounds, their escape attempt a success. Yet, the execution of the plan went awry. So many years, so many people doing the digging, so dark down in the tunnel, men becoming so tired. Mistakes were made. A few wrong turns were unknowingly taken here and there. All of this led to the plan's failure and the resulting disastrous outcome.

The prisoners had a good plan, but they wound up in the wrong place. Evaluation is necessary to help ensure that energies are being directed in accordance with the plan that has been developed and to determine whether the goals of the plan have been satisfactorily met.

IMPORTANCE OF PLANNING AND EVALUATION

Writers who have considered mental health and prevention are in agreement that planning and evaluation are critical functions. Morrill, Oetting, and Hurst (1974), in discussing their dimensions of counselor functioning "Cube" (see Chapter 3), emphasized that assessment and evaluation comprise one set of counselor functions that overrides all others. Wilson and Yager (1981) strengthened this perspective with regard to prevention programs:

> Our belief is that imaginative and competent planning of prevention programs requires a research orientation to the conceptualization, development, implementation, and evaluation of the task. Realistic and effective prevention programs are based on good research entailing a logical, systematic, developmental approach. (p. 590)

Cowen (1984) added additional support to this theme. He believed that although primary prevention is recognized as an attractive alternative to the insufficiencies contained in the present (remedial) mental health system, its conduct can be improved significantly through use of a sound program development model that contains concrete steps, including evaluation.

These observations cogently suggest that if prevention programs are to be delivered effectively and efficiently, planning and evaluation are essential applied research functions. In turn, as Price (1983) indicated with regard to the field of preventive psychology, what will cause it to develop from a "worthwhile aspiration" to an "accomplished fact" is the creation of new prevention-relevant knowledge. He pointed to various forms of prevention research as being essential in this evolution.

PLANNING AND EVALUATION IN PROGRAM DEVELOPMENT

If one thinks linearly about program development, planning and evaluation occupy the first and last points in that process. Planning identifies what to do and how to do it. Evaluation shows how effectively and efficiently the program achieved the desired goals, which, in part, is a measurement of how the program was administered. Sandwiched between planning and evaluation, of course, is the actual program implementation. These three steps of Planning-Implementing-Evaluating (PIE) account for most of the program development model but not all of it.

Program development is not a linear process. Rather, it is recursive and cyclical. What makes it so are the evaluation data that are produced not only at the conclusion of the program (summative data about program outcomes) but, importantly, all along the way. This latter kind of information, produced through formative evaluation, tells implementers whether the program is on target, whether activities are occurring according to plan, and other practical information related to whether or not the original plan is actually being carried out. When the program development process is working properly, evaluation data are fed back regularly during the project to keep it "on-course" and, at the project's conclusion, to determine whether outcome goals have been met. Thus, a total program development model includes four broad, generic elements: (1) planning, (2) implementing, (3) evaluating, and (4) feedback about both process and outcomes.

With regard to program development, however, training programs and practitioners place an overwhelming emphasis on program implementation. This book has followed suit by devoting considerable attention to the direct and indirect methods of preventive counseling.

While there are good reasons for adopting this approach, doing so unfortunately relegates planning and evaluating to a secondary position. The intent in this chapter is to locate planning and evaluating within the general program development model and to emphasize their important place in preventive counseling.

HOW PLANNING AND EVALUATION OCCUR

Three of the most incisive and difficult issues in determining whether or not an intervention was preventive are the following:

1. Was it offered "before-the-fact" or early in problem evolution?
2. Was the target group or situation "at risk," currently unaffected, or early in problem development?

3. Did the intervention actually prevent the identified dysfunction, or did it develop resources to aid positive future coping, that is, was it successful?

To resolve these issues, designers of prevention interventions must devote much more energy to the program development steps of planning and evaluation than is ordinarily given.

Any of the direct or indirect methods and interventions identified in earlier chapters of this book frequently are used for purposes other than preventive ones. Remediation is the most common reason. No preventive magic resides in the approaches themselves.

For instance, the indirect method of consultation is not exclusively a preventive one. Consultation becomes so only when it is conducted with reference to satisfying prevention goals, such as problem avoidance or health promotion. The same situation applies to all the other methods and interventions contained in the preventive counseling model that has been described. Only through planning and evaluation is the necessary information acquired to produce interventions that are preventive in purpose. Next, we will examine these essential program development steps of planning and evaluation as they relate to preventive counseling. Examples will be presented to highlight key points.

Planning

The planning step is important, and it is also complex. Only limited coverage can be provided in this short chapter. You are therefore encouraged to pursue other sources for in-depth coverage of this critical process (e.g., Bloom, 1996; Coursey, 1977; Cowen, 1984; Craig, 1978; Moore & Delworth, 1976; NIAAA, 1978; Patton, 1997; Wilson & Yager, 1981).

In general, planning includes six interrelated substeps:

1. Identify possible problems and potentials
2. Identify the generative base
3. Assess needs and targets
4. Set goals
5. Select strategy
6. Prepare for implementation

Identify Possible Problems and Potentials

Bloom (1996) suggested that planning should identify the problems and strengths faced by potential participants in their settings. This makes good sense because starting at this point allows for a prevention program to begin with the context being addressed and then proceed to the next steps.

Identify the Generative Base

A generative base provides the conceptual underpinnings for identifying what should be attempted. It is derived from pertinent theory and research. According to Cowen (1984), a generative base is necessary in planning primary preventive programs because "it provides prospective investigators with plausible leads about the types of interventions that hold promise for positive (primary preventive) payoff" (p. 485). Omitting this step can lead to doing entirely the wrong things or doing what the intervener likes to do or does well, regardless of the situation.

The generative base is influenced by previously gained knowledge. This knowledge may point to existing relationships between the presence of competencies and adjustment, or to the lack of competencies and maladjustment. For instance, considerable evidence exists to support the importance of interpersonal problem-solving skills in healthy functioning, and deficiencies in the same for unhealthy functioning.

Existing knowledge could also implicate the association of a situation, setting, or life circumstance with subsequent psychological dysfunction. Abundant evidence here implicates highly competitive and nonsupportive social environments, as well as such stressful life situations as divorce or unemployment, with a range of negative physical and psychological indices.

These and other kinds of knowledge bases have been developed. They can be drawn from to shape the direction of future preventive counseling projects.

Assess Needs and Targets

The generative base selected must correspond directly to actual issues in the community of interest. Assessing community needs and targets helps to determine what those actual local issues may be and which of them could profit from preventive counseling. This assessment of needs and targets involves analytic strategies (D'Aunno & Price, 1984), where the assessor assumes the role of a problem analyst (Price, 1983).

A number of analytic strategies are available for use in the assessment of needs and targets. These range from the highly qualitative, which emphasize observational, descriptive, and interview approaches, to the highly quantitative, which involve the collection and statistical analysis of numbers.

D'Aunno and Price (1984) have identified and described five broad analytic strategies for community research that span this qualitative to quantitative dimension. Beginning with the qualitative and moving to the quantitative end of the spectrum, these strategies are participant observation, ethnography, key informant interviews, network analysis, surveys, epidemiology, and social indicators.

Space does not permit defining these strategies, but the important point here is that the problem analyst ought to be able to draw competently from a range of qualitative to quantitative assessment methodologies (Price, 1983). The combination of data that emerges from different sources and perspectives can inform the most validity about peoples' needs and situations.

For instance, in student retention research at the University of Cincinnati, survey research was used to study the behaviors and experiences of freshmen students. Much was learned about these students' work hours, involvement with faculty, intention to transfer, academic and social involvement, and other matters of importance, such as the finding that there was no direct correlation between grade point averages estimated by the respondents and their intention to re-enroll.

In the second year of this study, the process compared dominant behaviors and campus experiences of the dropouts from the university (i.e., the "non-Sophomores") with those of students who did return for their second year. This information provided leads us to what "retenters" do versus what the "leavers" do not do, to remain at this one institution.

In addition to this quantitative approach, a complementary qualitative, ethnographic study was also conducted. A doctoral student closely studied the student lives of six freshmen as they moved through their first year. The researcher was attempting to learn firsthand what these students said about their experiences, the events that occurred in the various university settings they were a part of, and the meanings the students attached to these occurrences.

Information produced by both of these assessments gave fuller understanding about what constitutes a "holding" campus environment and about what specific student behaviors contributed to or detracted from becoming positive and attached. Assessment results contributed to subsequent program development steps aimed at reducing student attrition, such as developing learning communities of students around selected themes.

Set Goals

Goals indicate how a prevention program will respond to needs or problems that were identified during the assessment step. They describe what the program is to accomplish.

Preventive goals often include statements of "incidence;" that is, they are geared to lowering the number of new cases of certain disturbance. Reducing the number of new teen pregnancies in a population or averting depression among a group of newly divorced individuals illustrates how the concept of incidence is important in prevention goals. In addition, preventive goals may be directed at improving health status, for example, by programs to develop social support or problem solving. Still other prevention goals might address strengthening environmental systems so that they support human functioning more fully—for example, by installing ramps in an office building for disabled visitors or improving access to health insurance for workers in a school system.

The goal statements need to be as specific and concrete as possible. Concrete goals provide the guidance necessary to develop methods of intervention and evaluation. They should be based on action verbs that describe observable behavior; they should identify the situation or circumstances where the behavior will occur; and they should indicate the criteria for determining success (Mager, 1962).

The two statements of incidence given earlier go only part of the way necessary, for some vagueness exists. In the teen pregnancy instance, would reducing the number of new cases by one, or two, or by 3000 all be considered a success? What teenage population is being targeted? Is it teenagers of a neighborhood, a city, the whole state? Will resources be focused equally across the teenage years, or will a more specific set of years (such as 15 to 17) be targeted? Will teenage boys also become a concern of this project, or will the project be restricted to girls? A better goal statement might read: "to reduce the number of new teen pregnancies in Clinton County by 25%, by focusing on both boys and girls from ages 13 to 18."

A particularly useful method for developing prevention goals (and subsequent program steps) is found in the use of a representative task force. Although a task force is frequently assembled at the assessment step, it is more economical and just as effective to form it at the goal-setting step, after assessment data have been collected but before data analysis, discussion, and the determination of program goals have occurred.

Task forces are comprised of representative community members and professionals who have some special stake in the issue at hand. For instance, with the teen pregnancy case, members might be drawn from families of teens, some teenagers themselves, high school faculties, church staffs, and social service, political, legal, and medical agencies. Task force members join to form a core of representative knowledge and opinion. They guide the development, implementation, and evaluation of the primary prevention program, under the facilitation of the organizer who in this case would be the preventive counselor. (Parenthetically, consider the competencies this individual would need to effectively manage this task force.)

Working with these members provides some special advantages: (1) their information and views are cross-sectional, reality-based, and valuable; (2) they are aware of or may control sources of information and access to the target population; and (3) their cooperation and involvement can increase chances that the prevention program that is generated will not only be on-course but will also actually be put into practice.

Moreover, implicitly within these advantages lies a golden nugget. Collaborating with a representative task force can go a long way toward answering a very common concern about doing prevention: "I want to do it, but how do I get started; how can I get involved on the preventive end, before problems are entrenched?"

Select Strategy

If program planners have not already jumped ahead to developing a "solution" to the identified needs, they are likely to do so now. This premature tendency toward quick closure must be resisted.

The appropriate step called for here—select strategies—includes three parts. These are: (1) to generate a range of alternative strategies for reaching the identified goals that have been established; (2) to analyze each; and (3) to select the one strategy that realistically holds the greatest chance for success. Price (1983) referred to this process as "innovation design."

A strategy is simply a series or group of activities that is conducted to reach designated goals. Alternative strategies can be generated in a number of ways. Brainstorming, the Nominal Group Technique, and the Delphi method represent three of the structured ways that this can occur.

For instance, brainstorming could be used to produce alternative strategies for reducing the pregnancy situation mentioned earlier. Members could be asked to quickly and without evaluation generate as many competency-enhancement ideas (e.g., teach assertive skills) as possible, and then to do the same with system change ideas (e.g., introduce health clinics throughout the school district). Scores of such ideas can be produced by planning groups.

The next issue in strategy selection considers the feasibility of these brainstormed ideas. Some may be too expensive, some may be obvious political bombshells, and some just couldn't be done for whatever reasons. A useful exercise for determining the feasibility of the alternatives is force-field analysis. In this analysis, the promoting and the restraining forces affecting each proposed idea are carefully analyzed. Other approaches consider feasibility strictly in terms of resources that would be required to carry out each idea. A third method for determining feasibility is to check these ideas against specific evaluation criteria, such as their expected appropriateness, adequacy, effectiveness, efficiency, and side effects.

Finally, after the feasibility analysis is completed, program planners use the information to reach a decision about which strategy—or strategies—

they will use to reach their primary preventive goals. They then proceed to the step of preparing for implementation.

Prepare for Implementation

Note well: implementation has yet to happen! But the time and effort expended in these preliminary planning steps are absolutely critical to the effectiveness of whatever program will be implemented. Failure to plan thoroughly is virtually a guarantee of a failed prevention effort.

Once a strategy is selected to reach the desired prevention goal, the planners must turn to the very hard questions of who will do what, when, where, with what, and how? This is the "nitty-gritty" of planning. How many of you will admit to having been involved with creating a great plan that never was realized because concrete task assignments were left undone? Unfortunately, I have had such experiences, although less often now. When it happens, I'm always reminded of the good-hearted folks who spent lots of time and money planning a special party to which no one ever came. How deeply disappointing!

In my experience, professional counselors and counseling psychologists tend to avoid the kind of detail work necessary for programmatic success. In preventive counseling, however, an essential aspect is to become practical in designing a strategy and the set of activities that comprise it. This means (1) to determine what major activities are needed within the strategy and in what order they must occur, (2) to create a specific and public time schedule for completion of these activities, (3) to identify what resources (e.g., personnel, supplies) are needed, and (4) to assign precise responsibility to persons for completing each activity (Craig, 1978).

Let us assume that the planners selected the system-change strategy of establishing school health clinics throughout an entire school district in order to meet the teen pregnancy goal mentioned earlier. Think about the steps involved in "preparing for implementation" that you have just read about, and take a few moments to apply them to this strategy and goal.

Once this aspect of the plan is completed, implementation can occur. As you can plainly see, planning is complicated. Yet, it is fully capable of being mastered. Most importantly, as has been emphasized, effective planning is fundamental to success in preventive counseling.

Evaluation

Determination of success is an evaluative issue. Program evaluation is tied inexorably to program planning. It begins with the statement of goals and objectives, and it proceeds through all subsequent planning steps. It is a truism that the more precisely the primary prevention program is planned, the more easily and accurately the evaluation will be completed.

Basically, two major questions command the attention of the program evaluator: (1) Is the program being delivered according to plan? and (2) Is the program realizing the outcomes set out for it? These are issues of formative and summative evaluation, respectively.

Formative Evaluation

Formative evaluation is used to determine how an intervention is proceeding. That is, the resources, activities, strategies, and goals of the intervention program are closely monitored to ascertain whether they are being applied as designed and whether they need modification.

Narrative reports and diaries kept by the program planners and deliverers are often useful in determining whether the intervention is occurring as planned, whether any unexpected external events occurred (e.g., a large budget cut) that affected the program, and whether alternatives are required. Feeding-back formative evaluation data in a timely way to decision makers is essential if the information is to be effectively used to keep the program "on-track."

A course I teach, called "Program Development and Evaluation," is built around an actual project that students complete in small teams. Last quarter, the students were asked to analyze data collected to evaluate the effectiveness of an extensive Problem-Based Learning project and to design a plan for the next academic year that would improve upon the project they were studying. A centerpiece of that course always is construction of a Planning, Evaluation, and Review Technique (PERT) chart (Craig, 1978). The PERT chart requires planners to design carefully the relationships among objective, strategy, activities, tasks, responsibilities, resources, timelines, and evaluation. A PERT chart is created for the planners to post publicly and to follow as implementation of the plan occurs. The chart allows them to monitor the events and activities as they occur in relation to what was planned. With such a plan, accompanied by formative feedback, planners have an increased capacity to make adjustments to promote success.

Summative Evaluation

Summative evaluation is used to determine whether the planned outcomes were achieved. If they were, it is used to identify whether the realization of outcomes can be attributed to the prevention program or to some other cause.

Summative evaluation includes two levels. The first level can be considered midrange in scope. It is concerned with whether the intended behaviors or conditions that were to be produced by the intervention were attained. For instance, did participants in an assertiveness training workshop become more assertive by the program's end? Were the school health clinics established, and are they functioning? Measures of these midrange outcomes include observation, self-report, interviews, and behavior checklists.

In the second level of summative evaluation, long-range outcomes are examined. This level is of particular importance to primary prevention programs, for it allows judgments to be made that reductions in incidence did occur or failed to occur. At this level it is possible to learn, for example, if the gains in assertion skills led the workshop participants to experience fewer interpersonal crises at work and in their families, and if the installation of health clinics in the schools led to reductions in teen pregnancy for the targeted students.

Although long-range effects in prevention programs are difficult to measure, it is important to make the attempt. As has been observed (Bales, 1987), many programs stop collecting data too early, resulting sometimes in missing program effects. Only through the process of long-term data collection can incidence reduction, which is the ultimate goal of preventive counseling, be determined.

The evaluation methods to be employed in this effort are standard. Whenever possible, it is desirable to use experimental designs with randomization and control or contrast groups. Failing that, which is often the case in the "real world" of prevention, then quasi-experimental research designs (Campbell & Stanley, 1963) become very suitable. Gaining increasing favor these days is use of multivariate designs that enable researchers to examine multiple dependent measures simultaneously, and the use of qualitative, $n = 1$ designs, that provide for the intensive study of a few individuals over time.

Research issues in preventive counseling are generally the same as those found in many other field research (Price, 1983) and program evaluation areas (Cowen, 1984). However, in what is perhaps an understatement, the effort is "fraught with difficulties" (Wilson & Yager, 1981, p. 594).

Bloom (1977) and Baker, Swisher, Nadenichek, and Popowicz (1984) identified many of the difficulties facing prevention researchers, including: Are both goals and methods stated clearly? What is the relationship between program goals and methods? Is psychological growth in the target group assessed in relation to a no-program control group? Are the dependent measures being used appropriate to the task and to the population? Are these measures sensitive to the goals of the change program? Are a number of data sources being used? How do their results interrelate? Are long-range results examined? How important are the changes that have been found? And how does one measure the "nonoccurrence" of problems, which is a main goal of preventive counseling and other prevention efforts?

Bloom (1996) pointed to the importance of exiting a prevention project gracefully and being certain to leave behind a situation that has been improved. Sustainability is a critically important criterion so that participants can continue, and perhaps enhance, what has been put into place during the project.

Continuing with his examination of post-project responsibilities, Bloom (1996) pointed to the importance in planning and evaluation of incorporating civic, scientific, and professional responsibility. At the civic level, providing manuals and reports that can be used locally to guide action, or engaging appropriately with the local media about the program, might serve to buttress the project. At the scientific level, submitting papers and reports to refereed scholarly outlets is necessary to enter the project's process and results in the scientific storehouse of knowledge. Finally, Bloom suggests that a professional responsibility needs to be activated so that colleagues with whom one has worked or from whom one has borrowed ideas or practice approaches can learn what has and what has not worked.

BECOMING MORE SPECIFIC: HOW TO JUDGE EFFECTIVENESS IN PREVENTIVE COUNSELING PROGRAMS

What makes for an effective preventive counseling effort? Several approaches for evaluation are presented in this section. Look for the commonalities and the uniqueness across them.

Common Denominators of Success

Price et al. (1988) identified five "common denominators of success" that applied to the primary prevention programs that were identified as "excellent" in the 14 ounces of prevention study. These success barometers also are pertinent to preventive counseling. The programs are as follows:

1. Were targeted
2. Were designed to positively alter the "life trajectories" of participants
3. Provided new skills and social support
4. Strengthened natural support systems
5. Were able to demonstrate evidence of success

Demonstration of evidence of success (#5, above) relates directly to the process and outcome considerations discussed earlier in this chapter. Was the program delivered consistent with its plan (formative evaluation)? Were program goals realized (summative evaluation)?

The other three success barometers also relate to questions of effectiveness. Programs work best when they are targeted. That is, they need to be well planned and focused in relation to who might most benefit from them. For instance, a program in substance abuse prevention should contain elements that are attuned to a particular population and context, acknowledging relevant risks, protective factors, and cultural conditions.

Effective programs seek to change patterns of behavior and life conditions over time. Life trajectories are altered positively in such programs. For instance, children and families may create different rules of interaction to enable them to prosper over time, not just for the moment.

Program participants gain new skills and ways to provide support to each other. Skills in problem solving and communication skills, for example, can aid participants in interacting more successfully with their environment as well as in being better support to one another.

Natural support systems can be strengthened in effective preventive counseling efforts. Rather than importing expensive new resources or technologies, often the best way to produce and support change is for existing systems to become more naturally supportive. Schools, families, neighborhoods, and work settings can become increasingly responsive, stimulating social support for participants.

Resource Directories Containing Effective Prevention Programs

A number of wonderful resources have emerged over the last few years that continue the effort to evaluate prevention programs in relation to their quality. Programs that survive the evaluation process may be designated as excellent, as promising, and/or as model programs. I will provide two examples involving the Substance Abuse and Mental Health Administration (SAMHSA) and the Center for the Study and Prevention of Violence "Blueprints for Violence Prevention" project.

The Substance Abuse and Mental Health Administration (SAMHSA) produces a list of prevention programs with brief descriptions and follow-up information. SAMHSA uses the National Registry of Effective Programs (NREF) to identify programs that first rest upon a science base, meaning that they are deemed conceptually sound and internally consistent, with program activities that are related to program conceptualization and that are reasonably well implemented and evaluated. Upon that platform, prevention programs are then judged as being "promising" if they produce some positive outcomes, as being "excellent" if they consistently produce positive outcomes and are strongly implemented and evaluated, and as being "model" programs if they also are available for dissemination and if technical assistance is available from the program developers. See the SAMHSA Web site at http://modelprograms.samhsa for in-depth information and extensive listings of programs.

The Center for the Study and Prevention of Violence "Blueprints for Violence Prevention" Web site at the University of Colorado (http://www.colorado.edu/cspv/blueprints) also contains extensive information related to the evaluation of prevention programs. Evaluation criteria used in the Blueprints project include: (a) evidence of deterrent effect within a strong research design, (b) evidence of sustained effects that endure beyond the length of the prevention program of at least one year, (c) multiple-site replication, demonstrating that the prevention program can be replicated effectively, and (d) evidence of attention to important mediating effects (e.g., risk and protective factors) and whether the program is cost effective in relation to benefits. These are stringent criteria. Only 11 prevention programs have been able to fully meet them as of this writing.

Durlak's Criteria

Durlak (2003) discussed effective prevention and health promotion programming, suggesting eight generalizations that characterize successful interventions. Note that these points are highly consistent with those presented by Price et al. above.

According to Durlak, successful prevention and health promotion programming interventions:

1. Are data based and theory driven
2. Recognize that adjustment is affected by multiple factors at multiple levels
3. Emphasize behavior change and skill development
4. Are well timed
5. Use developmentally appropriate techniques and materials
6. Monitor to assure good program implementation
7. Are tailored and adapted for the particular population and setting
8. Are evaluated carefully

Effective prevention programs evolve intentionally from an intersection of data and theory. Theory serves to guide the overall direction of a program. Durlak suggests that certain theories, notably, social learning, behavioral, and ecological—are associated more than others with prevention, and often they are integrated. In addition, theories are applied in relation to data that have been collected that are either from the population setting itself or have bearing on it (e.g., demographic data). The point here is that good preventive counseling programs rest upon good data and theory and are not developed in a vacuum.

Adjustment and development are influenced by multiple factors, and program development/evaluation efforts need to be sensitive to them. These factors can be thought of in terms of risk and protective factors and how they combine and interact. It is not usually the case that one risk factor leads to a later dysfunction or that one protective factor can forestall it. Rather, factors combine, and it is the relationship between patterns of risk and patterns of protective factors that is salient. For instance, consider family life. Risk factors might include poor communication skills and high economic instability, while protective factors might include strong religious belief and warm social climate. How these risk and protective factors interrelate will affect ongoing family life.

Skill development and behavior change are critical to preventing dysfunction and promoting healthy functioning. Skill sets that have been important in prevention programs include communication and assertiveness, stress reduction, and interpersonal problem-solving. These skills are often taught using a social learning approach involving description, modeling, performing, feedback, and retrial. They also need to be set within the contexts for skill application. In preventive counseling, psychoeducation groups are used often to effect skill training (e.g., Conyne & Horne, 2001). Price, in his "Winning New Jobs: Path to the Future" program, has shown the value of skill development emerging from group participants. This empowering approach is fully consistent with preventive counseling.

Effective prevention programs need to be well timed. Although "before-the-fact" is ideal, that goal for timing may not always be possible. Yet, the attempt should be made to deliver these programs when most of an intended target population is problem free. Developmental transitions provide one means for timing preventive counseling so that later problems might be averted. Such developmental transition points include graduation, marriage, divorce, and retirement.

Prevention programs need to be pitched at a level that is developmentally and contextually appropriate. Younger age participants will not connect with overly complex or highly sensitive material. Group-based interventions for children need to be smaller, shorter, and more active than those for older participants. Participants' life experiences and culture need to be considered when designing preventive programs. What might be an appropriate prevention program on human sexuality for one group of teenagers may not be for another, depending on life experience, religious belief, and other factors.

Good program implementation is a part of effective prevention. This point addresses process evaluation/program monitoring, which we have discussed. The fidelity of the actual program as it is delivered in the real world in real time needs to be monitored, with feedback to program planners to help keep the program on course and make needed adjustments.

Summative evaluations are conducted to determine whether the program worked and what its effects on participants and systems were. Evaluation designs need to address many concerns, including: (a) fit the circumstances surrounding the program and that will allow important questions to be answered, such as what was promoted or prevented by the program; (b) have the design contain measures that are psychometrically valid and that address multiple levels, methods, and settings that comprise the program; (c) examine linkages between processes (e.g., group participation) and outcome (e.g., improved self-esteem); and (d) obtain both short-term and long-term results, as prevention often takes time to demonstrate effects.

Review of Reviews: What Works in Prevention

In a recent article in a special issue of *American Psychologist,* "Prevention That Works for Children and Youth," specific consideration was given to what works in prevention (Nation, Crusto, Wandersman, Kumpfer, Seybolt, Morrisey-Kane, & Davino, 2003). The authors used a review-of-review approach over four domains (substance abuse, school failure, risky sexual behavior, and juvenile delinquency), from which they derived a set of principles associated with effective prevention programs for families. In order of strength of support for each principle, the following emerged about effective prevention programs. These programs:

Are Comprehensive: Multiple interventions need to occur in multiple settings. Prevention programs need to contain an interconnected set of interventions, such as educational and organizational methods, to address protective and risk factors across domains and settings, such as family, school, and work.

Use Varied Teaching Methods: Effective preventive interventions involve active, skills-based, interactive instructional processes that often also include hands-on opportunities. Providing skill training, asking participants to role play, giving presentations, writing statements, researching topics, and so on all get participants involved and help to increase awareness, understanding, and skill acquisition.

Contain Sufficient Dosage: There needs to be enough of a preventive intervention, not too little or too much, in order to engage and to produce intended effects. Booster sessions may be helpful, and follow-up assessment is frequently lacking, the latter making the long-term effects of preventive programming largely unknown. In addition, participants with greater deficits and risk factors require more intense and higher dosage.

Are Theory Driven: Effective prevention programs follow a theoretical terrain, based on accurate information and empirical research. We have observed, however, that the etiology of cause and effect in prevention often is tenuous, at best. Frequently, one causal factor (e.g., poverty) can result in a range of both predicted (e.g., antisocial behavior) and unpredicted effects (e.g., resilience). It is also the case that one effect (e.g., academic failure) is the result of multiple and interrelated causes (e.g., family resources, ability, opportunities). These caveats, though important, do not dissuade from the importance of prevention programs being based on a theoretical system.

Include Positive Relationships: Strong, positive relationships with pro-social people are strongly related to effectiveness. Adult mentors, for example, as provided through Big Brothers and Big Sisters, speak to this issue, as does having bonds with peers, teachers, parents, and community members. The authors point out that their research review indicates the importance of having a strongly positive relationship with at least one adult.

Are Appropriately Timed: Prevention programs need to be timed so that they target "changeable precursor behaviors" (Dryfoos, 1990) before the full-blown problem behavior can be prevented. In addition, these programs need to be sensitive to the developmental needs of the participants.

Be Socioculturally Relevant: Prevention programs need to fit appropriately the cultural and community norms and values of participants as well as involved participants in program planning and implementation. One size does not fit all. These programs need to be translated substantially into the practical experience of those who will be part of them.

Include Outcome/Summative Evaluation: Prevention programs are characterized by clear objectives and processes, are documented, and examine how effectively goals were achieved. The programs presented in Section II of this book have undergone rigorous evaluation by various external sources (e.g., www.samhsa.gov/csap/modelprograms). Without outcome evaluation, it is not possible to determine program effectiveness.

Use Well-Trained Staff: Prevention staff need to be supportive of the program, understand it, and be trained and supervised sufficiently to be able to deliver the program faithfully and well.

When I teach students in my graduate-level Preventive Counseling course how to analyze the programmatic interventions we are discussing, I provide them with criteria to use in describing and evaluating the programs. These criteria were constructed to subsume those presented by Price et al. and by Durlak, as well as to be consistent with the preventive counseling model. The resulting 20 criteria, arranged into 7 categories (purpose, population, methods and settings, timing and appropriateness, skills and support, role, and planning and evaluation) are presented next.

Criteria for Evaluating Preventive Counseling Programs

Purposes

- What is being prevented or promoted?
- What is the program's purposive strategy (system change, person change, everyday prevention)?
- What are the program goals and objectives?
- How do they relate to methods?

Population

- What is the target population?
- How are the program participants functioning (well functioning, at risk, early stage of problem)?

Methods and Settings

- What methods of intervention are used (education, organization, media, consultation, advocacy, intended prevention within remedial methods, etc.)?
- What settings are involved (family, work, school, neighborhood, other)?
- How do methods and settings interact?
- How do they relate to program purposes?

Timing and Appropriateness

- How is the program timed (before-the-fact, early stage)?
- How is developmental and contextual appropriateness addressed?

Gradients

- How is the gradient of: Stressors + Organic Factors + Exploitation/Self-Esteem + Coping Skills + Support involved?
- How is the gradient of: Risk Factors/Protective Factors involved?

Skills and Support

- How are skills developed?
- How is social support developed?
- How do skills and support interact?

Role

- What is the program deliverer's role or roles (e.g., direct service counselor, group facilitator, consultant, evaluator)?
- To what degree is collaboration manifested?

Planning and Evaluation

- To what degree are program development and evaluation steps represented in the program?
- Does evaluation address both process and outcome?
- How sophisticated is the research design?
- Do results show evidence of goal accomplishment? Promise of eventual goal accomplishment?

In addition to using these criteria to analyze existing prevention programs, they can serve as a checklist for assisting in program development.

In the end, the real issue may not be how to do planning and evaluation at all, inasmuch as considerable recent progress in this area has been made. Rather, the real issue may be the valuation of it (Price, 1978; Wilson & Yager, 1981) as a process that is integral to service delivery of any type. The counseling heritage of helping leads to a natural proclivity to serve. This is as it should be, but sometimes in the drive to be helpful, planning and evaluation are given too low a priority. In today's world of accountability, showing evidence of effectiveness has become a survival skill (Hershenson & Power, 1987).

Finally we must remember, especially in preventive counseling, that planning and evaluation are integral parts of the intervention process, thus requiring both our valuing and our best energies.

CONCLUSION

This chapter has examined briefly the important planning and evaluation steps that accompany and support every intervention. The following planning substeps were considered: (1) identify possible problems and potentials; (2) identify a generative base, (3) assess needs and targets, (4) set goals, (5) select strategy, and (6) prepare for implementation. Program evaluation was then discussed, with attention given to its two main forms: (1) formative evaluation, or the monitoring and regular feedback of process results and events; and (2) summative evaluation, which is concerned with program outcomes of both a midrange and a long-term nature. Several criteria for evaluating preventive counseling programs were described to determine effectiveness. Excellent sources were provided to assist with accessing information about positively evaluated prevention programs. The overall point of the chapter was that planning and evaluation are integral and critical steps to preventive counseling projects.

ISSUES FOR REFLECTION AND DISCUSSION

1. The importance of planning and evaluation for preventive counseling has been stressed. Try to put this message into your own words. Having done so, do you agree?
2. What is the role of feedback in the planning-intervention-evaluation model? If you were a program planner, how would you want to use feedback?
3. How can a representative task force be useful in planning?
4. How do formative and summative program evaluation differ?
5. Explain the two main forms of summative evaluation.
6. Several sets of criteria were presented in this chapter that address how to determine if a prevention program is effective. Review that section of the chapter. Identify the commonalities and the uniqueness across the criteria. Develop your own "Top 5" criteria for determining effectiveness and their source(s). Write your "winners" in a two-page paper.
7. Suppose you were a school counselor employed in a rural setting. Your charge is to begin a program to reduce alcohol and other drug abuse among teens in the school. Use the planning and evaluation model presented in this chapter to design how you would fulfill this responsibility. Take 15 minutes to rough out some ideas and then hold a discussion with a partner for 30 minutes, comparing your approaches.
8. In the above situation (#6), how might you attempt to evaluate program effectiveness? What criteria might be important? Identify at least three criteria that would fit your situation, and then write some specific ways you might apply them.
9. It is said that it is difficult to evaluate prevention and preventive counseling. Do you agree? Why, or why not? Hold a discussion with others in a small group to explore this issue and to compare and contrast your ideas.

CHAPTER 5

Prevention Programs in the Family Setting

CONTEXT

The family is a critically important setting in American life. When a family functions well, it can guide and shape children's development positively and provide a continuing source of purpose, support, challenge, and enjoyment in the lives of all family members. When the family is not functioning well, its members can suffer a number of difficulties, ranging from disaffection to dysfunction and illegal behavior.

Prevention programs targeting the family seek to assist at the "ground level." Regardless of the traditional or nontraditional nature of a family, these programs address the most basic unit of importance in human development in our society.

The observation made in the Preface to this section—that effective prevention programs typically cross settings—is especially valid for the family setting. Reviews of prevention programs that are restricted to the family setting indicate that few such efforts exist. Rather, attention to the family setting is often incorporated within broader setting applications, such as the school or the community.

Prevention programs focused on family settings frequently emphasize parent training (e.g., Patterson, Chamberlain, & Reid, 1982) or parent involvement (e.g., Davis & Tolan, 1993). Parent training programs typically educate parents or other adult caretakers of children in parenting skills and strategies. Once trained, the caregivers are assisted in practicing these skills and strategies with their children. Parent involvement prevention programs typically involve families in the process of implementing the program through participating in events, activities, or strategies that are embedded naturally with learning principles—such as working with others, listening, sharing ideas, and talking about what works. These family programs take place in the home of the family, or they involve family members off-site in some intentional form of family involvement (Catalano, Berglund, Ryan, Lonczak, & Hawkins, 2002).

This chapter will examine three programs that have been evaluated as being effective:

1. Functional Family Therapy (FFT) (Alexander, Barton, Gordon, Grotpeter, Hansson, Harrison, Mears, Mihalic, Parsons, Pugh, Schulman, Waldron, & Sexton, 1998), which is focused on the family setting
2. FAST Track (Bierman, Coie, Dodge, Greenberg, Lochman, & McMahon, 1996; ConductProblems Prevention Group, 1992, 2000), which is focused on family, individual, and school settings
3. Houston Parent-Child Development Center (Johnson, 1988; Johnson & Walker, 1987,1991), which was identified in *14 Ounces of Prevention* (Price, Cowen, Lorion, & Ramos-McKay, 1988)

FUNCTIONAL FAMILY THERAPY

What Is Functional Family Therapy (FFT)?

Functional Family Therapy (FFT) (Alexander, Robbins, & Sexton, 2000; Sexton & Alexander, 2002) is a family-based prevention and intervention program that is used to target high-risk youths and their families (treatment) or at-risk youths and their families (prevention). Family-based, FFT uses a multisystemic and multilevel approach to treat and prevent the broad range of problems encountered by juveniles in relation to delinquent and criminal behavior. It focuses on the treatment system, individual and family functioning, and the therapist as key factors. FFT combines and integrates a number of components within its model, including clinical theory, empirically supported principles, and extensive clinical experience.

The original developers of FFT (Alexander & Parsons, 1973) realized over 30 years ago that the development and rate of juvenile delinquency, drug abuse, and violence were increasing much faster than were the successful treatment programs. FFT was created with the family at the center of treatment and prevention, and with the evolving belief that identifying and building family members' strengths was a critically important process. Moreover, Alexander, Robbins, and Sexton (2000) maintain that FFT can exert a so-called dual effect involving successful treatment of youth who are presently offending through changing risk and protective factors within the family system, while also exerting a primary preventive effect on siblings who are at risk but not yet offending.

How Is It Done?

FFT targets youth 11 to 18 years of age across a range of ethnic and cultural groups, while also providing assistance to younger siblings. It is a short-term, multiphase, goal-directed, systematic intervention involving an average of 8 to 12 sessions for milder cases and up to 30 hours of direct services for more challenging ones. FFT has evolved into an intervention model including systematic training, supervision, and process and outcome assessment.

FFT works first to identify and develop the inner strengths of family members, as well as a sense that they can improve their situations. This avenue is very consistent with positive psychology tenets. Also, centering initial activity around strengths provides the family with a "platform for change and future functioning" that can lead to greater self-sufficiency, lowered treatment needs, and much reduced costs.

Sexton and Alexander (1999) have further refined and systemized the phases of intervention in FFT. They have articulated intervention steps and considerations associated with each of three phases over time:

1. Early-phase intervention emphasizes engagement and motivation, where establishing a family focus to the work includes increasing hope and positive expectations for change.
2. Middle-phase intervention emphasizes behavior change, where special attention is given to using appropriate techniques that fit the family relational system.
3. Late-phase intervention emphasizes generalization, where the primary goal is to improve the family's capacity to impact the multiple systems in which it is embedded (e.g., school, community, juvenile justice system).

Sexton and Alexander (1999) described the early phase of engagement and motivation as typically including:

Goals: Develop alliances, reduce negativity and resistance, improve communication, minimize hopelessness, reduce dropout potential, develop family focus, increase motivation for change.
Risk Factors addressed: Negativity and blaming, hopelessness.
Protective Factors addressed: Credibility, alliance, treatment availability.

Assessment: Behavior (e.g., risk and protective factors presented), relational problems (e.g., needs), and context (risk and protective factors). Assessment is multilevel, multidimensional, and multimethod and focuses on family functioning, not on diagnostic assessment.

Therapist/Interventionist Skills: Interpersonal skills (e.g., validation, reframing), high availability to provide services.

What Works?

FFT is one of 11 "model" Blueprint prevention programs, as judged by the Center for the Study and Prevention of Violence, and it has been evaluated very positively by several other sources (e.g., as being effective by the American Youth Policy Forum, and as a Model 1 program in the Surgeon General's 2001 report). It always has required a comprehensive evaluation of process and outcomes. From 1973 to the present, research data demonstrate that FFT is highly successful when compared with residential treatment, standard juvenile probation services, and alternative therapeutic approaches. Indices such as reduced recidivism, lowered re-arrests, reductions in offending by the siblings of adolescents in treatment, and lowered costs of service have clearly favored FFT. For example, a study by Aos and Barnoski (1998) produced savings of $14,000 per family. These results all evidence of positive prevention outcomes.

Why Does It Work?

FFT derives its effectiveness from emphasizing factors that are essential to positive change and to their generalization. Its three phases are tied to specific factors associated with positive change. Strengths are recognized and valued. Risk and protective factors that are both person- and system-centered are incorporated within assessment and behavior change. The approach is oriented within the context of the family and attends methodically to connected systems. Care is given to nurturing the relationship between the family and the provider.

Implications for Counselors and Other Helpers

FFT occupies a unique place in prevention programs, aside from its validated effectiveness. It is both a treatment and a prevention program. FFT therefore illustrates how a powerful approach can be used, on the one hand to target offending adolescents and their families (treatment) or, on the other, at-risk adolescents and their families (prevention). It is a program that has been replicated across 15 states where thousands of adolescents and families are served each year. Moreover, a range of trained professionals are using this approach, both for treatment and for prevention—including licensed mental health counselors.

By spanning the treatment–prevention spectrum, FFT is highly compatible with counselors and other helpers who understandably are interested in identifying prevention approaches they can use which fit well with their ongoing work. FFT's focus on relational dynamics builds a natural bridge linking treatment and prevention. This proven program offers professional counselors who are prepared to work a prevention vehicle with families that can be used perhaps more readily than some other equally excellent prevention programs that we will examine next.

FAST TRACK PREVENTION PROJECT

What Is FAST Track?

FAST Track is a multisite, comprehensive, long-term prevention program that includes multiple settings: the family/home, school, and the individual (Bierman, Coie, Dodge, Greenberg, Lochman, & McMahon, 1996; Conduct Problems Prevention Research Group, 1992, 2000). The preventive intervention includes a universal-level classroom program and social skill training, academic tutoring, parent training, and home visiting aimed at improving competencies and reducing problems in a high-risk group of children selected in kindergarten. Its overall purpose is to prevent chronic and severe conduct problems for children at high risk for long-term antisocial behavior. The program seeks to reach its prevention goal by increasing communication bonds and interaction competencies among children and parents, by enhancing children's cognitive, social, and problem-solving skills, and by improving peer relationships. It can be implemented in urban and rural areas for girls and boys of varying social class, ethnicity, and family composition.

The program is premised on an ecological and developmental perspective that antisocial behavior has its origins in the interaction of multiple influences. Risk levels increase when children and families reside in low-income, high-crime neighborhoods where marital conflict and other forms of instability are more likely to occur. In such situations, consistent and positive parenting practice is difficult to maintain, especially if children may be impulsive. In turn, these children's readiness and preparation for performing well in school are threatened, and their repertoire is often inadequate for coping with social, emotional, and academic demands in school. In addition, parents from such situations often are unable to relate well to school staff and may find the school environment uncomfortable.

How Is It Done?

Based on the above developmental model, the prevention strategy includes providing intensive interventions during transitions located at school entry and from elementary to middle school. FAST Track also is predicated on a unified model of prevention that includes both universal intervention (teacher-led curriculum, called PATHS) and components administered only to high-risk students.

The universal intervention of a teacher-led curriculum (PATHS) continues from first through fifth grades and includes 57 lessons. These lessons were taught about three times a week, with each lesson lasting 20 to 30 minutes. The lessons addressed skills for understanding and communicating emotions (40%), skills for increasing positive social behavior (30%), and skills for self-control and social problem solving (30%).

The high-risk program spans grades 1 through 6 but is most intense during transitions occurring upon entry into first grade and from grade school to middle school. The program is multidimensional and includes:

1. Parent and child training groups meeting biweekly in second grade and then once per month for all other years
2. Biweekly home visits to reinforce parenting skills, foster parents' problem-solving capacity, and promote parents' feelings of efficacy and empowerment
3. Academic tutoring being offered three times per week to improve the reading skills of children, and child case management activities occurring as needed.

What Works?

The FAST Track Prevention Project has been evaluated very positively by several sources (e.g., as a Promising Blueprint program and as being effective by the Center for Mental Health Services). An evaluation by Greenberg, Lochman, and McMahon (1996) and by the Conduct Problems Prevention Research Group (1992, 2000) indicated that the FAST Track Prevention Project addressed 10 positive youth development constructs: social, emotional, cognitive, and behavioral competence, self-efficacy, resiliency, bonding, recognition for positive behavior, opportunities for prosocial involvement, and prosocial norms.

Research of the FAST Track program has yielded strong and consistent evidence for successive three-year cohorts favoring first grade program participants ($N = 448$) over controls ($N = 450$). The program children consistently showed better social skills, more positive peer relations, better reading skills, and more positive emotional and social coping skills, with some indication of fewer conduct problems. Parents of the program children were shown to be more involved in their children's schools, to be more positively involved with their children, and to use more effective discipline strategies. Observers of children's aggressive, disruptive, and oppositional behavior in the classroom reported fewer related problems for program children. In terms of process evaluation, several positive results were obtained, including the fidelity with which teachers delivered the PATHS curriculum. Over a life course, should these results continue, prevention effects of the FAST Track program will contribute to an improved life for both children and parents with fewer debilitating problems.

Why Does It Work?

The FAST Track Prevention Project is comprehensive and long term. Its conceptual base is well developed and focuses on a universal program as well as on a high-risk program organized around developmental transitions. Multiple sets of skills are addressed across three domains (social, cognitive, problem solving), parents and peers are involved, and multiple methods are incorporated (parent training, home visitations, social skills training, academic tutoring, and PATHS classroom curriculum). The prevention program is delivered within a carefully constructed research design, including program and control students. Both outcome and process evaluations are planned for and conducted. The prevention program is coordinated across family and school settings.

Implications for Counselors and Other Helpers

Mental health and school counselors frequently are confronted with child and family problems that often center around existing poor social skills, discipline problems, and disruptive behavior at home and in the classroom. Individual, group, and family counseling and therapy typically are the reactive responses, often with positive results. The FAST Track Prevention Project, however, illustrates how counselors and associated helpers could collaborate with others to create prevention programs aimed at both reducing the occurrence of these kinds of problems and developing competencies in children and parents. This kind of approach might engender even broader empowering consequences owing to its early stage and comprehensive focus.

THE HOUSTON PARENT-CHILD DEVELOPMENT CENTER

What Is the Houston Parent-Child Development Center (H-PCDC)?

The Houston program is one of three Parent-Child Development Center sites, the others being in New Orleans and Birmingham, Alabama. All three programs generally are directed at fostering positive relationships between parents and children by targeting low-income families and providing multi-dimensional interventions.

Designed for Mexican-American families below the poverty line in Houston, the H-PCDC seeks to help families optimize the competencies and school performance of their children. The program is based on the importance of parent-child relationships and on an ecological and transactional perspective that behavior problems (and growth) arise out of children's interactions with significant people in their environment. From this viewpoint, outcomes are a product of interactional history.

How Is It Done?

The H-PCDC offers a broad range of support services for Mexican-American mothers and children. Cultural sensitivity is taken very seriously, with the first year of the program held in the home and involving fathers, and with much of the verbal interaction conducted in Spanish. Considerable attention is given to program development processes that involve Mexican-American families in surveys and interviews conducted in the barrios, with representative families serving as discussants of evolving data. Other processes also are used to increase ecological validity, such as meeting with groups of Mexican-American professionals and using a Parents Advisory Council to help guide the program. In these and other ways, program development and its monitoring actively involve family members.

An important program premise is that mother–child interactions are of primary importance, especially in the early childhood years of 1 to 3 years. Through parent training, continuing education classes, and home visits, mothers learn about their children's intellectual, socioemotional, and physical development. Basic services also are provided to the family through transportation, health and social services, meals, sibling programs, and participant stipends for participation. Beyond that, the H-PCDC provides activities for children and structured play periods for children and mothers. These periods are videotaped, analyzed, and then used to improve the interaction and communication skills of families.

What Works?

This prevention program was described in detail (Johnson, 1988, 1990). It was cited as an excellent prevention program by the American Psychological Association (Price et al. 1988) and by the Substance Abuse and Mental Health Association as a Promising Blueprints program, and it was featured in the training video, *An Ounce of Prevention* (1992).

The H-PCDC is a large-scale, externally reviewed research program set within an experimental design. In one study, an experimental group of 97 mother–child pairs was compared against a control group of 119 mother–child pairs. Data were collected from observations made of mother–child interactions, of the home environment, and of infant development. Statistically significant results were found in a follow-up study, showing (a) improvements in mothers' use of affection, praise, criticism, and restrictive control; (b) increased parent–child interactions; (c) more verbalizations, (d) less destructive, overactive, and negative attention-seeking behavior for children between ages 4 and 7; (e) higher cognitive scores; (f) lower teacher ratings for children between 8 and 11 showing disruptive, hostile, impulsive, obstinate, and fighting behaviors; and (g) continued program effects five to eight years after program completion.

Why Does It Work?

The program requirement of 550 hours was rather extensive for typical parent–child programs; the amount of time is about the equivalent of a three-semester credit hour college course. The intensity of the program was a factor, with a myriad of activities (e.g., skill training, home visits, graduation ceremonies) and with the involvement of both mothers and of fathers. The program's cultural sensitivity contributed to success (e.g., use of Spanish), and its attention to providing basic needed services, such as transportation and child care, acted on environmental impediments that too frequently are not considered. The program itself became a continuing source of social support, where families could learn and count on each other. The development of skills in child management and knowledge of child development were centrally important. Teachers were paraprofessionals during the first year, which served to lessen status differentials that sometimes can occur between professionals and indigenous participants. Involving families in the program's creation and maintenance helped to shape the program to fit core values and to make it both acceptable and appropriate. Perhaps of highest significance was the focus of the program on developing positive patterns of mother–child interaction. Finally, the entire project was set within an externally funded experimental design to allow for testing of both process and outcome effectiveness.

Implications for Counselors and Other Helpers

Several implications for counselor practice can be noted. Counselors and other helpers can benefit from how a generative and theoretical base was translated effectively into applied practice. Home visits, which were a central part of this program, can be included more often as a delivery mode. Program development, which occurred in collaboration with participants, is a best practice that needs to be broadly replicated. As with other exemplary programs, an externally funded research design was used to monitor and test the program's utility. Funded research is often a key to being able to mount and deliver prevention programs, and to determine their effectiveness. A strong focus on social support and skill development led the program itself to become a nurturing place and space; better awareness of the ecology of settings is needed by practitioners .

All of these points, and more, represent areas for learning by counselors and other helpers as they become more involved with prevention programs. None of these kinds of involvements require training and skills that are presently outside the scope of most counselors' repertoires. However, students need focused training experiences that ask them to apply their knowledge and skills in real-world settings, under guidance and supervision. Putting it all together in a new way is what matters. The H-PCDC provides a concrete example of how this can be done to prevent disorder from occurring and to develop human strengths.

CONCLUSION

Each of the three family-based prevention programs described in this chapter demonstrates important ways to positively affect family functioning and to exert a preventive influence. Mental health and school counselors alike need to be aware of the role of family dynamics in the overall development of strengths and deficits found in the family members the counselors may be working with—remedially, developmentally, or preventively. Prevention programs that may be located in a different setting, such as a school, neighborhood, or workplace, usually can improve their effectiveness by incorporating family influences within their design and delivery.

Here is one example from my experience. We began to develop a collaborative working relationship with a school in a geographic area of the city that is heavily populated by persons from Appalachian descent, many of whom had only recently migrated from the mountains of Tennessee and

Kentucky. In the course of our work, we began to notice that services to family members in that district were minimal and costly. The cost of food at the local "mom-and-pop" grocery store seemed inflated and the food restricted in range. Although a large hyper-super market was only two miles away, members of this neighborhood did not shop there. When we began to discuss this matter with school and family members, we were at first surprised to learn that the hyper-market had by its own volition provided free bus transportation from the area to their store over a one-month period, but virtually no neighborhood member had used it! Why? We learned that family members did not appreciate a "handout" of this service when it was not requested. They perceived the bus as an intrusion, and so they ignored it. This story can teach us that families are affected by their environment, have their own important value systems, and need to be approached as partners in potential new interventions.

Common ingredients such as these have been identified that span effective prevention programs (as we have seen in earlier chapters) and family-based prevention programs in particular. Most recently, Kumpfer and Alvarado (2003) have reported on two federal studies (that of the National Institute of Justice, Office of Juvenile Justice and Delinquency Prevention project in 1989 and that of the Center for Substance Abuse Prevention's Prevention Enhancement Protocol System in 1998). Through this review process, the authors identified effective family preventive interventions (behavioral parent training, family skills training, and family therapy) and what accounted for this effectiveness. Effective family-focused prevention interventions were those that:

1. Were comprehensive, multicomponent programs that could modify a broader range of risk and protective processes in children than could single-faceted programs
2. Emphasize family strengths (e.g., resilience and protective processes) instead of deficits, are generally more effective in addressing families experiencing relationship problems than are programs centered more specifically on either parents or children alone
3. Address family relations, communication, and monitoring provided by parents
4. Produce enduring effectiveness results when they are able to change cognitive, affective, and behavioral dynamics within the ongoing family environment
5. Recognize that higher-risk families need an increased dosage or intensity of intervention (25–50 hours) than do lower-risk families (5–24 hours), due to the involvement of more risk factors and fewer protective factors

6. Recognize that age and developmental appropriateness are necessary for family programs
7. Introduce developmentally appropriate interventions when a family is receptive to change and growth
8. Introduce family interventions as early as possible in situations of greater dysfunction
9. Tailor the preventive program within the cultural traditions of the family, which improves recruitment, retention, and sometimes effectiveness
10. Build incentives, such as child care and transportation, into prevention programs in order to increase recruitment and retention
11. Use trainers and staff who are competent, warm, humorous, use empathy well, and are able to structure training so that it is organized and directive
12. Use interactive skills training methods (e.g., homework practice, role playing, active modeling, CDs/videos) rather than passive, didactic learning approaches to increase client satisfaction and program effectiveness
13. Employ a collaborative process with participants to foster empowerment and the identification of support and participant-based solutions

When working in the area of family-based prevention, these guidelines can be very helpful to counselors. No intrusive buses, no matter how well intended!

ISSUES FOR REFLECTION AND DISCUSSION

1. Let's return to the example given in the Conclusion concerning work with families primarily from Appalachian backgrounds. From this study, we know that the free bus service provided by the grocery store was not accepted. Although I discussed this topic, now it is your turn: Meet with a person with whom you have not yet held a discussion and explore this "matter of the unwanted bus service." What do you make of it? How does it apply to prevention counseling with families? Develop three suggestions that seem to fit well and be prepared to share them with others in the class.
2. How does family life affect functioning in other domains, such as school? Identify some ways. How can preventive counselors take advantage of that influence to develop effective family-based programs?

3. Which of the three family-based prevention programs described in this chapter resonates most with you? Why? Again, discuss your choice with a partner and compare notes. Pay close attention to what you may be saying about yourselves in the process.

4. Consider your own family history and dynamics (choose your family of origin, your present family, or another connection with people that feels like a "family"). How are you affected by this history and dynamics? What is the openness of your family culture to mental health service involvement? to preventive counseling? How might a prevention program best be introduced so that members of your family might be attracted to it? Write a one-page analysis paper to share with others later.

5. Pick three of the principles of effective family-focused interventions presented in the Conclusion which seem to make the most sense to you. Why those? How could they be incorporated within a family-based prevention program aimed at drug abuse prevention?

CHAPTER 6

Prevention Programs in the School Setting

CONTEXT

Perhaps the single best organized setting available for locating and delivering prevention programs is the school. A range of physical, environmental, and behavioral factors that may negatively influence a student's personal and academic development typically are found in schools (Meyers & Swerdlik, 2003). Moreover, schools present unparalleled opportunities for developing and supporting student strengths.

Schools are a valuable entry point and resource setting for prevention for many reasons. The most obvious one is that children and adolescents are required to attend school and thus can be found in one spot. Second, children and adolescents spend large, continuing portions of their everyday lives (at least from September through mid-June, some 5400 hours) in school. Third, the mission of schools and the goals and purposes of prevention programs coalesce around an intent to improve outcomes for students. Fourth, schools provide convenience and accessibility to parents and family members, in addition to students, allowing the capacity to include them in skill building and other activities. This is an important point, especially for families of limited resources whose children may be at elevated risk for academic and personal difficulties. Fifth, schools provide an ongoing structure through which prevention programs can operate (Branden-Muller & Elias, 1991; Brown & Bolen, 2003; McMahon, Ward, Pruett, Davidson, & Griffith, 2000; Ross, Powell, & Elias, 2002).

Therefore, the school setting affords a significant opportunity for engaging students and important others, such as teachers and parents, in prevention activities. In addition, the school is an organized setting that can be coordinated with other settings, such as family and community, for prevention programming (Kolbe, Collins, & Cortese, 1997).

Schools provide an ecology that incorporates students and adults in important ongoing processes and structures. These processes and structures include a complex organizational structure, cultural norms and values, social and peer groups, classrooms, clubs, athletics, music, cafeterias, faculty lounges, temporal patterns, and physical structures, among others (Oxley, 2000, 2001). Settings within schools and schools themselves as settings are naturally occurring, ecological units of activity that provide rich milieus for prevention programs. Also important are the contextual relationships of schools with other systems, such as the community and with state and national policies and legislation.

It may not be surprising, then, that schools are frequent sites for prevention programs and that a number of school-based prevention programs have been recognized for their quality. Greenberg, Weissberg, O'Brien, Zins, Fredericks, Resnik, and Elias (2003) recently observed that school-based prevention and youth development programs are most beneficial when they simultaneously can increase students' personal and social assets while also enhancing the quality of the school environment itself. The term SEL (social and emotional learning) spans this effort, and information about it can be found through the Collaborative for Academic, Social, and Emotional Learning (CASEL) (see www.CASEL.org).

In this chapter, we will examine three programs that have demonstrated impressive evidence of effectiveness:

1. Life Skills Training (Botvin & Kantor, 2000; Botvin & Tortu, 1988; Botvin, Schinke, Epstein, Diaz, & Botvin, 1995)
2. School Transitional Environment Program (STEP) (Felner & Adan, 1988; Felner, Brand, Adan, Mulhall, Flowers, Sartain, & DuBois, 1993; Felner, Felner, & Silverman, 2000)
3. Seattle Social Development Project (Hawkins, Catalano, Morrison, O'Donnell, Abbott, & Day, 1992; O'Donnell, Hawkins, Catalano, Abbott, & Day, 1995; Hawkins, Catalano, & Kosterman, 1999; Lonczak, 2002)

LIFE SKILLS TRAINING

What Is Life Skills Training (LST)?

You may recall that the discussion in Chapter 2 on "everyday prevention" drew on the Life Skills Training program developed by Botvin and his colleagues. LST is a three-year program intended for middle and junior high school students (sixth–seventh grades). Its goal is to prevent drug use among these students, and it makes use of a carefully developed training regimen in life skills and social resistance. Psychoeducation groups are a main vehicle for conducting the training, which includes attention not only to specific resistance skills but also to enhancement of generic personal and social skills.

The program takes as a conceptual touchstone the research of Jessor (1984) indicating that health-compromising behaviors appear to be positively correlated. This condition suggests that a number of problem behaviors may be caused by the same set of basic factors. Thus, the set of underlying factors that lead to substance abuse, for example, may also lead to other problem behaviors such as academic difficulty and depression. Therefore, the Life Skills Training program seeks to target factors that are linked to a range of later dysfunctions and problem behaviors through training in skill sets that are both specific to the behaviors to be prevented (in this case, substance abuse) and aimed at increasing general personal and social competence.

Social learning theory (Bandura, 1997) and problem behavior theory (Jessor & Jessor, 1977) theoretically undergird the program components. Substance abuse is conceptualized as being socially learned and functional, resulting from an interaction of personal and social-environmental factors and where modeling and social reinforcement play important roles. Learning new specific and generic life skills and how to apply them—that is, gaining personal and social competence that can be acted on—is the basic fulcrum for prevention in this program.

As cited in Botvin and Tortu (1988), the objectives of the Life Skills Training program are to: (a) provide resistance skills against direct and indirect social pressures to drink excessively, smoke, or use marijuana; (b) help students to manage anxiety, especially social anxiety; (c) increase self-esteem, autonomy, self-confidence, and self-mastery; (d) increase awareness of the negative consequences of substance abuse; and (e) enhance attitudes and behaviors that support not using substances.

How Is It Done?

The Life Skills Training program includes three major parts: (1) general self-management skills, (2) social skills, and (3) information and skills specifically related to drug use. Each part contains a number of 45-minute sessions that can be delivered as an intensive mini-course or once a week. Skills are taught in a psychoeducation group format using strategies of instruction, demonstration, feedback, reinforcement, and practice.

Areas covered within the three major components include:

Knowledge and information: Sessions address knowledge and information specific to substances and substance abuse.

Decision making: Sessions address making decisions and independent thinking and also how the media and advertising influence decisions.

Self-directed behavior change: Sessions address self-image and self-improvement. An eight-week self-improvement project is started at this point.

Coping with anxiety: Sessions address common anxiety-arousing situations and practicing skills and techniques for coping.

Social skills: Sessions address verbal and nonverbal communication skills, social skills aimed at overcoming shyness, social skills dealing with boy-girl relationships, and assertiveness training.

LST is delivered in 15 sessions in year one, 10 sessions in year two, and 5 sessions in year three. A critically important facet of the program is incorporation of booster sessions following the main program (10 sessions for eighth graders and 5 sessions for ninth graders). These booster sessions are used to help thwart tendencies to regress and to reinforce the skills and their application.

What Works?

LST is one of the 11 prevention programs evaluated by the Blueprints project as being both an excellent and a model program, and by OJJDP and SAMHSA as a model program. LST also has been evaluated by NIDA as an effective program and by the Department of Education-Safe Schools as exemplary. In terms of program outcomes, over a dozen studies consistently demonstrate that LST dramatically reduces gateway drug use. That is, the program has been shown to reduce the rate of increase in target behaviors (e.g., smoking) in program participants, or in the proportion of adolescents in the program manifesting the behaviors, compared to those in comparison groups. Cross-cultural studies show that LST is effective with a diverse range of adolescents from different cultures. Moreover, results indicate that the program results are durable and that the program is effective whether it is delivered by teachers, peer leaders, or health professionals.

More specifically, averaging outcomes over several studies, LST has been found to cut tobacco, alcohol, and marijuana use from 50 to 75%, with long-term follow-up results (six years post-program) showing that LST cuts polydrug use up to 66%, reduces pack-a-day smoking by 25%, and decreases the use of inhalants, narcotics, and hallucinogens. Last,

LST is cost-effective, amounting to about $7.00 a student per year, not including the cost of training, which is a minimum of $2000/day for one or two days (Botvin, Mihalic, & Grotpeter, 1998).

Why Does It Work?

LST is a carefully constructed program that matches its objectives with its methodology. It is set within a sophisticated research design that allows for testing immediate outcome effects as well as durability and replicability, and it has included both pilot studies and large-scale prevention trials. A variety of outcome measures is used, including self-report questionnaires and saliva samples. The inclusion of training and education in both drug-specific and generic competencies acknowledges that trying to prevent one specific set of behaviors alone is but a partial approach; rather, programs need to be more comprehensive as there is no single and direct route between etiology and effect in mental health and educational prevention programs. The use of psychoeducation groups that include peer participation resonates well with adolescents. The program curriculum is clearly developed, training for group leaders is thorough, parental support for the program is intentionally sought and maintained, and ongoing support and consultation is made available for program implementers.

Implications for Counselors and Other Helpers

The LST program relies on methods and intervener skills that are central to counselor training, role, and function. The use of psychoeducation groups connects with a dominant group work application for counselors in all settings (Conyne, Wilson, & Ward, 1997). As Albee and Gullotta (1997) observed about group methods in general, "Group can provide a simple, sustained kind of human friendship *where the act of genuine, honest, trusting, and empathic caring has great growth-promoting power*" (p. 18).

Training and consulting with others, such as teachers, and training and supervising others, such as students and paraprofessionals, are critically important activities for counselors in the schools. Collaborating with parents, so important in the LST program, is a mainline counselor function within the schools. Fitting the program within the ongoing school environment is a task that school counselors are educated to do as part of any comprehensive and developmental school counseling program. In short, the LST prevention program affords a close and comfortable match with the school counseling mission.

SCHOOL TRANSITIONAL ENVIRONMENTAL PROGRAM (STEP)

What Is the School Transitional Environmental Program (STEP)?

The School Transitional Environmental Program (STEP) is based on the transitional life events model. The premise of this model is that stressful life events occurring around life transitions, such as changing schools or moving into retirement, places people at higher risk for dysfunction. The significant transition, then, becomes the risk condition around which the prevention program is applied.

STEP (Felner & Adan, 1988; Felner, Ginter, & Primavera, 1982) is focused on the life transition of changing schools. Research has documented that many students find that changing schools can lead to lower academic achievement, elevated anxiety, increases in school absences, and classroom behavior problems. In turn, these kinds of problems can track with dropping out of school and to larger behavioral and social problems. STEP takes as its main focus altering a school's ecological context, rather than trying to change any individuals directly (Felner, Felner, & Silverman, 2000).

How Is It Done?

STEP seeks to reduce the complexity of school environments for targeted incoming students, to increase teacher and peer support, and to reduce students' vulnerability to emotional and academic difficulties. Students involved in the program are those who generally were coping adequately prior to the school transition but who may be at elevated risk. Some risk factors include low socioeconomic or minority status, entering puberty, lower levels of coping skills or family support, and the co-occurrence of other life transitions or stressors.

STEP can be applied at transitions from elementary to junior high school and from junior high school to high school. It is targeted to students usually coming from multiple and smaller feeder schools who will be entering a much larger new system; most applications have been in large, urban schools serving primarily non-White, lower-income students. In such situations, the sudden and far greater complexity of the new school environment, in combination with its more limited capacity to respond to the needs of the entering students, make it more difficult for the developmental transition to occur without significant challenge.

The prevention program is used to create smaller, developmentally enhancing social contexts within the large school that will reduce continual flux in the system and increase the support available. The program components are straightforward and focused on environmental modifications.

STEP students are assigned to core academic classes containing between 60 and 110 students. These students proceed together to take the necessary classes, thereby limiting the exposure to large numbers of other students. Moreover, to continue to control for flux, these core academic classes are scheduled in adjacent classrooms so that students do not need to traverse long corridors to locate their classes. Finally, the role of the teacher in these classes is changed to include an administrative-counseling link among the student, the school, and the family. Teachers advise and guide students regarding course selection, school, and personal issues, and they liaison with parents to explain the project and communicate about any other issues affecting school participation (such as absences). Teachers receive special training and support to prepare them for this new role, which is geared to be much more responsive and supportive to student needs and to helping with negotiating school and family demands. All aspects of STEP are aimed at smoothing the developmental transition into the more complex setting and at preventing sets of negative consequences from occurring.

What Works?

STEP has been identified as successful through different external reviews. The APA Task Force on Prevention selected it from 900 other programs as being effective, and it was a featured program in the Price et al. (1988) *14 Ounces of Prevention*. STEP also has been judged as being effective by the Center for Mental Health Services and by Communities That Care, among other sources. It is listed as a Promising prevention program in the Center for the Study and Prevention of Violence Blueprints compendium, in the Surgeon General's Report of 2001, and as being Highly Promising by Title V (OJJD).

A number of program evaluations of STEP have been conducted. These evaluations include the original program and replications in middle schools, high schools, in both urban and rural settings. A five-year study of students in the original STEP trial showed that the dropout rate for program students was 50% less than for control students. In addition, compared to program students, control students in a second evaluation were shown to have developed significant negative movement across a broad range of developmental outcomes, including in self-concepts and behavioral and emotional problems, delinquent behavior, and the reported likelihood of illicit substance use (Felner, Felner, & Silverman, 2000). Evaluations conducted at the close of ninth grade demonstrate that STEP students, compared to controls, showed reductions in absenteeism, increases in GPA, stability of self-concept, and more positive feelings abut the school environment. Similar outcomes were found in replication studies conducted in lower and lower-middle-class high schools and in three junior high schools (Felner & Adan, 1988; Reyes & Jason, 1991).

Why Does It Work?

STEP is a good example of a first-order prevention program that is aimed at improving developmental pathways (new school) and reducing developmental hazards (e.g., excessive organizational flux). Leveraging improved pathways can prevent poor transitions by students through these pathways that can lead to negative consequences (e.g., dropping out) and can yield positive benefits, such as improved self-concept and liking school more. Note that the targets of the prevention program—the students—are not directly addressed. Conditions are addressed, and through those modified conditions, students are affected. Thus, STEP illustrates that sound and systematic environmental change can be used effectively for prevention purposes. The relative parsimony of this program, compared with more costly and time-consuming personal change or enhancement efforts, provides another compelling argument for its use, perhaps as a first-choice approach and/or as part of a more comprehensive effort.

More specifically, STEP works because structural and role changes are made in the host school in relation to targeted incoming students who, it is anticipated, will face specific transition difficulties. Providing these students with a niche and the ongoing opportunity for instrumental and social support are primary contributors to this program's success.

Implications for Counselors and Other Helpers

As we have seen, counselors can intervene in a variety of ways (see the discussion of the Counseling Cube in Chapter 3). Preventive counseling captures a number of ways, all devoted to preventing dysfunction and promoting strengths. Working with clients directly to enhance their competencies is a time-tested approach used frequently, and well, by counselors and other practitioners. However, the particular value of STEP in terms of practitioner implications is that it shows clearly how environmental conditions can become the focus of a prevention program, with the beneficiaries being students who interact with those conditions.

Counselors and other helpers can augment their intervention potential and effectiveness through prevention programs that adopt and/or incorporate environmental foci (Conyne & Cook, 2004). These efforts are aimed at altering basic important life conditions—developmental pathways—through which a targeted group must pass. Examples include changes in policy and procedures, classroom management, physical redesign of space, and providing mentors. This kind of preventive counseling often can be less costly and simpler, thus more parsimonious, than more traditional direct services. It certainly warrants increased application by counselors and other helpers and for inclusion within professional training programs.

SEATTLE SOCIAL DEVELOPMENT PROJECT (SSDP)

What Is the Seattle Social Development Project (SSDP)?

The Seattle Social Development Project (SSDP) began in 1981. It is a universal, comprehensive school-based preventive intervention that targets multiple-risk and protective factors in both home and school. The program intends to reduce risk factors in childhood for drug abuse, school failure, and delinquency, while seeking to increase protective factors, such as pro-social bonds, commitment to school, and attachment. It also is based on the conception that many of the same risk factors (e.g., poor and inconsistent family management practices, peer rejection) predict multiple poor outcomes, such as substance abuse, teen pregnancy, and school dropout. That is, as has been observed several times earlier in this book, when preventing academic and socioemotive problems there is no single and direct linkage between one cause and one effect; rather, multiple casual factors may interact to yield any of a range of outcomes.

SSDP is based on the Social Development Model (Hawkins, Catalano, & Miller, 1992), where strong bonds (attachment, commitment, and belief) are considered to be essential protective factors that serve to moderate social norms about childhood maladaptive behavior, such as delinquent acts. According to the model, the positive bonding of children is a function of opportunities provided within the family and classroom, possessing necessary skills to interact successfully in these environments, and for pro-social behavior to be recognized and reinforced. The Social Development Model further holds that changing the developmental trajectory toward negative outcomes is dependent on early and sustained programmatic intervention.

How Is It Done?

SSDP can be used for the general population of young children in the first through sixth grades. It is also appropriate for use with high-risk children from low socioeconomic conditions and with low school achievement.

SSDP emphasizes a combination of parent and teacher training. The program is intended to be developmentally appropriate throughout the application period and to reduce early conduct problems, academic failure, and peer rejection. These factors are all considered as antecedents for future dysfunctional behavior and other negative outcomes.

Parental training is presented in parent classes offered optionally in first through third grade, in collaboration with school and parent councils. During first and second grades, seven sessions of the Catch 'Em Being Good program is provided. This family management program assists parents to set appropriate expectations for child behavior, improve their monitoring of child behavior, and support parents' use of consistent disciplinary practices. During the second and third grades, the four-session How to Help Your Child Succeed in School program is provided to encourage parents to improve their own communication practices, their involvement with their children, and their interaction with teachers. These sessions also address how parents can better support their children's learning, mastery of math and reading skills, and create positive learning environments in the home. During the fifth and sixth grades, five sessions are made available to help develop family positions on drug use and to reinforce children's application of refusal skills they are learning.

Teachers receive training that focuses on proactive classroom management, cooperative learning, and interactive methods. They learn strategies for establishing clear expectations and rules, along with rewards for compliance. They learn how to organize small-group learning activities, where heterogeneity is included, as an important method for increasing students' social skills and their participation and connection with peers. First grade teachers also learn how to teach students better communication skills, negotiation, decision-making, and conflict-resolution skills through the Interpersonal Cognitive Problem Solving (ICPS) curriculum developed by Shure and Spivack (1988). Sixth grade teachers learn how to present refusal skills training as related to peer pressure and substance abuse.

What Works?

SSDP has been evaluated positively by several external sources. It has been accorded excellent status by the American Youth Policy Forum, the Center for Mental Health Services, Communities That Care, and the National Institute of Drug Abuse (NIDA), among others. It has been judged as Promising by the Center for Substance Abuse Prevention (CASP) Blueprints, by the Department of Education-Safe Schools, as Highly Promising by Title V (OJJDP), and as a Model 1 program by the Surgeon General's Report of 2001.

The SSDP has conducted a number of program evaluations. These evaluations have tended to show that the project improves school performance, family relationships, and student involvement with drugs/alcohol at various class grades. Some sample results follow.

Evaluations conducted at the end of second grade of project students compared to controls, showed that White boy students exhibited lower levels of aggression and externalizing of antisocial behaviors and that White girl students exhibited lesser amounts of self-destructive behaviors. At the end of fifth grade project students, compared to controls, engaged in lower initiation of alcohol use and of delinquency behaviors, realized closer attachment to their family and to school, and improvements were realized in family management practices and family communication. Continuing with this longitudinal developmental study, at the end of grade 11 project students, compared to controls, demonstrated reductions in drunk behavior and in drinking and driving, as well as reduced involvement in sexual activity and in violent behaviors. Presently, the SSDP is involved with an intergenerational study, a five-year project aimed at understanding the effects of SSDP participation on the children of those participants. This example of longitudinal study over many years is a very positive aspect of the SSDP.

Why Does It Work?

The SSDP is based on a well-developed underpinning theory, connected with bonding and the understanding that a set of risk and protective factors may be associated with a range of potential outcomes. The project is carefully constructed to articulate the theory in practice, with an interconnected application of both school and family preventive activities. It is set within a developmental longitudinal research design allowing for tracking of long-term changes. The SSDP has established itself solidly as a competency-enhancement approach, integrated within multiple contexts and levels. The knowledge, attitudes, and skills that the project focuses on are pertinent to situational needs and to developmental age progression.

Implications for Counselors and Other Helpers

The importance of competency enhancement as a route to wellness and prevention of deficits is naturally attractive to counselors and many other practitioners. Serving in a training and consultative role is becoming more familiar and more important. For instance, students of mine are providing consultation and training to university faculty in how to establish and maintain classroom environments that support small-group instruction, and they also are teaching the faculty how to facilitate small-group interaction. Seeking to improve classroom and family systems as well as students/children as they move between both of these important settings reinforces the importance of ecological connections. Following the progress of trainees across a developmental time period is a research approach that preventive counselors need to take increased advantage of as they seek to document the durability of growth and change.

CONCLUSION

Many in our society blame the schools for the problems of children. Others blame families for the problems of children that are brought to school. Neither is totally right and neither is totally wrong. The difficulties with each position are that blaming others is unproductive and harmful, and the problems of concern germinate from multiple sources in a variety of interconnected ways. It might be more accurate to state that the problems of many youth—manifested in such domains of academic performance, social relationships, physical health, attitudes toward self and others, management of feelings—arise from the mesosystems of life, the intersections and disconnects between main units such as the home and the school.

Therefore, in this and the other chapters of Section II, we are engaged in a somewhat arbitrary analysis. Examining prevention programs aimed at the family (Chapter 5), and the school (this chapter) separately fails to appropriately acknowledge the dynamic interplay between school and family that contributes so strongly to health and disorder. The same observation holds for community and work settings, the subjects of the next two chapters of this section.

Yet, we know that the school setting itself can be critically important to youth development, and preventive counselors can make a significant contribution at this level. Within the schools, certainly school counselors (and to a lesser degree, school psychologists, school social workers, and an increasing number of counseling psychologists) are the natural role occupants who are in position to make such a positive difference in their work with others, both in and out of the school. It is no secret, however, that in many school districts school counselors do not exist, being the victims of budget cuts and/or of misplaced priorities. In other situations, the ratio of students to school counselors is abysmal, far exceeding well established guidelines. In still other situations, school counselors are performing tasks that are inconsistent with their desired role. They should not, for instance, be tied to clerical record-keeping, supervising study halls, and performing disciplinary actions (among many other inappropriate activities).

The American School Counseling Association (ASCA) has developed a national model to provide a framework for school counseling programs (see www.schoolcounselor.org). This model contains four interrelated components: (1) foundation, (2) delivery system, (3) management systems, and (4) accountability. The model is an organized, systematized, and comprehensive effort to produce student development in interconnected domains (academic, career development, personal/social development). One responsibility set forth for the school counselor in this model is to collaborate with teachers to present proactive, prevention-based guidance curriculum lessons. Taken in total, the systematic and developmental role called for in this model should be expected to yield preventive effects.

The programs examined in this chapter would fit very well within the school counselor role and function and are consistent with the ASCA developmental model. Providing life skills training for students, organizing the school environment to promote organization and clarity, and training teachers and parents in important family and school-based skills offer school counselors (and other school personnel) tested designs that can be adapted to fit local circumstances. The injunction is: just do it!

ISSUES FOR REFLECTION AND DISCUSSION

1. Help me! A colleague and I have just received a Safe and Healthy Schools grant for three years. This is a dropout prevention grant to occur in three inner-city middle schools, with attention to the high school to which these middle schools feed. We are intending to combine aspects of student life skills training, teacher-parent training, and ecological transition. All is well and good, except today is October 10, the funding is yet to be released, the public schools have been in session since August 27, and no staff can be hired until the grant contract is finalized! Organize with a partner, or with a small group (whichever best fits your situation). Discuss this situation, in general, and then more specifically develop ideas about the questions below (30 minutes):

   • What do you think my colleague and I should be doing during this lull in the action? How could aspects of the three programs discussed in this chapter be interconnected?
   • What might be some challenges we could face, given the information I have provided?
   • Finally, share your ideas with others and look for commonalities and differences (30 minutes).

2. How can school counselors counter the forces so strongly in place in many school systems that serve to keep them from doing preventive counseling? What do you know about this situation? What do you need to know? How can you find it out?

3. There has been some work done that supports the idea that a whole school and its surrounding community should be viewed as one unit of change, that is, where school and community are in complete partnership. Is this a feasible approach to take? What are some pros and cons? Develop a list to capture these competing factors to share with others.

CHAPTER 7

Prevention Programs in the Community Setting

CONTEXT

When considering preventive programs at this level, I am thinking of both neighborhoods and communities, that is, those more or less loosely organized levels that lie outside more tightly organized settings, such as work, school, and church. For the sake of discussion, I will refer to these as the community setting. Community settings strongly affect many aspects of everyday life. They make a difference in health, participation, and satisfaction.

Community-level interventions combine individual and environmental change strategies (multicomponent) across multiple settings to promote well-being and prevent dysfunction among population groups in a defined geographic location (Wandersman & Florin, 2003). These interventions typically include aspects of grassroots involvement, interorganizational linkages, and improving community problem solving.

Social organization (Mancini, Martin, & Bowen, 2003) is a term describing "the collection of values, norms, processes, and behavior patterns within a community that organize, facilitate, and constrain the interactions among community members" (p. 319). The social organization of a community directly impacts the capacity of a community to promote the health and well-being of individuals and families living within it. Thus, we see in popular magazines various discussions of those communities considered to be the best places to live, or the most attractive places to retire, or the safest communities in America, and so forth.

Mancini et al. (2003) suggest that prevention and health promotion effectiveness within communities is influenced substantially by "community capacity," a concept involving the willingness and ability of community members to connect with each other, to assume mutual responsibility, and to exert a collective competence aimed at reducing risks and promoting assets associated with health and with health promotion. Community capacity is realized through demonstrating a shared responsibility to produce obtainable health and prevention benefits.

In this chapter you will read about three award-winning prevention programs that are located at the community level:

1. Big Brothers/Big Sisters of America (see McGill, Mihalic, & Grotpeter, 1998), which uses both mentoring and case management approaches to assist youth from single-parent homes
2. Quantum Opportunities Program (see Lattimore, Mihalic, Grotpeter, & Taggart, 1998), a development program for disadvantaged youth from 9–12 years of age
3. Communities Mobilizing for Change on Alcohol (CMCA) (Wagenaar, Gehan, Jones-Webb, Wolfson, Toomey, & Murray, 1999; Wagenaar et al. 1998; Wagenaar, Murray, & Toomey, 2000), a community-organizing program to reduce adolescent access to alcohol through changing community policies and practices

BIG BROTHERS/BIG SISTERS OF AMERICA (BBBSA)

What Is Big Brothers/Big Sisters of America (BBBSA)?

This prevention program is a national youth-service community-based organization that has been providing volunteer-based services to children and adolescents (age range from 6–18, typically) since its initiation with the Big Sisters program in New York City in 1902; Big Brothers followed in 1904. Through a network of some 500 agencies located throughout the country, BBBSA includes around 70,000 youth and adults in one-to-one mentoring relationships. The overall purpose of BBBSA is to help at-risk children, generally from single-parent homes, to cope more effectively with their environment. BBBSA established basic requirements (called standards) in 1922 to guide the one-to-one relationships of volunteers with children, as well as for how local agencies should operate. Eventually these standards evolved into a set of Standards and Required Procedures for One-to-One Service. Compliance with these standards and procedures provides the foundation for how each agency throughout the country is to operate and lends consistency to the work of mentors with individual youth.

At the heart of the BBBSA approach to serving at-risk youth is what might be thought of as a nonprescription individual mentoring process. That is, this form of mentoring is not based on manually driven steps and procedures, but on the development and maintenance of friendship and trust, a mining of the mutually shared experiences of everyday life that may later lead to learning and growth. Here, the quality of the mentoring relationship is vitally important. A caring adult who is not part of the family seeks to maintain a consistent availability and presence with a youth who is growing up in what might be thought of as adverse circumstances (e.g., one-parent family, low SES). The BBBSA belief is that the frequent and consistent involvement of a caring volunteer in a youth's life can serve a powerfully positive influence.

In this way, the conceptual framework for BBBSA is aligned with social control theory, where attachments to positive role models, commitment to socially appropriate goals, and involvement in conventional activities and experiences can serve as a protective factor for youth. Such positive social bonding can buffer negative pressures and assist youth to refrain from involvement in problem behaviors and delinquent pursuits.

How Does It Work?

BBBSA is a community mentoring program accomplished through the careful construction of thousands of one-to-one mentoring relationships. In the program, an adult volunteer mentor (Big Brother or Big Sister) is intentionally matched with an at-risk child (Little Brother or Little Sister), with the goal of creating a warm, positive relationship that might then exert preventive effects. Two aspects of this match are important: (a) the appropriateness of the match itself, and (b) the ongoing supervision of the match relationship that is provided by a professional staff member, whose role is known as a case manager.

The volunteer mentor generally meets with the child for 3 to 5 hours a week throughout the course of one year and sometimes longer than one year. What occurs is not specified, except that activities need to be in accord with the goals that were set when the match was created. These goals emerge from an extensive interview conducted by the case manager with the child and the parent/guardian. The overarching goal is to develop and maintain a mutually positive relationship through regular meetings between the mentor and child. Other more specific goals may be set as well, related to such areas as general hygiene, peer relationships, learning a new skill, and academic performance. These goals and progress toward them are stipulated in an individual case plan that is maintained and updated by the case manager over time.

The case manager oversees all aspects of the mentoring relationship, from forming the match through monitoring and terminating the relationship. An important part of the case manager's role is to communicate about how things are going in and around the mentoring relationship with the volunteer, the child, and the parent/guardian. The Standards and Required Procedures for One-to-One Service establish the regularity of case manager contacts and communication. For instance, early in the match case manager contacts with volunteer and parent occur frequently, followed by monthly contacts during the year, and contact is made with the child at least quarterly. In all aspects of their role, case managers are guided by the Standards, mentioned earlier.

What Works?

BBBSA has been evaluated by external reviewers very positively. It has been judged as one of eleven model programs by the Blueprints for Violence Prevention and has been rated as Effective by the American Youth Policy Forum, the Center for Mental Health Services, Communities That Care, and Title V (OJDP), as well as a Promising program by the Center for Substance Abuse Prevention (CSAP).

Much of the evidence supporting the program is in the form of anecdotal reports from a range of parties over decades, including parents, children, teachers, and case managers. Indirectly, support emerges from sets of resiliency studies examining the role of caring adults. For instance, Werner (1996, 1997) found in her long-term longitudinal study in Hawaii that high-risk boys and girls who interacted with caring adults outside the family provided an important protective factor contributing to successful transition to adulthood.

Historically, research on mentoring programs has not shown effectiveness. However, research conducted by Public/Private Ventures (P/PV) demonstrated that the BBBSA program provided many concrete benefits. P/PV conducted an 18-month (1992–1993) comparative study of randomly selected BBBSA children compared to non-BBBSA children. Results showed that youth participants in the program (i.e., Little Brothers and Little Sisters) were 46 percent less likely to have initiated use of drugs or alcohol (26 percent), felt more competent about doing their schoolwork, attended school more frequently, obtained better grades, maintained better peer relationships, and were about one-third less likely to have hit others. In terms of cost, the BBBSA program, which matches one adult with one youth, is estimated to cost about $1000 per year. In relation to outcomes summarized above, this cost seems very acceptable (McGill, Mihalic, & Grotpeter, 1998).

Why Does It Work?

Mentoring and its supervision are the hallmarks of this program. The idea of matching to create a warm relationship is a simple but elegant one. The basic simplicity of the program's underpinning (albeit, being connected to more sophisticated theory related to positive social bonding) is one important reason why this program works. It is understandable. It is feasible. It is not complex. It is not costly. All of these characteristics promote successful application, replication, and adaptation. Moreover, the very careful monitoring of the matching relationship through case managers, following clearly articulated standards and procedures, helps to ensure that the central program component functions well and appropriately, and stays targeted on agreed-upon goals. The ongoing communication process that the case manager implements keeps the program moving ahead and allows key partners to be involved and to contribute.

Implications for Counselors and Other Helpers

Often community-based prevention requires multiple layers and systems of involvement, and is necessarily complex and comprehensive in scope. The Big Brothers/Big Sisters of America program shows that a community prevention program can be very simple conceptually. This one has established well-developed procedures to provide support and communication while allowing for the inventiveness and creativity of the mentoring process to emerge—consistent with goals and agreed-upon rules and procedures. Nothing can be more simple and direct than one-to-one relationships.

Of course, counselors are well trained in this basic delivery approach, whether expressed through direct contact, training and supervising of others, consulting about these programs, or developing and evaluating mentoring programs. For instance, we are employing a "near peer" voluntary mentoring component within our counseling program, where returning students and first-year students are matched. Results are very favorable, actually going both ways, with mentors and mentees alike gaining.

The challenge for counselors and other practitioners is to connect this standard delivery method within a system that is geared toward the prevention of problems. Here is where the BBBSA has provided a model that works.

QUANTUM OPPORTUNITIES PROGRAM (QOP)

What Is the Quantum Opportunities Program (QOP)?

The Quantum Opportunities Program (QOP) is a comprehensive, long-term prevention effort to help youth from families receiving public assistance to make a "quantum leap" to new opportunities. The QOP was first developed and implemented as a pilot project from 1989 to 1993 by the Opportunities Industrialization Centers of America (OIC of America), with additional grant funding by the Ford Foundation. OIC is a nonprofit organization serving the poor, unemployed, underemployed, and youth. OIC operates through a national network of 58 local affiliates located in 30 states and the District of Columbia. It seeks to prepare people for today's workforce following a philosophy of self-help and with attention to the whole person.

The QOP pilot project was implemented in five different urban sites. It involved 125 youth participants (called Opportunity Associates) in an intensive variety of coordinated services, including building a sustained relationship with a peer group and with a caring adult over four years of high school. Twenty-five youths at five sites across the country were recruited from poverty neighborhoods and the high school nearest the participating OIC. Each high school provided a listing of students meeting the eligibility requirements, from which 25 were randomly selected. A Coordinator was assigned to each site, and to each youth, thus having responsibility for both the program and each youth involved.

The Quantum Opportunities Program initiated by the OIC employs a comprehensive, long-term youth development model that was designed by Lattimore and Taggart. It is based on two central conditions: (1) the lack of opportunities that are available to poor teenage youth such as in education, training, and employment, and (2) the deficiencies, such as poor coordination and inattention to developmental issues, that were present in many existing programs offered through governmental and nonprofit organizations.

Theoretically, the program is most closely aligned with the Social Development Model (Catalano & Hawkins, 1996), which holds that development of a positive social bond is essential to youth development. This theory suggests that a positive social bond can emerge through consistency in: (a) perceived opportunities for involvement in activities with others; (b) becoming involved and interacting with these opportunities; (c) necessary skills to allow for this kind of participation; and (d) being reinforced and acknowledged for participation. A positive social bond allows people to attach, connect, comply, and commit with the norms and values of the socializing unit.

How Does It Work?

The QOP applies these Social Development Model concepts with the Opportunity Associates (youth participants from poverty situations) by instilling hope in the youth, opening up opportunities for involvement, providing skills training to help youth in the program to be successful in their involvement, and by offering a program of reward and positive reinforcement for successes achieved, as follows:

1. Instilling hope, the program seeks to help the Associates perceive that opportunities are possible for them, to develop optimism and a belief that upward mobility and success are attainable goals, and that opportunities are available to help them to progress.
2. Becoming involved, the program provides Associates with involvement and interactive opportunities (e.g., with a Coordinator who holds positive values and fulfills multiple roles such as role model, adviser, surrogate parent, and disciplinarian).
3. Skills, training is provided for each Associate to equip them for success.
4. Reinforcement, frequent feedback, and positive reinforcement are given by instructors and the Coordinator and others in the program to recognize individual effort and achievement.

The prevention intervention itself is wrapped around a year-round program extending for the four years of high school. QOP intends to offer a balanced and sequential set of opportunities (educational, development, and service) to small groups of youth and their families who are receiving public assistance.

The Associates participated in a coordinated set of activities each year, including 250 hours in each of the following areas: (a) education activities (e.g., peer tutoring, computer-assisted instruction) to increase basic academic skills; (b) development activities (e.g., cultural involvement, skill building), aimed at planning for advanced training and college and in job preparation); and (c) service activities (e.g., volunteering in agencies), intended to broaden experience and develop a sense of contribution to a larger good. In addition, the Associates are motivated through performance-based incentives, including modest cash awards and scholarships. A high degree of bonding within the program is sought, evidenced by the motto for QOP: "Once in QOP, always in QOP."

What Works?

The QOP has been judged by several external review committees as being a sound program. Blueprints for Violence Prevention assigned it as one of its 11 model programs. It was evaluated as being effective by the American Youth Policy Forum, Communities That Care, and Title V (OJJDP), and it was judged to be a promising program in the Surgeon General's Report of 2001.

Program outcomes result from comparing QOP members with a control group, and from a one-year follow-up study (Hahn, Leavitt, & Aaron, 1994). Associates (especially from the Philadelphia site) realized more positive outcomes in educational attainment and scholarly achievement than those in the control group, and were less likely to become teen parents. More specifically, Associates were more likely to graduate from high school than controls (63 to 42 percent), were more likely to move ahead to postsecondary schools (42 to 16 percent), were less likely to drop out of high school (23 to 50 percent), were more likely to have received an honor or award in the past year (34 to 12 percent), were less likely to be arrested (19 to 23 percent), and were less likely to become a parent as a teen (24 to 38 percent).

Why Does It Work?

The QOP clearly identifies an at-risk target and setting and sets specific goals for accomplishment. The program is set in the community and in settings of the participants, taking advantage of familiar contexts. It works with small groups of youth and develops all activities around a pro-social bonding theme, while also attending intentionally to individual needs and circumstances. The close, ongoing monitoring of a site Coordinator, who works very closely with each Associate, contributes to continuity and to the development of social bonds among the Associates. The program is instituted prior to problems taking hold in the at-risk students' lives, and this "before-the-fact" application allows for time for prevention to occur.

The program includes sets of everyday opportunities (that have been previously unavailable to the participants), rather than expensive and complicated interventions that would need to be specially created. The QOP includes multiple dimensions and is comprehensive, seeking to integrate skill training, development opportunities, and service engagements. The participation of Associates is recognized through various incentives, such as rewards for hours worked and bonuses for completion of projects. The Coordinator and other staff are committed to daily involvement with the Associates, evidenced through monitoring ongoing activities, providing feedback, making home visits, and offering guidance and discipline as needed.

The program has been able to capture its effects through program evaluation and research, contributing to the multiyear funding support that has supported overall program continuity and effectiveness. Finally, QOP is cost effective, with a calculated cost over four years of $10,600 per participant, or $2650 per year for each Associate.

Implications for Counselors and Other Helpers

The Quantum Opportunities Program demonstrates how an effective prevention program can be mounted to address youth living in poverty who are at risk for a host of negative consequences, such as dropping out of school, early pregnancy, criminal behavior, and drug use. Counselors and other helpers often work "after-the-fact" with youth who already seem intractably involved with these and other kinds of problems.

Using QOP as an example, practitioners can work with others to apply preventive interventions that are aimed at contravening the anticipated negative trajectory of many at-risk youth, instead helping them move toward positive development. Preventive counselors can draw upon their knowledge and skills in the method of organizing naturally occurring opportunities that may be otherwise out of reach for many at risk students, setting those within a learning framework. In a real sense, the larger community becomes an experiencing resource for providing opportunities for participation and learning. Going to ball games, taking a ride in the country, visiting the zoo, touring a college campus, or learning how to use a computer through the local library are examples of such naturally occurring opportunities. A youth opportunities program in Cincinnati, for instance, with which our Counseling Program has been involved, links learning to play tennis with academic support to assist inner-city adolescents in pro-social choices and involvement.

Making these opportunities consistently and appropriately available to at-risk youths, coupled with strong support, monitoring, and rewards, offers a powerful and relatively inexpensive avenue toward improving social bonding and reducing future negative consequences.

COMMUNITIES MOBILIZING FOR CHANGE ON ALCOHOL (CMCA)

What Is Communities Mobilizing for Change on Alcohol (CMCA)?

CMCA is a broad community initiative intended to reduce access to alcohol by teenagers. It was developed and evaluated in a 15-community randomized trial by the Alcohol Epidemiology Program at the University of Minnesota School of Public Health. CMCA is based on theory and research that emphasizes how important the social and policy environment is in promoting or in retarding youth drinking of alcohol. This viewpoint reinforces the understanding that long-term prevention success is dependent on changing the social and policy environment in a community to support the prevention goals. Therefore, this initiative targets the whole community for change, rather than individual young people. Community factors receiving specific prevention attention are the policies and practices of major community institutions.

Most prevention interventions to reduce youth drinking and its negative consequences have focused on reducing the youth *demand* for alcohol, typically through school-based programs. Prevention programs that are based on information-delivery and on affective change strategies have demonstrated no lasting positive effects, while some programs based on life skills and resistance skills have shown beneficial effects. Yet, the latter seem to require intense implementation, many sessions, and booster sessions.

Reducing the *supply* of alcohol represents another way toward prevention of youth alcohol used. Examples of supply reduction include increasing the legal age for purchase or consumption of alcohol, or reducing availability of alcohol via raised excise tax. Both of these approaches have shown success (Wagenaar, Murray, Gehan, Wolfson, Forster, Toomey, & Perry, 1998).

CMCA falls within the supply reduction approach to youth alcohol drinking prevention, with its intent being to reduce youth access to alcohol. Effectively limiting teen accessibility to alcohol can directly reduce teen drinking and also communicate within the community a clear social norm that underage drinking is both inappropriate and unacceptable.

How Is It Done?

As mentioned, CMCA seeks to engage community citizens to change local public policies to affect the practices occurring within major community institutions in relation to youth alcohol drinking. Examples of these community institutions include law enforcement, schools, licensing departments, community events, the local mass media, civic groups, and churches and synagogues. The objective of CMCA is to reduce youth drinking through limiting the accessibility of alcohol to them, such as through illegal sales by retailers and by adults who may provide teens with alcohol.

Community organizing is the major intervention method used in CMCA, which involves activating grassroots citizens in a community to pursue policy and institutional change. Those involved usually constitute a group independent from the existing power structure in a community, even if some members may hold leadership positions in community organizations.

The project aimed to reduce youth access to alcohol through a community organizing preventive intervention. This intervention was accomplished through a 15-community group-randomized trial to change the policies and practices of major community institutions, resulting in reduced commercial and social sources of alcohol to youth below the age of 21.

The community organizing intervention involved hiring a community organizer within each intervention community. The community organizer worked for a 2.5-year period (completing a total of 1518 one-on-one meetings) with a wide variety of persons in policy or policy-influencing positions and with retailers. These meetings accomplished several ends by: (a) assisting the organizers to better understand the community, including its history, culture, and the patterns of influence and power; (b) building personal and political relationships with people across the community; (c) gaining an understanding of the interests, views, and commitments of community members; and (d) providing recruitment leads of individuals to the core strategy group to be formed. During this phase, the community organizers also reviewed existing alcohol control policies, procedures, and enforcement practices.

During the second phase of the CMCA preventive intervention, a strategy team was formed, comprised of a local core leadership group. In addition, a larger base of active and diverse citizens was created. These groups worked to develop a base of community support and to design specific community organizing strategies, which included identifying specific alcohol policy and enforcement targets for change and plans for mobilizing citizens in the community to advocate for these changes.

What Works?

The CMCA project has received an Exemplary evaluation from the Center for Substance Abuse Prevention and is listed on the National Registry of Effective Prevention Programs. The Web site of the Alcohol Epidemiology Program (www.epi.umn.edu/alcohol) contains many resources related to the CMCA project and to strategies for reducing youth access to alcohol. These are available at no cost.

Many communities have adapted ideas and components of the CMCA project, following its original implementation and evaluation. The CMCA was evaluated in a fully randomized trial across 15 communities in Minnesota, with 7 communities assigned to intervention and another 8 to controls. Baseline surveys were conducted in each community and repeated three years following. A multiple time-series design was implemented. Data collection included pre-and post-test surveys of twelfth grade students conducted in schools, telephone surveys of 18- 20-year-olds and of alcohol retailers, use of direct tests of retailers' propensity to sell alcohol to young buyers, and monitoring pertinent changes in the community practices of community institutions.

Results demonstrated that CMCA favorably and significantly affected the drinking behavior of eighteen 20-year-olds. They were less likely to try to buy alcohol, less likely to gather at bars, less likely to drink alcohol, and less likely to provide alcohol to other teens. Arrests for driving under the influence of alcohol also were significantly reduced. Younger adolescents were not significantly impacted by the program. Alcohol merchants reduced sales to minors and increased their checks of age identification.

Another study (Wagenaar, Murray, & Toomey, 2000) was conducted, using the CMCA to affect arrests and traffic crashes. Arrest and traffic crash data were collected from 1987 to 1995, providing a six-year baseline and for three years of intervention data. Results showed net declines in the preventive intervention communities for all arrest and traffic crash indicators.

Drawing from the two studies summarized, the researchers observed that the CMCA approach to limit youth access to alcohol may be effective but that a longer intervention period is necessary.

Why Does It Work?

Community organizing aimed at policy change represents an important prevention strategy; this strategy was intentionally used to guide the design, implementation, and evaluation of this project. This relationship between guiding precepts and program development, implementation, and evaluation is an important reason for the program's success.

Moreover, CMCA effectiveness is tied to careful development of the community organizing function and matching the preventive method with a sensitive evaluation regimen. In terms of the first point, CMCA community organizers spent considerable time and effort getting to know people in the community and to learn about the community itself. They formed personal relationships and connected both with influential community members and with a diverse range of citizens. They worked intentionally to create a strategic plan for mobilizing community members to seek desired change. In that sense their efforts were infused by the goal of empowerment, where people gain increased control and power in effecting changes that are important for improving their condition and that of others.

Regarding evaluation, the preventive intervention was set within a solid community-based research design, allowing for proper evaluation to occur. Data resulting from the preventive intervention were collected that were synchronized with the intervention itself. A variety of measures was used, including surveys of relevant groups, archival data, alcohol purchase attempts, and drinking behaviors.

Last, the CMCA approach to preventing underage drinking through limiting the access of minors to alcohol has been disseminated through a variety of means, and the program is being adapted in many communities. This dissemination function is important for effective prevention programs.

Implications for Counselors and Other Helpers

CMCA provides a crystal-clear example of a community-based prevention program that is purely environmental and systems oriented. (Compare this approach with those that have focused just as strictly on person-oriented variables.) It is important for counselors and other helpers to be aware of how prevention can be accomplished through leveraging environmental variables; in this case, the community policies affecting underage access to alcohol.

In an extensive university project I was involved with, we gathered campus environmental assessment data about the effects on students of a number of campus conditions, such as policies, the physical space, and opportunities for socializing. We then consulted with campus administrators about the results. Two major environmental changes occurred from this effort: (1) because personal safety at night on campus emerged as a consistent concern, a new lighting system was installed to improve the visibility, and (2) because high levels of stress were consistently reported at about the midsemester points, a midsemester break was incorporated within the academic calendar (Conyne, 1975; Conyne & Clack, 1981).

Practitioners can collaborate with others in environmentally oriented prevention programs in various ways, such as helping to shape the interaction processes to be engaged in by community organizers. In addition, counselors and other helpers can add unique components to such programs, helping them to expand beyond a reliance on environmental change, only to also include attention to person-oriented change methods. In the case of the CMCA program, for example, might incorporation of skill-building workshops for community organizers be beneficial to assist them in doing their work more effectively?

CONCLUSION

The three community-based prevention programs presented in this chapter demonstrate different approaches. The Big Brother/Big Sister Program shows the power of ongoing and carefully monitored mentoring relationships that, with broad-scale application across many mentors-mentees, has the capacity to elevate the quality of life in a community. Quantum demonstrates that piquing hope and linking it to naturally occurring opportunities in the community that the target population had ever perceived as being possible can have startlingly positive effects. Communities Mobilizing for Change on Alcohol illustrates how environmental change (policy), arrived at through appreciable attention to collaborative relationships, can result in positive change within one focused area of concern (reducing alcohol problems).

In these and other community-based prevention programs, the need is to blend two sometimes competing approaches: (1) community-driven and (2) research-driven (Wandersman & Florin, 2003). The grassroots tradition (community-driven) needs to be informed by the prevention science tradition that is now emerging (research-driven), and vice versa.

Community counselors (e.g., Lewis et al., 2003) and community psychologists (e.g., Rappaport & Seidman, 2000) have long been focused on how the community context can provide the fulcrum for substantial, meaningful, and durable change. Both of these perspectives have contributed in important ways to the delineation of what prevention is today and to preventive counseling as well.

Involvement at the community level is critically important for preventive counselors; they need to increase their knowledge and skills in how community-driven and research-driven approaches can be integrated. It is not necessary, however, for one preventive counselor to know absolutely everything! What is necessary is that counselors learn what they know and can do well, what they need to know and do, and how they can satisfy any discrepancies. Here is where collaboration across specialties can be very helpful in allowing the community-research nexus to be joined appropriately and effectively.

ISSUES FOR REFLECTION AND DISCUSSION

1. In many ways, the concepts of community and prevention have been linked. Why do you think this is so?
2. Communities are rather complex, however. They are characterized by competition and cooperation, political dynamics, ethnic and racial issues, resource questions, and many other factors. Communities also can be supportive and nourishing or unfriendly and toxic. For some counselors and psychologists, this messiness is perceived as an attractor; for others, it is a detractor. Where do you stand on this dimension? How appealing—or unappealing— is community-based prevention for you?
3. You have now read about a number of prevention programs and have access to many more (see References). Pair up with a partner. Together discuss the three programs outlined in this chapter. Select one for further study. Identify what each of you might look for— for example, program goals, program methods, program results, and participant involvement. Learn more about it through your research and come back in two weeks ready to share what you have learned.
4. Get back with your partner. Continue with that same program. Now ask yourselves this question: "How could such a program be introduced/adapted into the local community?" (Define this so you both agree.) That is, identify what factors should be considered in any plan to try bringing this program here.
5. Finally, how do you see the setting of the community relating to other settings in which preventive counseling might occur? What are some other important settings? How might these be interconnected, and what might this mean for your practice?

CHAPTER 8

Prevention Programs in the Work Setting

CONTEXT

Working is a central part of most adults' lives; indeed, they spend much of their lives at work. Work is not uniformly agreeable for all employees, of course. On the positive side, work provides income, offers a route to satisfaction and happiness, provides a way to contribute and be productive, develops opportunities for social interaction, and can give a general purpose and organizing structure for life. Along with love, Freud identified work as a major feature of a healthy life (Freud's *lieben und arbeiten*: to love and to work).

Work also can be a significant source of stress and an engine for generating psychological disorders and distress. Work-related stress has many causes (Quick, Quick, Nelson, & Hurrell, 1997), including excessive demands, economic instability, job ambiguity, unabated routine, rapid technological change, lack of control over work, and international economic competition, to name just a few.

Work-related psychological dysfunctions constitute one category in the top 10 occupational health risks in the United States (Quick et al., 1997). Not confined to the United States alone, work-related stress is the major health and safety issue for most employers in the Western world. For instance, in the United Kingdom, more than 6.5 million working days are lost each year at a cost to companies of almost £400 million. The cost to society in human as well as financial terms is greater still; the financial costs have been estimated at some £3.75 billion annually. Preventively oriented organizations have been seeking not just to control these costs but to establish work systems that positively enhance mental health. The motivation for these systems has derived from the understanding that improvements in organizational health show up on the bottom line (Miller, Lipsedge, & Litchfield, 2002).

Sauter, Murphy, & Hurrell (1990) proposed a national strategy for the prevention of work-related psychological distress that was based on public health prevention precepts (see also Sauter, Lim, & Murphy, 1996). Their proposed strategy contained four parts: (1) work and job redesign; (2) surveillance of stressors and distress in the work setting; (3) education and training programs; and (4) mental health service delivery for distressed employees. The key principle underlying this national strategy is "to encourage the development of psychologically healthy occupational work environments" (Quick et al., 1997, p. 14).

The Institute of Medicine's definition of prevention applied to the workplace identified the following three types: (1) universal preventive interventions that focus on the entire workforce and families; (2) selective preventive interventions that target members of the work setting or their families who are at high risk; and (3) indicated preventive interventions that are aimed at high-risk workers or their family members who are showing signs or symptoms of problems.

One type of work setting prevention program is in the area of substance abuse prevention. Substance abuse is a significant issue in many work settings. Most heavy drinkers (77 percent) and illicit drug users (70 percent) are working adults, and alcohol and drug use or abuse among employees is strongly correlated with accidents, turnover, absenteeism, and work performance issues.

In terms of prevention program delivery, the work setting provides many advantages. For instance, the work setting affords a locale where large numbers of parents can be reached with messages related to prevention of children's use of alcohol and other drugs, and where substance abuse prevention can be integrated into a standard health promotion and wellness program. In terms of concrete benefits, work setting prevention programs addressing substance abuse can reduce costs in such areas as Workers' Compensation claims, injury, litigation, and health insurance, among others. Although the work setting is a major one in most adults' lives in this country, relatively few preventive programs are in place there, compared with other settings addressed earlier (i.e., family, school, community). More progress needs to be made in this area.

In this chapter, we will focus on three preventive programs that are conducted in work settings:

1. The Healthy Workplace (Cook, Back, Trudeau, & McPherson, 2002; Cook & Schlenger, 2002), which incorporates substance abuse prevention within a general health promotion format

2. Yale Work and Family Stress Project (Kline & Snow, 1994; Snow & Kline, 1995; Snow, Swan, Raghavan, Connell, & Klein, under review), which develops and evaluates preventive interventions that are based on relationships between risk and protective factors for female employees

3. JOBS Project for the Unemployed (van Ryn, & Vinokur, 1992; Vinokur, Price, & Schul, 1995; Vinokur, Schul, Vuori, & Price, 2000), which seeks to prevent recently unemployed persons from further psychological distress and to promote self-efficacy in relation to the job search

Note that each of these excellent prevention programs tends to emphasize a competency-enhancement approach. More will be said about that emphasis at the end of this chapter.

THE HEALTHY WORKPLACE

What Is the Healthy Workplace?

The Healthy Workplace (Cook, Back, Trudeau, & McPherson, 2002) is a universal prevention program containing a set of workplace substance abuse preventive interventions that are intended to reduce unsafe drinking, illegal drug use, and the abuse of prescription drugs. Importantly, the Healthy Workplace program simultaneously seeks to improve the healthy practices of adult workers, because it is based within a health promotion framework. Integrated with health promotion activities, this program adapts and adds to Social Cognitive Theory (SCT) (Bandura, 1997), the health belief model (Rosenstock, Strecher, & Becker, 1988) and to form its conceptual base. Therefore the program is positive, emphasizing the benefits of healthful behaviors and not the dangers of substance abuse (although these are covered). Program materials are designed to appeal, rather than to scare, by featuring healthful activities that are rewarding and fun and by presenting the program in interesting ways.

The Healthy Workplace program has been tested in a variety of work settings (e.g., large and medium-size companies, with construction workers, in manufacturing and printing facilities), and with ethnically diverse workforces (e.g., Latino, African American). Central components of the Healthy Workplace program include: (a) reaching the mainstream of workers in a work setting through the positive vehicle of health promotion; (b) raising awareness of the benefits of healthful behaviors and practices, as well as the hazards of using tobacco, alcohol, and illegal drugs, and in misusing legal drugs; (c) teaching specific techniques to employees for improving health and reducing use of tobacco, alcohol, and illegal drugs; and (d) using carefully developed videos to raise self-efficacy and provide models for how healthful practices can be incorporated and substance abuse reduced.

The Healthy Workplace program is designed to increase protective factors and to decrease risk factors at the individual and organizational level. Individual level protective factors to increase include stress-coping abilities, belief in the benefits of a healthful lifestyle, and skills to reduce alcohol and drug abuse. Organizational level protective factors to increase include management support for health promotion and low-to-moderate job stress. Individual-level risk factors to decrease include the levels of personal and work stress, denial of the benefits of a healthful lifestyle, and inadequate skills for alcohol and drug abuse reduction. Organizational level risk factors to be reduced include lack of management support and high levels of workplace stress.

How Is It Done?

The Healthy Workplace program consists of five preventive interventions that are delivered in small-group sessions incorporating tailored videos and print materials. These interventions can be used in any sequence. They are chosen to best fit an organization's goals and the composition of its workforce.

The "SAY YES!" intervention is a classroom series with a multisegment video and accompanying booklet. It is a general health promotion that contains substantial sections addressing alcohol and drug abuse. SAY YES! can be used within organizations that desire a general health promotion program that focuses on substance abuse prevention. The purpose of this preventive intervention is to improve health attitudes and practices and to reduce substance abuse.

The intervention can be delivered by a trainer in three sessions, each lasting about an hour. Session 1 (45 minutes) is the introduction, addressing central concepts including healthful lifestyle and well-being, personal choices and lifestyle, and the impact of alcohol and drug use on health and well-being. Session 2 (1.5 hours) focuses on drugs, alcohol, and healthy choices. Media messages are examined, and a variety of means are used (e.g., didactic presentation, video vignettes, group exercises) to compare drug and alcohol use with healthful choices involving relaxation, physical exercise, and recreational activities. Behavioral guidelines for appropriate use of alcohol or for refusing it are provided. In Session 3 (45 minutes) the emphasis is on healthy choices and action, including a stepwise process of behavior change and the setting of realistic health behavior goals.

The Working People program consists of four 30-minute small-group sessions over a period of four weeks. It focuses on alcohol abuse prevention and is intended especially for a blue-collar workforce of 18- to 35-year-olds. Less attention is given to improving health practices. Session 1 is entitled "A Closer Look at Drinking." This introductory session overviews some health and safety risks and the potential negative social and lifestyle effects of irresponsible and/or heavy alcohol use. Session 2 presents some important facts about alcohol, centered on a lecture-style video. Session 3 is entitled "One More Pitcher?" It focuses on decision-making processes and alcohol consumption, on setting personal limits, and on practical ways to reduce drinking. Session 4 emphasizes positive alternatives to alcohol abuse.

The "Make the Connection" intervention is a three-part series of video and print materials, with each part consisting of three 45-minute sessions: (1) The Stress Management Connection; (2) the Healthy Eating Connection; and (3) the Active Lifestyle Connection. The program is intended to be included in workplace health promotion programs on stress management, weight management and nutrition, and fitness.

The "Power Tools" intervention consists of three 45-minute sessions that was developed specifically for young, blue-collar men. The intervention combines general health issues with sessions particularly devoted to alcohol and drug abuse.

The "Prime Life 2000" program contains layered interventions consisting of a series of small-group sessions on stress management, healthy eating, and fitness. In addition, print materials and videotapes are mailed to all employees. All components include preventive information on alcohol abuse, illegal drug use, and prescription drug use.

For each of these five interventions, small-group sessions of 10 to 20 employees are essential for implementation. These sessions are generally held on-site, in the work setting's training or conference room. Each intervention has a training guide and backup materials. A trainer who is familiar with the appropriate guide and has the necessary support resources (i.e., print and videotape materials) can implement the intervention. Materials can be obtained at www.centerforworkforcehealth.com and the training program can be accessed at www.PrevConn.com.

What Works?

The Healthy Workplace program has been evaluated as a model program by the Substance Abuse and Mental Health Services Administration (SAMHSA). The program has evolved over several years of developmental, implementation, and evaluation trials. Training guides, videos, and print materials for its preventive interventions have been implemented in many work settings throughout the United States, Australia, and Canada.

The Healthy Workplace preventive interventions have been field-tested in five different worksites, using pre-post repeated measure designs. Random assignment to program or control groups was accomplished in three of the five studies, and a quasi-experimental design was used in two studies. Sample sizes ranged from 108 workers (in "Working People") to around 1500 workers (in "Prime Life 2000"); sample sizes in the other studies were approximately 300 to 400. The Health Behavior Questionnaire, containing multiple measures of health and substance use practices and attitudes, was used for assessment. Analysis of covariance and hierarchical regression were the main statistical analytic methods employed.

Generally, these research studies have demonstrated reductions in alcohol and drug use among participants, accompanied by improvements in related health measures, such as coping with stress, and in dietary practices. More particularly, in the "Working People" intervention, alcohol consumption was decreased by 47 percent and the number of binge drinking days was decreased by 60 percent. In the "Make the Connection" intervention, participants showed increases in awareness of perceived risks associated with alcohol and drug use and between health and alcohol and drug abuse; they also showed reduced use of alcohol and drugs for relieving stress. In the "Prime Life 2000" intervention, reductions were found in binge drinking and heavy drinking.

The Healthy Workplace program results suggest that substance abuse prevention in work settings can be accomplished within health promotion offerings without lessening the impact. Stress management health promotion programs seem to provide an especially useful vehicle *(note:* material taken from a draft "Fact Sheet" summarizing the Healthy Workplace program).

Why Does It Work?

Health promotion and disease prevention efforts are being used with increasing frequency within work settings. Employers and managed care organizations are interested in improving employee health and productivity, while healthcare costs are contained. Preventive programs that address health promotion in the work setting are an attractive choice and so are beginning to find a niche that can only be expected to grow in the future.

The Healthy Workplace program fits within this evolution of care in the work setting. Moreover, combining attention to substance abuse prevention with general health promotion offers a delivery system that is acceptable to workers without diminishing program effects. The capacity of the program to grow strengths and assets, as well as to reduce negative behaviors, contributes to overall effectiveness.

Making use of group methods for delivering the program, along with other well-constructed modes (such as videos) connects well with the general theory on which the program intervention is based and with best practice emerging with prevention programs. The training and support resources provided by the program developers afford the possibility of adequate delivery of these methods amidst good, ongoing communication and support.

The program has been carefully studied and has evolved consistent with successively obtained research data. The program has been tested and applied in numerous types of work settings, at differing levels, and with a range of ethnic diversity.

Implications for Counselors and Other Helpers

Work settings are an untapped resource for preventive counselor involvement. A program with various interventions, such as the Healthy Workplace, provides evidence that a technology exists for helping employee participants to realize specific and general prevention goals and means to achieve this. Group-based preventive methods such as this one tap into a decided skill set of most counselors and many other practitioners.

Counselors need to expand their horizons to consider the workplace as an actual setting for counselor participation. Mental health and school settings, though critically important, are not the only settings of importance in people's lives. Taking the skills that counselors possess, for instance in group work, and applying these skills preventively in the workplace affords a potential for change that needs to be joined. The Healthy Workplace program provides a means for organizing and delivering such preventive counseling projects.

YALE WORK AND FAMILY STRESS PROJECT

What Is the Yale Work and Family Stress Project?

This project includes studies in two broad areas: (1) conducting evaluations of work-based coping interventions aimed at reducing negative behavioral and psychological consequences of work and family stressors; and (2) examining relationships between particular risk and protective factors in relation to psychological symptomatology, work adjustment factors, and substance use.

The conceptual framework for the project is based on a stress, social support, and coping paradigm (Lazarus & Folkman, 1984). In this model, work and family stressors and poor coping strategies serve as risk factors and perceived social support and adaptive coping strategies operate as protective factors. It is suggested in this model that psychological symptoms arise from multiple contexts (such as the workplace), and are influenced by the interaction of individual and situational risk and protective factors over time.

Project and other research has shown that occupying multiple roles, such as those contributed from family and work sources, does not necessarily exert a greater risk for negative health outcomes and that there is evidence that multiple roles and the accumulation of social roles may assist well-being (e.g., Thoits, 1986). Moreover, multiple roles may serve a protective factor for women because females appear to be susceptible to unique vulnerabilities in their role of spouse or partner. The protective factors of coping skills and social support in relation to work and family stress are essential to investigate, as is the role that gender difference may play in this equation.

How Is It Done?

The Yale Work and Family Stress Project has conducted several studies to examine preventive programs and their effects on women. The typical intervention to be summarized here (Snow & Kline, 1995) was intended to teach participants new strategies to decrease the negative influence of specific risk factors while increasing the beneficial aspects of protective factors. The women who participated in the preventive intervention, as compared with the control participants, were expected to report: (a) lower levels of role, work-family, and work environment stressors; (b) higher perceived social support from both work and from no-work sources; (c) higher behavioral and cognitive coping and lower avoidance coping; (d) less psychological symptomatology; and (e) lower tobacco, alcohol, and illicit drug use.

A 15-session workplace coping-skills intervention was conducted for female employees located at one of four corporate job sites in Connecticut. Intervention participants met in small groups of about 10–12 employees led by a facilitator for 1.5 hours per week over 15 weeks. Sessions occurred during work hours, using release time, and were held at the company site. The preventive intervention was based on Pearlin and Schooler's (1978) hierarchy of coping mechanisms: (a) responses to change a situation (i.e., proactive measures to eliminate sources of stress); (b) responses to control the meaning of the stressful experience (i.e., cognitive restructuring); and (c) responses to control the stress after it has emerged and cannot be removed at the source (i.e., stress management techniques, such as relaxation).

The preventive intervention sessions to improve coping with work and family stress with the female participants in this study included:

Session 1: Focus on women, multiple roles, and stress
Session 2: Identifying and examining stressful situations

Session 3: Problem solving

Session 4: Managing stress (Part A): Deep breathing and muscle relaxation are learned and used throughout the whole program

Session 5: Attacking the problem (Part A): Effective communication skills are discussed and practiced

Session 6: Attacking the problem (Part B): Empathic listening and responding are learned as skills

Session 7: Attacking the problem (Part C): Direct expression of needs and identifying how to overcome communication barriers

Session 8: Attacking the problem (Part D): Integration of communication skills

Session 9: Personal networks and social support

Session 10: Group strategies

Session 11: Rethinking the problem (Part A): Self statements are explored

Session 12: Rethinking the problem (Part B): Alternative thinking modes are reviewed

Session 13: Managing the stress (Part B): Visualization and self suggestion are developed

Session 14: Personal stress management plan (Part A): Problem solving, cognitive restructuring, and stress management are integrated in relation to family and work experiences

Session 15: Personal stress management plan (Part B): Implementation of the plan in gradual steps is discussed, participants review their accomplishments during the program, and process termination issues

What Works?

The Yale Work and Family Stress Project has been evaluated by the Substance Abuse and Mental Health Administration as an Effective program. The program described above sought to assess the effectiveness of workplace coping skills intervention by teaching participants strategies to reduce negative influences of risk factors and to enhance beneficial effects of protective factors. Experimental and no-treatment control conditions were established. Participants were 239 female clerical staff members who were assigned randomly to either the preventive intervention ($n = 136$) or control ($n = 103$), within a pre-, post- and delayed post-test design. The experimental condition involved the weekly 15-session coping skills intervention. The control condition involved completion of surveys only. Variables included demographic and background factors, role stressors (employee, spouse/partner, parent), work and family stressors, active and avoidance coping strategies, work and nonwork social support, and substance use and psychological symptoms. A repeated measures analysis of variance was conducted, including time periods of post-test and a six-month follow-up.

All findings favored the coping skills intervention, supporting the risk and protective factor model that was used. Certain risk and protective factors were modified positively, with corresponding reductions in alcohol use and reliance on alcohol for reduction of tension. Overall, the project results indicate that preventive interventions in the workplace that focus on coping skills enhancement can substantially benefit women working in secretarial and clerical positions.

In longer-term follow-up (22 months), results indicated that program effects were attenuated by the follow-up. The researchers note that it is reasonable to assume that a person-centered coping skills intervention such as this one holds more potential for changing individual behavior than to decrease risk factors that are linked to organizational variables. A valid criticism is that such person-centered programs may teach participants how to adapt successfully to stressful conditions in the workplace instead of implementing strategies to change system-level conditions that lead to stressors.

Implications for Counselors and Other Helpers

The Yale Work and Family Stress Project again demonstrates that well-constructed psychoeducation group coping skills interventions can produce positive preventive effects, with enhanced skills for coping with life demands and for dealing with the more specific challenges targeted in the program (e.g., reducing future substance abuse). Counselors are well prepared to engage in such programs, as are many other professionals. In addition, these results point to the importance of including system-level change approaches within workplace prevention programs. A more comprehensive program, with both person- and system-change components, may yield more enduring preventive effects. Finally, as observed earlier, prevention programs in work settings are relatively infrequent compared to family, school, and community settings. Counselors can make a special contribution by adding the work setting to their repertoire.

THE JOBS PROJECT FOR THE UNEMPLOYED

What Is The JOBS Project for the Unemployed?

The JOBS Project is a prevention program intended to assist unemployed people to reenter the labor market. JOBS was developed by researchers at the Michigan Prevention Research Center (MPRC). The MPRC focuses on a program of prevention research on problems of employment, economic stress, and well-being over the life span. In addition, the MPRC scientifically examines relationships between employment conditions and mental and physical health, while also expanding policy and practice opportunities to the public and private sector.

The JOBS Project is funded by the National Institute for Mental Health. It seeks to develop job-seeking skills in the recently unemployed in order to prevent feelings of anxiety, helplessness, and depression and to promote reemployment.

The JOBS Project is based on a theoretical rationale taken from several areas. Vigilant coping holds that people under pressure frequently restrict their search for solutions and directions, tending to invest prematurely on one single course of action. To counteract this orientation, the JOBS Project works with unemployed persons to open up their orientation through learning how to explore, diagnose, and understand their situation and how to generate alternatives for reemployment. JOBS adapts a stress inoculation strategy from cognitive-behavioral theory, based on the concept that setbacks in the job search are inevitable and people need to learn how to inoculate themselves against these setbacks through a reserve on inoculation coping skills. JOBS also focuses on self-efficacy, the powerful belief that one can succeed in attempts rather than fail, as providing a strong motivational force for trying out new and/or difficult behaviors. A last component of the JOBS Project is derived from theory identifying the critical importance of social support in behavior change. Confiding in and drawing support from others can provide a needed buffer against the adversity of job loss and the challenges of moving forward to seek and find reemployment.

How Is It Done?

The JOBS Project is concerned with questions about unemployed persons, such as: How can social support be enhanced? How can a sense of mastery be increased? How can motivation be kindled? What is the impact of a preventive intervention that is designed to be sensitive to these kinds of questions? What can be learned about preventive interventions by studying such a program applied to unemployed persons?

Participants in the project were selected carefully and in accord with its prevention goals. Thus, participants included those who were free from diagnosable mental health disorders and who had been "recently" unemployed, that is, within the previous four months.

A central feature of the JOBS Project is using psychoeducation group learning. In groups of 15 to 20 persons, recently unemployed participants engage in a training program facilitated by a male-female team. The group-based program is delivered in five 4-hour sessions during one week. Group activities are constructed to involve participants actively in discussions, to elicit social support among each other, and to enhance their mastery through developing effective job search skills.

The JOBS Project group activities include: (a) addressing reemployment obstacles; (b) identifying marketable skills; (c) identifying sources of job leads; (d) using social networks to discover job leads; (e) conducting an information interview; and (f) managing emotions related to unemployment. The project seeks to maximize opportunities for the participants to engage actively throughout the process, operating with the contention that participants are much more likely to accept what they come up with themselves. For example, they brainstorm diagnoses of problems, alternative solutions to those problems, and ways to overcome barriers. They role play employment interviews. They give and receive feedback. They are led to identify what meaning they are taking from their training experiences. As Price observed in relation to a follow-on program to JOBS, called "Winning New Jobs," "The idea is to send the message to trainers that people have strengths inside themselves and the trick is to bring them out rather than opening up people's heads and trying to pour skills in, which doesn't work as well from a motivational view" (Price, Personal Communication, May 1, 2003). In adition, the group setting allows participants to learn from each other within a supportive environment.

What Works?

The JOBS Project was cited as an Excellent prevention program by the APA Task Force and described in detail in *14 Ounces of Prevention* (Price et al., 1988), and as Effective by the Substance Abuse and Mental Health Services Association. The project also is featured in the video, *An Ounce of Prevention* (Annenberg, 1992). Studies of the JOBS Project have demonstrated that it produces preventive impacts on mental health while maintaining favorable cost-benefit results. Effects also were differential, with more positive benefits accruing to women, to those with less formal education, and to those at highest risk psychologically.

The following summary of results is taken from an update of the project provided by the Michigan Prevention Research Center (MPRC, 2003). Eight sets of outcomes have been identified, indicating that the JOBS Project, compared to a control group, promotes:

1. Lower levels of depression. Two and one-half years following a randomized trial evaluating the JOBS Project showed that participants experienced significantly fewer depressive symptoms (Price, van Ryn, & Vinokur, 1992).

2. Skills, support, and inoculation. Results support that a carefully designed preventive intervention, such as the JOBS Project, can assist the recently unemployed (and especially those who are at risk) to acquire new job skills and a sense of mastery, provide social support, and inoculate against the setbacks that may occur in the job search.

3. Social resources that reduce vulnerability. Attention to social support and acquiring a sense of mastery through skill building contribute to a set of social resources that can serve as protective factors against the mental health risks of involuntary job loss (Price, 1992).

4. Positive outcomes especially for unemployed women and workers with less education. Results indicated clearly that mental health and economic benefits were strongest for those at higher risk and those who would be most disadvantaged by job loss (Vinokur, Schul, & Price, 1992).

5. Higher paying jobs with cost-benefit. Results showed that people in the JOBS Project obtained higher paying jobs and higher quality work than others, yielding more income while generating increased tax revenues. Thus, the intervention appears to develop preventive mental health benefits while being cost effective. For instance, this program can be implemented in unemployment offices in the United States at approximately $300 per participant. In addition, estimates suggest that the JOBS intervention can pay for itself through increased tax revenues in as few as seven months following reemployment.

Another reasonable test of a prevention program is the degree to which it has spread successfully. The JOBS prevention program has been implemented in social service agencies in Michigan and Baltimore, Maryland; in community service agencies in California (including the "Winning New Jobs" program), and in China. A comprehensive implementation manual also is available to guide the program's implementation (Curran, Wishart & Gingrich, 1999).

Why Does It Work?

The JOBS Project for the Unemployed is grounded in a strong theoretical base and ties its method directly to it. It carefully selects participants who have not yet begun to experience the conditions that the program seeks to prevent, such as depression, and who can benefit from the active ingredients of the program, including social support and self-efficacy. The program uses small groups as the engine to drive the intervention, and these groups are facilitated in such a way as to empower participants to identify and develop their own solutions and directions. A trainer's manual is available to help facilitators guide the process and to maintain a level of treatment integrity. The program is set within a research design that is sensitive to identifying the prevention of dysfunction (e.g., of depression), competencies developed for the job search (e.g., skills and inoculation strategies), job search outcomes (i.e., securing reemployment), and cost benefits.

Implications for Counselors and Other Helpers

As with most of the preventive programs that have been reviewed at the family, school, community, and work setting levels, the JOBS Project requires provider roles and skills that are well within the repertoire of counselors and other helpers. Its emphasis on small-group intervention that is both guided and seeks to draw out the resources of participants for mutual problem solving fits directly with counselor training and role. Again, as with other prevention programs reviewed, the question is not, "Can counselors and other professionals do prevention?" Rather, the question is, "How can counselors and other professional helpers become more involved in doing prevention?"

CONCLUSION

This chapter examines three workplace prevention programs with the observation that they tend to emphasize competency-enhancement, that is, the building of skills and knowledge among employees, as the primary route. This certainly is a worthy approach that we have also seen featured in many other prevention programs, and it should be very attractive to counselors.

It is also important to consider how prevention can occur at the level of the work setting itself. Becker and Steele (1995) have developed a workplace focus that they term *organizational ecology*. This is an approach to creating healthy workplaces that centers on the totality of the workplace, all the places where one works. Organizational ecology seeks to consider an integrated workplace strategy that integrates two parts: the scope of the physical settings and the social processes that are used to plan, manage, and link the physical settings over time. See Conyne and Clack (1981) and Rapin (2004) for applications of this general approach.

Quick et al. (1997) have addressed a workplace approach, as well as competency enhancement, from the perspective of preventing stress within organizations. In what these authors refer to as "organizational prevention," two major approaches can be taken: (1) job and physical demands can become the target for improvement; and/or (2) work relationships can be enhanced. In either case, the aim is to modify and shape the organization/work setting, altering demands placed on employees, so that sources of stress are removed or minimized. This approach is addressed in earlier chapters as a Level 1 change.

In terms of altering job and physical demands, Quick et al. describe five strategies for improving job and physical demands: (1) job redesign, to improve person-job fit; (2) participative management, to increase employee involvement and control in decision making; (3) flexible work schedules, to provide greater flexibility for employees in managing their work and personal demands; (4) career development, where career paths and opportunities are opened; and (5) design of physical settings, where noxious elements are reduced and nourishing ones are increased, thus better supporting task functioning.

With regard to enhancing work relationships, Quick et al. identify addressing role and relationship demands. Once again, five strategies are described: (1) role analysis, where an employee's work role is assessed and clarified to better connect the expected role with what is enacted; (2) goal setting, where the employee–supervisor relationship is addressed in terms of performance goals; (3) social support, which can buffer work stress, through emotional, informational, appraisal, and instrumental support; (4) team building, where an intact work group's functioning is assessed and enhanced; and (5) diversity programs, where various talents and perspectives are valued and used.

Programs with the organization/work setting that are aimed at stress prevention seek to contribute to a healthy organization. They can focus on the organization itself (for which fewer documented programs of excellence exist), or they can focus on individuals in the organization (these programs tend to dominate).

Rapin (2004) (a counseling psychologist and counselor educator) has reported on a fascinating 17-month organization development intervention she delivered within an in-house laboratory of a large medical center. The nature of this preventive and ecological work centered on assessing the laboratory's social climate, using the Work Environment Scale (Moos, 1974), and integrating these data with other sources of information about the work setting. Organization change interventions were implemented, including team building within the management staff and between the management staff and line staff, and a number of communication-enhancement measures, including both skill development and reconfiguring communication patterns. An example of the latter was the creation of a monthly laboratory newsletter to better distribute information and to increase awareness of ongoing events.

Not in References.

Work setting prevention is an area underpopulated by the efforts of counselors, counseling psychologists, and other professional helpers. Work is an important, abiding life context, as Freud underscored. Counselors are well prepared to enter this setting and contribute to prevention efforts in it. What blocks this from happening?

ISSUES FOR REFLECTION AND DISCUSSION

1. Let's continue, from the last sentence, above, which I will ask in another way. If work is so central to the lives of most Americans, and if counselors and counseling psychologists are well prepared to function within the work setting, why do these helpers play such a minor role in work settings? What are your thoughts? See if you can identify some barriers to work setting involvement by counselors. Be prepared to share them in a class discussion.

2. Many work setting programs are focused on substance abuse prevention. What other areas for prevention do you think would be important to address—and which counselors would be able to contribute?

3. You may work now, or have in the past. In addition, you have some awareness of your academic program and how it functions. What has been your experience within work settings as an employee or in viewing those settings and how they function? Pick one work setting. Close your eyes and connect with that work setting emotionally, what it is like, how people relate within it, how it values task and process, its physical characteristics, and so on. Draw a picture of it, free-style. Go back and put words to the picture. What do you come up with? Share your picture and your narrative with a partner.

4. How might a preventive counselor function in relation to work settings? What kinds of roles come to mind? List three roles. Pick one and expand it. How could a preventive counselor make such a role "come to life"? What would that look like?

5. In reading this chapter on prevention in work settings, what did you most notice? What grabbed your attention? Or did nothing really grab your attention? Why do you suppose either might be the case? Explain this to a small group. See how the others are thinking and feeling about this topic.

Training and the Future

Education and training in preventive counseling may be the ultimate issue confronting interested parties. For the individual student, it takes the form of, "How can I get the training I need for this when my academic program is so tightly prescribed and when I need so many other courses?" Academic program faculty, for their part, experience the issue as, "We hold many things dear: Therapy, career development, group work, research, prevention. Given the demands of accreditation and licensing bodies, how can we accord more resources to training in primary prevention?" On top of these concerns, no one (including authorities in the field) can say for sure what full education and training in prevention, or in preventive counseling, should look like.

Recognizing all that, Chapter 9 contains a proposed concept about appropriate education, training, and skills in preventive counseling. The intent is to be helpful to both students and faculty as academic preparation is actively considered. Chapter 10, which concludes this book, seeks to sum up preceding content through a look at the future.

CHAPTER 9

Education, Training, and Skills

CONTEXT

If a hale and hearty preventive counseling is to exist, it will emerge from the professional academic preparation programs of tomorrow. In reviewing the subject of prevention training in depth, Zolik (1983) cast the following long shadow:

> As the knowledge required for prevention is not always the same as that required for treatment, the need for modification in training programs is a paramount concern if training is to be improved.... New training formats must be explored; interdisciplinary dimensions must be introduced; current guidelines for accreditation must be challenged. Otherwise training obtained at the predoctoral level will by necessity have to be completed at the post-doctoral level into the indefinite future. (p. 287)

Zolik's words will be drawn upon to generally shape the directions of this final chapter. Therefore, education and training (E & T) in preventive counseling will be examined in terms of (1) required basic knowledge and skills, (2) interdisciplinary contributions, (3) training formats needed, and (4) external and internal forces. A Preventive Counseling Skills Checklist also will be presented and used to guide much of the discussion on training.

This discussion of education and training will be pitched at the doctoral level, although elements of it are appropriate for the master's level as well. Yet, the doctoral level is where the best opportunity would seem to exist for building on core counseling knowledge and skills that have been gained through earlier graduate study.

BASIC EDUCATION AND TRAINING

Although preventive counseling is still an evolving approach, what constitutes the "right stuff" for education and training is beginning to emerge. The basic knowledge and skills needed for preventive counseling are both similar to and different from those necessary for conducting remedial counseling. The similarities are traceable to the fact that preventive counseling, after all, is a type of counseling. Therefore, it should rely upon a core of basic knowledge and skills that are common to all counseling types. But as Cowen (1984) observed about mental health professional training, it is important to realize the differences. The "normal stuff" of remedial counseling is insufficient by itself for work in preventive counseling; supplementation is needed. Let us take a look at the basic knowledge and skills needed for preventive counseling.

The Counseling Core

As Price (1983, p. 295) has emphasized with reference to preventive psychology, it "would be a serious strategic and intellectual error" for departments of psychology to create separate programs. Prevention does not stand apart in isolation from existing psychology specialties and, in fact, it is being embraced by many (e.g., community, school, counseling, developmental) as an important direction for training, research, and practice."

The same situation holds for preventive counseling within professional counseling and counseling psychology. Carving out another independent specialty in preventive counseling would make as little sense as making one, let us say, for remedial counseling.

A more feasible approach would be for faculty to include in core courses those that are focused on prevention issues and for students who are especially interested in prevention to select courses accordingly, whenever a choice is possible. For instance, in the counseling program at the University of Cincinnati, the master's level specialties of school counseling and mental health counseling each provide attention to prevention. In addition, the preventive counseling course I have taught since 1984 is required of all mental health students and is an elective for others. Therefore, all of our students at the master's level are exposed to prevention, and some (those in mental health) are receiving a more concentrated dose.

This approach recognizes that preventive counseling is but one form of counseling while also supporting its uniqueness. Examples will be provided later in this chapter. This position further underscores the importance of tying preventive counseling into a core of counseling courses that is consistent with the CACREP or with APA, depending on the relevant accreditation body, and with the licensing board requirements in counseling or in psychology that apply.

In addition, specific courses in prevention, such as the one I teach at the University of Cincinnati, are beginning to appear in Counseling and Counseling Psychology curricula around the country. The Prevention Section of the Society of Counseling Psychology of the American Psychological Association has noted a trend in this direction, and members have provided support to faculty at institutions who are developing these courses.

Note that usually the more closely a training program adheres to meeting the standards and guidelines of external bodies, the less flexibility exists for students in the program to design their own program. An uncomfortable tension results in such situations that must be continually monitored by the faculty.

And yet, the core courses can be constructed so that they can fit with external considerations and be at least partially sensitive to prevention needs. For example, in our doctoral program students must take courses or meet prerequisites in consultation, professional orientation to counseling, program development and evaluation, and career development, among others, all of which are naturally suited to preventive counseling.

Other required courses, such as advanced practicum and internship, can be tailored specifically to address preventive counseling needs and settings. Thus, students can meet their advanced practicum or internship requirements through working under supervision in a university alcohol education center or in a consultation and education unit of a community mental health center, engaging in programs that are preventive in scope. For maximum exposure to prevention, faculty would need to locate field training sites that provide adequate supervised experience in both person-centered and system-centered approaches to preventive counseling. Doctoral programs in counseling that seek to prepare their students for licensure as a professional counselor or as a psychologist will need to require a set of courses that meet specific sections of the relevant state licensure regulations. In addition, they usually require a cognate support area or areas. Developing a doctoral support area with preventive counseling as a theme provides a means for advancing knowledge and skills. Pertinent courses might come directly from the counseling program but also might be taken in other departments, such as sociology, public health, and urban planning—examples of disciplines that contribute uniquely to a preventive orientation.

PREVENTION SUPPORT AREA

A student with preventive counseling interests should be able to dedicate several credit hours of courses strictly to prevention. We use a rough guideline of 24 credit hours (eight courses) in our counseling program to constitute a "support area" for purposes such as this one. These courses, as well as those with a prevention focus that reside in the core curriculum (especially the advanced practicum and internship), provide a minimum level of specialized training in preventive counseling.

Certainly, eight courses cannot begin to cover all that is needed, but they constitute a step in the right direction. What kind of knowledge and skills should be represented in the eight courses selected?

According to Lewis and Lewis (1981), a preventive counselor should be able to exercise three basic sets of skills: (1) educational, (2) program development, and (3) change agent. Their thinking is that educational skills are necessary for the counselor to enhance the competencies of a target group, through such means as courses, seminars, workshops, and media forms that are based on carefully designed instructional formats. Change agent skills are required for getting involved with human systems and empowering them to positively change. And program development skills are necessary for the effective implementation of either educational or change agent efforts; the counseling practitioner must be able to convert an idea into concrete, attainable goals and methods. Later in this chapter more attention will be devoted to an expanded set of skills that are needed by preventive counselors.

Cowen (1984), in examining training for prevention in mental health, identified much the same set of knowledge and skills. Moreover, he indicated content areas that can most readily address their development, and from which a primary prevention support area could be constructed. This information is presented in Table 9.1, followed by a brief discussion in the text of each area.

Education

Cowen saw education, defined broadly, as critical for promoting strength and competencies in individuals, with mass media approaches becoming more important. The kind of knowledge needed can be obtained from developmental psychology (for a generative base), educational psychology, and education (for writing sound curricula and how to present their contents), and perhaps the social psychology of mass communication (for effective development and use of media).

Table 9.1 Interdisciplinary Content Areas for a Prevention Support Area

Content	Discipline
Education	Developmental Psychology, Educational Psychology
Structural Change Support Groups	Social Science cluster: Social Psychology, Social Work, Sociology
Program Development & Evaluation	Psychology (Dev, Soc, & Educ), Social Ecology, Social Work, Epidemiology
Community Mental Health	Community Psychology, Counseling Psychology, Counseling, Planning, Management
Training	Preventive Counseling, Practicum and Internship

Knowledge of Structures and of Their Change

This is very similar to the change agent skill area suggested by Lewis and Lewis. In order to reduce the sources of stress in peoples' lives, some form of system change is often necessary. This kind of knowledge can best be obtained from the social-psychological sciences: sociology, social ecology, social and environmental psychology, architectural planning, political science, and economics.

Support Groups and Networks

Because stress seems more highly deleterious to those who are isolated and lack interpersonal support, a growing body of research suggests that support groups and networks can be helpful as stress buffers. The knowledge base for this kind of approach can be found in social psychology, sociology, educational foundations, social ecology, and social work.

Program Development and Evaluation

A major form of preventive counseling involves the development, implementation, and evaluation of intentional programs that are delivered before the fact to groups of at-risk or healthy people. The skills of program development and evaluation are essential to any prevention activity, as observed in Chapter 4. Cowen saw this knowledge base deriving from the areas of developmental, social, and educational psychology; social ecology; and epidemiology. Social work is another good source for this material.

Community Mental Health

Prevention programs occur in organized settings, such as work, family, and neighborhoods. The community mental health skills of entree, negotiation, consultation, and crisis intervention are essential to this end. Although Cowen did not mention it, these skills can be found in community psychology, social work, counseling, planning, management, and other programs.

Training Centers

Cowen strongly suggested that a limited number of field training centers be established to model and catalyze cutting-edge work in primary prevention program development, research, and the training of future leaders in this area. Not enough can be said for academic program faculty locating, or helping to create, community field training sites that are appropriate for students in preventive counseling. Funded grants in prevention (e.g., in dropout prevention, substance abuse prevention, and health promotion) can provide superb involvement in a wide range of prevention activities. It is in such sites and involvements that students will best be able to begin testing and integrating preventive counseling concepts and methods.

INTERDISCIPLINARY CONTRIBUTIONS

The content and methods for conducting preventive counseling, by definition, must be drawn from a variety of disciplines. In fact, when considering intervening at the systems level, it may be observed that sociology and the social sciences are as valid as psychology and the behavioral sciences.

Does one have to be a Renaissance person in order to engage in preventive counseling? The answer is no, and three implications of that question are especially important.

First, preventive counseling must be recognized as a complex endeavor that taps a wide range of academic and practical content. No one academic program can be expected to supply all the necessary instructional resources. Thus, students who are interested in preventive counseling must look to other disciplines for designing their plan of study. Although education and psychology will be strong contributors, so could sociology, social work, planning, and others.

Second, the "home" program should facilitate and help integrate this interdisciplinary process for students, while attempting to include a preventive focus wherever possible and appropriate in the existing program.

Third, no one student can possibly learn all that is necessary! Rather, as Cowen rightfully pointed out, students need assistance in learning where the relevant knowledge can be found and in gaining access to it effectively. Resourceful graduates—those who know some of the "right stuff" and, importantly, how to find the rest of the information they need—stand by far the best chance of functioning successfully as preventive counselors.

TRAINING FORMAT CHANGES

Even though most existing doctoral programs in professional counseling and counseling psychology are very tightly organized—especially if they are attempting to meet external guidelines, such as licensing—students can obtain at least a minimum level of education and training in preventive counseling. Hopefully, the material previously presented in this chapter will assist in that effort.

Thoroughly training professionals to do this kind of work, however, would require adjustments in training programs, as many have observed. In addition to the critical aspects of training in preventive counseling that have been already mentioned, let's begin with some of the additional training formats that might be needed

Ecological Perspective

An ecological perspective is most appropriate for preventive counseling. In an ecological perspective, persons are viewed within context, and the reciprocal interactions between people and their environments provide the fulcrum for change and growth. Many excellent prevention programs are aligned with an ecological perspective. As just one example, recall the School Transition Environment Program (STEP), which placed primacy on environmental change. Preventive counseling interventions always are nestled within person–environment interfaces and do less well when associated either with persons at the avoidance of environment or with environment at the avoidance of persons.

Early on, I dubbed an ecological perspective in counseling, "counseling ecology" (Conyne, 1985). Since then, we have reversed the order of this term (to ecological counseling), have oriented our counseling training at the University of Cincinnati around it (see Conyne & Cook, 2004 for an elaboration of ecological counseling), and have created a Center for Ecological Counseling at the University to assist in generating research and applications. This ecological orientation is what Hershenson and Power (1987) identified as the counseling model most closely linked philosophically to mental health counseling. If, indeed, these authors are accurate, preventive counseling will benefit greatly.

Prevention Perspective

Here, the historic individual-reparative understanding of help-giving is relaxed to allow for help-giving that is before the fact, aimed at presently healthy groups of people or those who are at risk in some real way. Again, as with the ecological perspective, this is a watershed kind of mind-set change that has a host of practical applications, as discussed in this book.

Expanded Conception of Counseling

When summed up, the first two items mentioned require a broad conception of counseling, one that comfortably permits work with systems and the indirect provision of services, for example. Faculty need to allow for such a perspective in order to give genuine support to the education and training of preventive counselors.

Training Program Flexibility

As a commitment to preventive counseling increases, possibly greater flexibility can be injected into training programs. For example, as has been mentioned, infusion can be used to include prevention in existing courses, a new preventive counseling course can be tried out as a special topic or an elective course, and students can be referred to other courses at the university that may address prevention. These kinds of changes could lead to more substantial training in prevention.

INCREASING PROGRAM RESOURCES

Increased resources is a corollary to the provision of greater program flexibility. Survey results have shown that the commitment of faculty resources to prevention is relatively low compared with that to remediation (e.g., see Zolik, 1983; also, Matthews later in this chapter). Counselor training programs would need to increase and strengthen the faculty involvement with prevention. Attention would need to be given, too, to all other facets of the counseling program to assure adequate support of preventive counseling.

Marketing

Far too many prevention programs "die on the vine" due to a failure to attract and hold target people. When the issue is clearly one of attraction, program designers need to examine ways in which they made the program known to potential participants. These are marketing questions. Counseling and counseling psychology training programs typically do not address issues of marketing, for a variety of reasons. The preventive counselor, however, must be as able to market programs as he or she is able to design, conduct, and evaluate them. Turning to the Marketing Department for courses in social marketing is recommended.

Qualitative Research Designs and Approaches

Research and evaluation methods traditionally taught in our training programs tend to emphasize quantitative experimental design and counseling process studies. Of course, other reputable research methods are available which may be even better suited for certain preventive counseling projects. These methods include epidemiology, naturalistic studies (e.g., ethnography), qualitative modes (e.g., case study), action research, and other related modes. Certainly, research design and modes have expanded since this book's first edition when I titled this section "Non-Traditional Research."

Perceptions

Note that three of the seven changes in training formats I have discussed involve alterations in perceptions: For program faculty and students:

1. To accept as valid an ecological orientation to help-giving
2. To subscribe to the concept of prevention as a legitimate avenue for providing help
3. To allow for an understanding of counseling that is set within an inclusive framework

As stated in the 1987 edition of this book, once these three perceptions are endorsed, then resources and curricular matters can be handled more effectively and efficiently.

SKILLS IN PREVENTIVE COUNSELING

What skills do preventive counselors need? In 1987 there was not much to write about in terms of skills for preventive counselors. Again, as the field of prevention has evolved, it has become possible to identify an associated set of skills for counselors to use when engaged in prevention programs. It also is a very important area, especially given Matthews' findings that prevention skills tend to be unaddressed.

As mentioned earlier, Lewis and Lewis (1981) began to address necessary prevention skills when they identified educational, program development, and change agentry skill clusters. I added several more skill clusters, including a primary prevention perspective, group facilitation, and social marketing (Conyne, 1997); the "Self-Assessment in Preventive Counseling" checklist below is associated with these clusters.

Romano and Hage (2000) described eight training domains relevant to prevention in counseling psychology, which include:

1. Community and multidisciplinary collaboration, where the ability to form effective partnerships is needed.
2. Social and political history, where knowledge of major current social problems, including racism and poverty, is necessary.
3. Protective factors and risk reduction strategies, where both personal and social risk and protective factors are important.
4. Political and social environment, where understanding the social context surrounding prevention activities is obligatory.
5. Systemic intervention, where institutions in which people live and work, as well as their interconnections, are valuable.
6. Psychoeducation groups, which are common strategies to use in conducting prevention.
7. Prevention research and evaluation, where students become exposed to participation on multidisciplinary and collaborative research teams, contextual influences, systemic change, and dissemination strategies, among other approaches.
8. Prevention ethics, including traditional ethical and more special concerns, such as equity and social justice, privacy, and entering and leaving systems appropriately.

The course, "Preventive Counseling," which I have taught in the University of Cincinnati Counseling Program since 1984, began as an experimental "special topics" offering that perhaps three students were brave enough to take! After about three years the course began to attract student interest, becoming a declared elective course in the curriculum. Again, enrollment began to increase from within the Counseling Program and also from some other related disciplines (e.g., School Psychology, Nursing, Social Work, Planning). In about 1994, the course was made a requirement for the Mental Health Counseling students (our largest program) and—all of a sudden—enrollment leaped from 10–12 graduate students to 25–30.

Over all these years, I developed the Self-Assessment in Preventive Counseling Checklist. This Checklist emerged from the original work of Lewis and Lewis (1981) and is intended to provide a means for trainees to self-assess their skills in preventive counseling. I added areas and items drawn from various sources in the interdisciplinary literature. I also asked my students toward the end of each course offering to complete the Checklist and to add any items and/or areas they thought might be lacking. Thus, this Checklist was created and modified over a period of some 12 years through more than 1600 suggestions from students. Today's version of the Checklist contains 13 preventive counseling skill clusters and 81 skills (see below). The Checklist content that addresses skills reinforces education and training issues that were discussed earlier in this chapter (also see Conyne, 1994, 1997).

A complex and interrelated set of skills is necessary in preventive counseling. As we have seen throughout the book, effective applications consist of comprehensive components and methods. For instance, a substance abuse preventive counseling program might include information about drugs and drug use, training in life skills, a media campaign, consultation to community caregivers, and formation and facilitation of family support groups (Conyne, 1997). The preventive counselor needs to be able to either deliver the necessary skills or, more likely, collaborate with others to produce them.

The preventive counseling checklist skill clusters include the following (note that the Checklist itself follows, containing all 81 skills):

1. *Primary prevention perspective* addresses a worldview for counseling, and it may be the most important skill set of the entire collection. Among its other characteristics is holding to a "before-the-fact" mind-set for counseling interventions.
2. *Personal attributes* and behaviors for preventive counselors are consistent with those for all counselors. However, because preventive counseling is a longer-term and programmatic intervention that often occurs within community systems, certain personal attributes and behaviors are particularly salient, including patience, perseverance, and flexibility.
3. *Educational skills* provide a familiar foundation for preventive counselors, involving teaching, training, leading, and other direct instructional and guidance functions.
4. *Program development skills* are centrally important to preventive counseling as most interventions are developed and delivered within a programmatic context.
5. *Change agent skills* are needed by preventive counselors in order to situate interventions within contexts, such as families, schools, communities, and workplaces, where they are needed. In addition, advocacy for and with target populations is an essential function.

6. *Ethical skills* are required; in preventive counseling, all the ethical codes and standards of behavior apply. Moreover, certain challenges exist, including being able to enter and leave community settings where programmatic intervention occurs, designing intervention with the involvement and support of local target population members, not infringing on privacy issues, and delivering preventive counseling interventions that are consistent with the dominant cultural values within the setting.

7. *Marketing skills* are especially important for preventive counseling because "prevention programs are too frequently offered in vacant space, such as an empty school auditorium or community center" (Conyne, 1997, p. 265). Social change and social marketing processes need to be appreciated, if not learned, and to be fit within stages of change.

8. *Multicultural skills* need to be mastered by preventive counselors because interventions are often constructed and delivered within community settings, and preventive counseling frequently is conducted with underserved populations.

9. *Group facilitation skills* are fundamental to the delivery of nearly every type of preventive counseling program. Most planning occurs in teams, and most delivery of programs is through group formats, such as psychoeducation groups.

10. *Collaboration skills* are basic to preventive counselors because solo work is now virtually nonexistent. Teamwork runs deep in preventive counseling, with the creation, delivery, and evaluation of programs typically accomplished through people working together. Often team members come from different disciplines and life situations, making collaborative participation even more necessary.

11. *Organization and setting skills* are connected to change agent skills. Preventive counselors need to understand individuals and groups, as well as organizations, neighborhoods, and communities. They also need to develop effective and appropriate ways to become involved in these settings and to work with members sensitively and effectively.

12. *Trends and political dynamics skills* are becoming essential for preventive counselors. They need to be aware of not only present and past practices and conditions but also impending ones. Moreover, they need to be attuned to the community and neighborhood politics and power structures because so much of their work is located in those settings.

13. *Research and evaluation skills* are not just "tack-on" skills for

counselors, and certainly not for preventive counselors. Preventive counseling programs need to be based on documented local needs, informed by research, and set within the best evaluation designs possible under existing conditions.

The Checklist comes next. Please scan it and, perhaps, complete it. Also, let me know what really seems to connect for you and what seems to be missing!

PLACE OF PREVENTION IN COUNSELING AND COUNSELING PSYCHOLOGY

What is the present status of prevention courses and prevention skill training in Counselor Education and in Counseling Psychology? Matthews (In review) investigated this question through a mailed survey, which contained the 29 items listed below. She was interested in the extent to which prevention courses are included in CACREP-accredited counselor education programs and in APA-approved Counseling Psychology programs. Her survey explored both prevention-specific courses and other courses in which prevention might be infused, and was adapted from previous work by Romano and Hage (2000), Conyne (1997), and Lewis and Lewis (1981). The items were:

Definition, history, and scope of prevention
Risk and protective factors—individual level
Risk and protective factors—group level
Prevention theory
Role of counselor in primary prevention
Place of prevention in counseling
Ethical issues specific to prevention
Culturally sensitive prevention
Planning and facilitating psychoeducational groups
Group facilitation skills relevant to community organizing
Assessing community needs
Identifying and articulating goals and objectives—community
Identifying and articulating goals and objectives—program
Prevention program evaluation
Evaluating and selecting prevention program materials
Creating effective prevention program materials
Systems theory
Systems-level interventions
Organizational dynamics

Consultation skills
Advocacy skills
Cross-disciplinary collaboration skills
Social marketing skills
Assessing social trends
Etiology of social problems
Role of social system in etiology of individual problems
Political ramifications of prevention
Empowering individuals and systems
Grant writing skills

Counselor Education Results

In Counselor Education, the survey was sent to 173 CACREP-approved programs, with one followup, yielding 89 responses. (The response rate to the survey was 52 percent.) Results showed that one-third reported offering specific prevention courses. While this seems like good news for prevention, many course titles did not appear to be specific to prevention (e.g., Human Growth and Development). Seven courses in six programs carried prevention-oriented titles (e.g., Preventive Counseling, Health Psychology, Holistic Wellness Counseling) and eight other courses had titles suggesting a specific prevention emphasis (e.g., At-Risk Solutions and Strategies).

When asked about the place of prevention in the counseling field, 54 percent of respondents indicated it was integral, and 0 percent said it was unimportant. (Other response categories are not reported here.) In terms of prevention being addressed adequately in counselor training, 28 percent judged it to be sufficiently covered, 72 percent said it should receive greater emphasis, and no respondents indicated that it receives too much attention.

Respondents indicated clearly that students could not specialize in prevention (94 percent). Only 2.2 percent responded that a prevention specialization was open to doctoral students. Related to specializing is the question of how much attention is focused on developing skills in prevention. Here, findings suggest that, while general prevention concepts may receive coverage, specific prevention skills such as in social marketing, grant writing, and assessing social trends, tend not to be covered.

Counseling Psychology Results

The survey was sent to the training directors of all APA-accredited Counseling Psychology programs ($n = 74$); 27 surveys (36 percent) were returned, after two follow-ups with reminders. The findings were as follows: 74.1 percent of respondents indicated that their programs do not currently offer prevention courses, while 11.1 percent reported that they do offer such courses. With regard to the infusion of prevention into other courses, results suggest that prevention does not tend to be routinely covered or is not clearly linked to prevention. On the positive side, Matthews observes that programs seem to be connecting counseling psychology and prevention; yet many of the competencies that are most particular to prevention tend to be addressed less often. These competencies include prevention theory, community organizing, and evaluating prevention programs, to name just three. When asked about the place of prevention in the field of counseling psychology, 80.8 percent indicated that it is integral to the field or it is historically important, but that the field is mistakenly moving from it. A total of 70.4 percent of the respondents responded that prevention should be given an increased emphasis in counseling psychology training.

Matthews states that the results obtained from these two sources are similar to the observations made earlier by others—that many consider prevention central to the field of counseling psychology, but that it is largely neglected. She suggests that we have a good idea of what should be included in prevention training within counseling psychology, but she challenges us to figure out *how* to move ahead on delivering this training.

How to interpret these results is a function of one's point of view. The relatively low response rates—especially with counseling psychology—should give us pause against generalizing too far. In addition, because we do not have previous empirical data, there are no statistical comparison points.

Although it would be comforting to find more prevention courses being offered and a greater attention to prevention skill development, for example, it is encouraging to note that prevention is being addressed and that there are examples of prevention courses in both counselor education and in counseling psychology curricula. This was not the case in 1987, when virtually no courses or emphases were available. Progress is being made, but its rate needs to be accelerated. Converting what may be a broadly held viewpoint that prevention is integral to counseling into an equally broad-scale application is still needed.

EXTERNAL AND INTERNAL FORCES TO BE CHALLENGED

Students can now be minimally trained in preventive counseling by attending to considerations presented in this chapter. To do so, a strong interdisciplinary orientation, committed faculty, interested students, and considerable creativity are required.

Realistically, however, one must recognize that most graduate counseling and counseling psychology programs are inflexible, dominated by standards and guidelines required by various accreditation, licensing, and credentialing bodies. Moreover, the main thrust of these bodies is the reinforcement of counseling for remediation, even though signs are all around us that prevention, wellness, and health promotion represent a growing trend. What results for many students and faculty, of course, is an uncomfortable tension and a sense of powerlessness about how to resolve these conflicting realities.

Although faculty may seek to influence external regulation in the field, no quick relaxation of guidelines can be expected. That's not to suggest that efforts to produce greater flexibility about what constitutes "proper" counseling and counseling psychology training should not continue with enthusiasm.

To bring about change, however, the faculty in each academic program must squarely face the question of where prevention ought to be in their curriculum and how many resources, if any, should be devoted to it. It can no longer be claimed that prevention does not work! Prevention can be done and done well. There are now many examples of excellent prevention programs in schools, communities, and other settings, and these can be easily located in the professional literature.

A major purpose in writing this book was to contribute to discussions of these contributions by faculty and students. This attention is a necessary precursor to professions and professionals taking an active role in preventive counseling.

CONCLUSION

This chapter addressed the thorny issue of education and training in preventive counseling. What has been provided is a possible means to provide minimal training in this new type of counseling by creatively selecting courses in required categories and by building an interdisciplinary support area in preventive counseling. Courses in the support area might address education, structural change, support groups and networks, community mental health, and practica/internships. These courses would be selected from a wide range of departments.

In-depth training is yet another matter, requiring program faculty to come to hard decisions about the actual place that prevention will occupy in their programs. Further evidence of commitment to preventive counseling would be found in the endorsement by program faculty of perspectives in ecology, prevention itself, and an expanded concept of counseling. Moreover, these faculty would provide for increased program flexibility and resources, while recognizing the importance of marketing and qualitative, "nontraditional" research in preventive counseling.

Yet, if a commitment to create a preventive counseling course is made, it is now possible to gear the course around skill development. Sets of preventive counseling skills now have been identified, and the means exists to teach them. In addition, ample illustrations of excellent prevention programs are readily available in the literature, which instructors can access in their teaching. But, as Matthews' survey results indicate, much remains to be done before what is generally held to be integral to counseling and counseling psychology becomes realized in the curriculum.

ISSUES FOR REFLECTION AND DISCUSSION

1. Preventive counseling is similar to, but also different from, remedial counseling (therapy). What basic knowledge and skills are compatible with both approaches, and what are unique to preventive counseling?
2. Describe an advanced practicum or internship experience that you think would fit well with preventive counseling. What would you do? Where might this be located? Share your ideas in a small group, which then will give a brief presentation to the whole class.
3. Carefully assess your academic program in terms of its offerings. What seems consistent with preventive counseling? Do you think that any modifications could be made to increase the preventive counseling focus? Identify any such possibilities.
4. Now, take a look at yourself in terms of skills, using Table 9.2. Carefully complete the questions, noting your strengths and areas for improvement. Make suggestions, where these are requested. Then, reflect on your responses: What do they mean? Finally, pair up with another student to share your results.
5. What kinds of counseling positions/jobs exist in relation to preventive counseling? Are there specific jobs, or is preventive counseling embedded within existing positions, such as mental health counselor or school counselor? What about functions and roles, such as trainer, consultant, or group facilitator? How might those fit? If you don't know the answers to these questions, how can you find out? Explore this area prior to the next class session, do some research, and come back with some information to share with the class.
6. How can prevention be viewed generally as being integral to counseling, while at the same time being a much less important part of the curricula? What do you think could be done to lessen this discrepancy?

Table 9.2 Self-Assessment In Preventive Counseling

Instructions: Circle the relevant response for each question in Sections A-M. Write any self-assessment comments after Section M. In Section N, suggest for possible future inclusion any skills that you think are presently missing.

	OK Now	Needs Growth
A. Primary Prevention Perspective		
Understand and appreciate:		
1. Before-the-fact orientation	x	x
2. Reduction of incidence	x	x
3. Ecological/systems viewpoint	x	x
4. Healthy/at risk targets	x	x
5. Wide scope target	x	x
6. Multifactorial interventions	x	x
7. Multidisciplinary contributions	x	x
8. Team functioning	x	x
9. Collaboration	x	x
10. Empowerment	x	x
B. Personal Attributes & Behaviors		
Ability to:		
1. Be patient	x	x
2. Be persistent	x	x
3. Be flexible	x	x
4. Be creative	x	x
5. Be organized	x	x
6. Be passionately involved	x	x
7. Be an effective helper	x	x
C. Educational Skills		
Ability to:		
1. Set educational goals	x	x
2. Select appropriate training materials and formats	x	x
3. Create appropriate training materials and formats	x	x
4. Involve individuals in active learning	x	x
5. Involve groups in active learning	x	x
6. Provide clear instructions	x	x
7. Provide clear feedback	x	x
D. Program Development Skills		
Ability to:		
1. Assess ecological needs	x	x
2. Define the problem	x	x
3. Identify attainable objectives	x	x
4. Develop a variety of intervention options	x	x
5. Plan and coordinate detailed implementation	x	x
6. Evaluate process and outcomes of program implementation	x	x

Table 9.2 Self-Assessment In Preventive Counseling *(continued)*

	OK Now	Needs Growth
7. Communicate ideas orally	x	x
8. Communicate ideas in writing	x	x
E. Change Agent Skills		
Ability to:		
1. Recognize the need for change in a given system	x	x
2. Analyze system resources for change	x	x
3. Analyze system barriers to change	x	x
4. Work effectively as a member of change-oriented teams	x	x
5. Select specific change strategies	x	x
6. Implement specific change strategies	x	x
7. Advocate for target	x	x
8. Negotiate for change	x	x
F. Ethical skills		
Ability to:		
1. Implement ethical code	x	x
2. Protect privacy of targets	x	x
3. Involve target members ("user participation")	x	x
G. Marketing Skills		
Ability to:		
1. Appropriately Promote	x	x
2. Use telecommunications	x	x
3. Use media	x	x
4. Involve marketing experts	x	x
5. Appreciate/apply social marketing approaches	x	x
H. Multicultural Skills		
Ability to:		
1. Be aware of own cultural values	x	x
2. Be aware of own cultural biases	x	x
3. Be aware of target's worldview	x	x
4. Be knowledgeable of target's worldview	x	x
5. Apply multicultural awareness and skills appropriately	x	x
I. Group Facilitation Skills		
Ability to:		
1. Perform core group work skills	x	x
2. Perform psychoeducation group work skills of:		
a. Provide developmental information	x	x
b. Train in competencies	x	x
c. Balance content & process	x	x
3. Lead a team	x	x
4. Be a good group member	x	x

Table 9.2 Self-Assessment In Preventive Counseling *(continued)*

	OK Now	Needs Growth
J. Collaboration Skills		
Ability to:		
1. Function interdependently	x	x
2. Problem solve with others	x	x
3. Exchange resources	x	x
4. Include others' expertise	x	x
5. Synthesize diverse inputs	x	x
K. Organization & Setting Skills		
Ability to:		
1. Be aware of organizational behavior	x	x
2. Apply consultation principles and processes	x	x
3. Apply organization development principles and processes	x	x
4. Gain access to environments	x	x
5. Function in various environments	x	x
L. Trends & Political Dynamics Skills		
Ability to:		
1. Recognize current emphases	x	x
2. Predict future trends	x	x
3. Relate prevention to managed care systems	x	x
4. Understand public policy	x	x
5. Respond to system supports and barriers	x	x
M. Research & Evaluation		
Ability to:		
1. Understand criteria of effectiveness, efficiency, side effects, appropriateness, and adequacy	x	x
2. Assess	x	x
3. Design research	x	x
4. Apply statistical methods	x	x
5. Use data programmatically	x	x
6. Use strategic planning	x	x
7. Write grants	x	x

Overall Comments:

N. Add Any Skills You Think Are Missing:

CHAPTER 10

The Future of Preventive Counseling

CONTEXT

This last chapter sums up major content themes by looking at the future of preventive counseling. Ten different needs that weave in and around prevention will be presented. The chapter will conclude with calls for action.

It is imperative that the issue of action steps be joined, for preventive counseling is at the threshold of our professions. The doors need to be opened more widely, if you will, for it to become a more available option for students, practitioners, and the public. Certainly, those who have the most to gain from this step are all those who can be reached through preventive programs, becoming empowered to improve their lives through more effective participation in systems and settings.

THE TEN NEEDS FOR ADVANCING PREVENTIVE COUNSELING

Need # 1: Address the Problem of Huge Needs, Limited Resources

Faculty and students in our counseling program at the University of Cincinnati are involved in a variety of applied projects. Among them is service delivery in a health resource center within the inner city, a project where doctoral students provide Problem-Based Learning instruction to academically underprepared university students, and service in a new charter school serving students, most of whom come from Appalachian (African American and White) families. In each of these cases, the type of counseling service provided is light years removed from preventive counseling. Although each of these situations is different, they all share one common theme: needs are significant and resources are scarce.

Here is one example. I recently attended (with faculty colleague Mei Tang) an intervention team meeting in the charter school mentioned above. I participated in the meeting in order to become better acquainted with school personnel through beginning to participate in an important ongoing activity of the school. In this way, we eventually hope to build a strengthened partnership where prevention programming, and perhaps funding, can be developed—benefiting both the school and the students in our program. The school was facing a great crisis as we were meeting (a middle school student was missing), and it was decided that the intervention team should meet with the parents immediately as one way to address the crisis. This was both an appropriate response and an illustration of everyday life in the school: much time every day in the school is spent responding to crises. Basics (such as student records) are not in place, and there is insufficient staff on hand to satisfy the developmental and preventive needs of students or the setting.

Similar scenarios could be written about the inner-city health center as well as the university program for underprepared students. It is very difficult to do prevention when one is always responding to crises. Moreover, the danger exists that a crisis response mode will become a chronic operational style. However, counselors and other professional helpers who have been trained in prevention are in a position to avoid this danger. They can break through the crisis response mode by envisioning additional possibilities and by helping others around them to do so as well.

Academic programs need to develop the kind of placements referred to above, even if they are not currently evidencing best practice preventive counseling. These placements (through practica, internships, grants, class projects, voluntary involvement, etc.) allow students to experience the realities faced within settings that, though greatly in need of preventive counseling, may not be ready for it presently. With good guidance and supervision, however, helping students to move with others in the setting toward prevention—to "break through" or to proceed in "baby steps," if needed—can be a powerful learning experience.

Need #2: Close the Training Gap

Counselors and other helpers need to be trained in prevention to possess the capacity to break through, or to work with baby steps. As has been pointed out, prevention can be introduced into a curriculum through providing a focused course on prevention, through infusing prevention concepts and methods in existing courses, through taking prevention courses that may be available in other disciplines (e.g., public health), or through arranging combinations of these approaches. The news is both good and bad. Although an increasing number of academic programs are developing courses in prevention and infusing it in other courses (the good news), the number of such courses remains low, and attention to developing specific prevention skills needs to be catalyzed and nurtured.

The low base rate for focused attention on prevention in counseling and counseling psychology sustains a gap between what is needed in terms of service delivery and what can be provided. Too few of our students are being systematically exposed to prevention concepts and applications. When they find themselves in situations such as those described briefly in Scenario #1, they are ill equipped to contribute a prevention mind-set and accompanying competencies. Consequently, partially as a result of this failure, settings tend to remain stuck in a crisis orientation.

Need #3: Continue the Advancement of Prevention

The prevention field is evolving positively, if slowly. Agreement about how to define prevention is increasing. Methods for conducting prevention have emerged. Preventive counseling skills have been identified and can be taught. Numerous prevention programs have been developed, implemented, and evaluated as being effective. Sources for learning about effective prevention programs have been developed and are readily available in text (e.g., journals and books) and on-line (e.g., Web-based resource directories) formats. Courses have been developed, with syllabi available for sharing. Continuing education training in prevention is becoming more noticeable. A prevention section has been established within the Society of Counseling Psychology of the American Psychological Association.

Training programs and practitioners must begin to avail themselves of the resources on prevention that are abundantly available. More current and future counselors, as well as students in other helping fields, need to be trained and supported in this area.

Need #4: Recognize and Counteract the Powerful Conditions That Inhibit Prevention

What keeps counselors from doing prevention and faculty from educating their students in preventive counseling? One answer is that present faculty have not themselves been educated in prevention science or interventions. This is no fault of their own, of course, because their training programs tended to omit prevention as a component. Another answer is that accreditation and licensing standards are silent on prevention training. If something is not mandated in counseling training, then it just may not occur. So much is required that there is little room (or energy) to develop other foci. A third reason is that mental health always has venerated the treatment of dysfunction, the repair of damage, and the rescue of human sufferers. Treatment is what is rewarded through mental health reimbursement (however inadequate it may be!), as are better salaries, wider job opportunities, available external funding, and, yes—the emphasis of training programs themselves. And, as has been observed, the high demand for remedial service can depress attempts to get ahead of the curve through prevention services and to encourage students to want to learn about prevention.

However, once barriers are identified, then goals and strategies for positive movement may become more possible. Collections of professionals, such as those in the Prevention Section of the Society of Counseling Psychology of the American Psychological Association, are working on these matters currently. Publications, such as the special issue of the *American Psychologist* on prevention that works for children and youth (Weissberg & Kumpfer, 2003), are becoming more available. Faculty in increasing numbers of academic programs are designing courses in prevention. Training in prevention is also beginning to be offered through continuing education workshops. All of these initiatives, and more that have not been mentioned here, resonate with decreasing inhibiting forces and with advancing supportive forces for prevention.

Need #5: Connect Prevention and Remediation

When remediation and prevention are placed in a competitive, either/or position, there is no gain. Yes, remediation predominates and garners the bigger share of resources and attention. Yes, prevention is negatively affected by this situation. However, attacks against one or the other of these two important goals for helping people serve to weaken both.

Indeed, many preventionists used to attack remediation and treatment—including myself when, in the first edition of this book I, too, suggested that prevention and remediation were at odds in a zero-sum kind of game. It is far healthier, and more accurate, to acknowledge that prevention and remediation are important realms coexisting along the same mental health services continuum. Rather than being in competition, prevention and remediation need to be perceived as harmonious goals that often can reinforce and supplement each other as comprehensive services are provided to people in systems and settings. The APA electronic journal, *Prevention and Treatment,* exemplifies this more integrated approach.

Need #6: View People in Systems and Settings, Not as Separate from Them

Counselors are naturally drawn to theory and applications that focus on improving and changing people. We work with people in different systems and settings: family, school, community, and work. It is the naive counselor who fails to consider, at whatever level of intervention, the conditions surrounding people's lives, their settings, both proximal and distal influences, and how people interact and draw meaning from all these sources. In another book (see Conyne & Cook, 2004), we have termed this approach to counseling *ecological counseling).*

Separating people from systems and settings is inimical to this ecological perspective. Prevention programs that are restricted to teaching skills, for example, without consideration for these skills being embedded and applied within settings lack the ability to effect substantive and lasting change. Conversely, prevention programs that seek a setting change alone (e.g., to create new rules and policies within an organization without involving and attending to organizational members) also limit their impact.

Those involved in counseling and counseling psychology are increasingly recognizing the importance of conceptualizing and addressing people in systems and settings. Taking a people-in-systems and settings approach maximizes opportunities for prevention programs to take hold and succeed. Yet, as Matthews' assessment data indicate, teaching students the skill sets that address setting and setting change occurs only infrequently. Skill areas accorded the lowest values on her assessment survey included those related to setting and social issues: assessing social trends, the etiology of social problems, and the political ramifications of prevention. Although we may be on the right track, then, much work needs to be done in this area.

Need #7: Help People to Empower Themselves

It is audacious to believe that counselors can directly empower people and systems, as the subtitle to the first edition of this book may have implied. At best, counselors and other helpers try to help people *to become* empowered— that is, *to empower themselves* within systems and settings. This concept is central to preventive counseling.

Here is an example of this concept. As mentioned in Chapter 3, at the University of Cincinnati's counseling program we have been working with Problem-Based Learning (PBL), both within some of our courses and in consultation with other faculty in the university who are trying it. In a recent project (PBL Pilot Project), we were asked to link our doctoral students, who are trained in group work and have exposure to PBL, to provide consultative assistance faculty in another college who were having particular trouble with the group facilitation aspects of PBL (Conyne et al., 2003). In one classroom situation that had been going especially well, the faculty member asked his counseling student consultant if she would conduct a training session for students in the class on the topic of group participation. Instead, the student consultant redirected the request, suggesting that the faculty member was able to do this now and to do it well, and supported the faculty member as he prepared to provide this training. It turns out that the training went very well! Moreover, that faculty member and his graduate assistants have become so empowered that they have submitted a proposal to a national convention of group workers based on their work with small groups in the classroom. This is a concrete example of becoming empowered.

Need #8: Find Ways for Prevention to Become Essential

Matthews' recently collected survey data provide some evidence of positive movement in prevention curricular training but also confirm past hesitancies to advance in this area. A large discrepancy appears to remain between a value that prevention is integral to the field and the actual investment in prevention training. As Matthews (in review) succinctly observed with regard to counselor education curricula:

> No CACREP-accredited program would graduate a student without providing skill development in both individual and group counseling, yet many programs seem ready to graduate students who have not developed skills in creating and evaluating prevention programs or in understanding ethical considerations unique to prevention (p. 12).

Developing special topics courses and electives in preventive counseling, leading eventually to a required course (as was done at the University of Cincinnati), may provide a way for a program to take developmental steps. Adding preventive concepts and strategies intentionally within existing courses offers another way. Developing a listing of prevention courses from other disciplines and referring students to those courses is yet a third. All such strategies are needed to narrow the discrepancy between valuing prevention and acting on that value through the curriculum.

Need #9: Educate Professional Colleagues about Prevention

Our training programs need to reflect prevention so that future practitioners will be adequately prepared to deliver preventive services. In addition, current faculty are an important resource. Continuing education and consultation and training are vehicles that should be explored to educate today's professionals about prevention. An example is the four-hour Teaching Prevention continuing education workshop sponsored by APA at the 2003 Toronto convention (Matthews, Conyne, Kenney, & O'Neil, 2003). When APA asked us if we would be interested in presenting this workshop regionally, we quickly agreed because this kind of opportunity allows wider dissemination of necessary knowledge and skills in prevention to other counseling psychologists.

Need #10: Advocate for Prevention

Advocacy is an important counselor competency area, and it is particularly important within prevention. Professional advocacy on behalf of prevention in counseling and counseling psychology is also critically important. If the standards set by licensing and accrediting bodies sometimes serve as disincentives for including prevention within training programs, then preventionists may want to try influencing those important sources. If mental health reimbursements are targeted away from preventive services, then preventionists may try influencing third-party insurers to change their practices. If colleagues are unconvinced that prevention is desirable and/or feasible within local curricula, then once again preventionists may attempt to nudge them toward acceptance.

ACTION STEPS

Nested in the previous discussion of needs are some directions for possible changes aimed at improving the spread of prevention to counseling and counseling psychology. Below are specific recommendations and suggestions that have been produced previously: (a) from the Task Force of the Use of Groups in Prevention (Conyne & Wilson, 2001) within the Division of Group Psychology and Group Psychotherapy (Division 49 of APA); (b) by Conyne (2000) within the special section on prevention in counseling psychology, edited by Romano and Hage (2000); and (c) by Romano and Hage (2000) as a conclusion to that special section. Presented first are recommendations related to using groups for prevention.

Recommendations of the APA Division 49 Task Force for Use of Groups for Prevention

Division 49, as a premier international association for the advancement of group training, practice, and research, should assume leadership in educating its members, mental health providers, third party payers, and the general public about the importance and benefits of using groups for prevention. The Using Groups for Prevention Task Force of Division 49 makes the following recommendations for consideration and action by the Executive Board in the areas of training, practice, research, and advocacy.

Training

Psychology training programs that concern themselves with group training should expand their training regimen to include use of the group medium for prevention purposes. This emphasis is intended to augment, not replace, other existing training emphases. Potential training foci could include prevention concepts, psychoeducation formats, evaluation of prevention designs, and supervised practice in group-based prevention activity.

Therefore: The Division should develop training materials and educational efforts that could be used by psychology training program personnel.

Practice

Practicing psychologists need resources and support for their work. They frequently are called upon to deliver groups intended to prevent dysfunction and/or to enhance well-being, but may possess insufficient training and resources for effectively planning, performing, and processing such groups.

Therefore: The Division should develop and make available resources to practitioners and researchers that will serve to guide and support efforts in the field. Training efforts might include pre-convention workshops and continuing education offerings. Resource materials might include design and implementation guides and compendia of model intervention programs for specific prevention efforts.

Research

Available research on the process and outcomes of group work, and especially on groups being used for prevention, is severely limited in quantity and quality. Practitioners, educators, and consumers all need evidence-based information about what works. Such information is vital for examining and advancing groups being used for prevention.

Therefore: The Division should encourage psychologists to conduct quality studies of group work in general, and of groups for prevention in particular.

Advocacy

Despite evidence that group-based delivery of preventive interventions is an effective and efficient methodology for advancing mental health and wellness in both educational and community settings, support for training, research, and practice of preventive group work is limited. Few training programs for psychologists include group-based prevention in their training objectives. The quantity of experimental and field studies of preventive group work lags behind research in many other aspects of group psychology. Practitioners often are discouraged from engaging in preventive group work because it is only rarely considered to be a reimbursable activity by third party payers.

Therefore: The Division should take the lead in disseminating information (e.g., 49 Web page, brochures, press releases, scholarly productivity, inter-association collaboration, public education) about the value and importance of groups used for prevention. Focused advocacy encouraging support and involvement should be directed to psychologists and other helping professionals, to managed care and third party payers, and to the public at large.

Recommendations of Conyne, in Romano & Hage (2000, pp. 842–843)

Resolving to Incorporate Prevention in Counseling Psychology

> *Whereas,* prevention has been shown to work and to offer benefits that can exceed treatment, yet treatment and its ethos predominate in counseling psychology
>
> *Whereas,* counseling psychologists occupy professional roles that naturally allow them to incorporate prevention in their service delivery, teaching, and research repertoire, yet most have generally not begun to realize this potential
>
> *Whereas,* by neglecting to apply prevention in their training, research, and/or practice counseling psychologists inadvertently truncate the extent to which they can be broadly helpful to larger numbers of people
>
> *Whereas,* counseling psychology training programs tend to be organized around a quasi-medical framework exemplified by diagnose-treat functions, thereby generally failing to include a prevention perspective
>
> *Therefore, be it resolved* that a preventive perspective will be integrated fully within counseling psychology practice, research, and training.

Recommendations of Romano & Hage (2000, pp. 855–856)

Call-to-Action Proposals

1. Modify the archival definition of counseling psychology to clearly state prevention as a fundamental activity of the profession.
2. Integrate prevention concepts, perspectives, and skills in core counseling psychology courses.
3. Require students to list prevention activity on practicum and internship applications.
4. Influence graduate training programs, accreditation bodies, and state licensing boards to recognize prevention science and practice as necessary competencies for psychologists.
5. Advocate for systemic change and political action for social justice.

CONCLUSION

A set of 10 needs and three action recommendations were presented in this final chapter. Their adoption would greatly increase the capacity of practitioners to provide the kind of help that is in such demand today. Although the recommendations themselves emerge specifically from a momentum occurring within counseling psychology, I also suggest that a similar set of recommendations could be forwarded for counselor education and the counseling profession, as well as for associated professions, such as social work.

Preventive counseling can add substantially to the armamentarium of professional helpers. It can be used to complement important remedial helping approaches through its unique goal of alleviating disorder and promoting health. The theoretical, research, and skills knowledge base is in place, and numerous examples of effective preventive programs have been documented. The personal and societal needs are substantial. Indeed, the time has come for counselors to adopt a preventive orientation to their work, helping people to empower themselves in the systems and settings of their lives.

ISSUE FOR REFLECTION AND DISCUSSION

There is just one issue to be addressed at the conclusion of this book. It is as follows:

Now that you have read and thought about preventive counseling, you know what I think. But the really important question is: What do *you* think? I ask that you—right now—while you are thinking about it, fire up your computer (or take out a piece of paper, whatever is your way to write) and respond to the question below in a 500-word essay to be shared with your class.

What are your thoughts about preventive counseling and how do you see yourself connecting with it in your professional future?

I am very interested in feedback and in all of your ideas about preventive counseling and its future use. It would mean a lot to me if you would send your essay to me at:

> conynerk@email.uc.edu

for those of you with Internet access,

or via U.S. mail at:

> Bob Conyne
> Counseling Program
> Teachers College
> University of Cincinnati
> Cincinnati, Ohio 45221–0002

Thank you.

Highly Recommended
Supplementary Reading

This section presents highly recommended supplementary reading for Chapters 1, 2, 3, 4, and 9. A source particularly recommended for Chapters 5 through 8 is: R. Weissberg & K. Kumpfer (Guest eds.), Special issue, Prevention that works for children and youth. *American Psychologist, 58,* 425–496.

CHAPTER 1

Publications

Albee, G. (1986). Toward a just society: Lessons from observations on the primary prevention of psychopathology. *American Psychologist, 41,* 891–898.

In this article, Albee, who is one of the prime movers behind primary prevention in mental health, explains why system-level change is critical to primary prevention efforts, and how social justice can be increased through redistribution of social power.

Albee, G., & Gullotta, T. (Eds.). (1997). *Primary prevention works.* Thousand Oaks, CA: Sage.

This edited book provides a review of primary prevention, featuring the "Albee incidence formula," and describes several programs in detail that cut across the life span.

Albee, G., & Joffe, J. (Eds.). (1977). *Primary prevention of psychopathology. Vol. 1: The issues.* Hanover, NH: University Press of New England.

This volume, and the other annual books emerging from the Vermont Conference on the Primary Prevention of Psychopathology, document trends and progress in this field.

Bronfenbrenner, U. (1979). *The ecology of human development: Experiments by nature and design.* Cambridge, MA: Harvard University Press.

This book is the seminal contribution to ecological understandings applied to human development.

Caplan, G. (1964). *Principles of preventive psychiatry.* New York: Basic Books.

For the initial thinking on the subject of primary prevention in mental health, turn to this book.

Conyne, R., & Cook, E. (Eds.). (2004). *Ecological counseling: An innovative perspective on person-environment interaction.* Alexandria, VA: American Counseling Association.

An examination of how ecological principles can guide counseling activities across varying levels and utilizing personal derived meaning.

Cowen, E. (1985). Person-centered approaches to primary prevention in mental health: Situation-focused and competence-enhancement. *American Journal of Community Psychology, 13,* 31–49.

Cowen, who was another important thinker in primary prevention in mental health, develops a very useful framework in this article for conceptualizing what he calls person-centered approaches in primary prevention. He details their empowerment capabilities and provides ample examples. The contents of this article are especially promising for professional counselors and counseling psychologists.

Durlak, J., & Wells, A. (1997). Primary prevention programs for children and adolescents: A meta-analytic review. *American Journal of Community Psychology, 25,* 115–152.

A thorough meta-analytic review of primary prevention programs for children and adolescents examining what works.

Felner, R., Felner, T., & Silverman, M. (2000). Prevention in mental health and social intervention: Conceptual and methodological issues in the evolution of the science and practice of prevention. In J. Rappaport & E. Seidman (Eds.), *Handbook of community psychology* (pp. 9–42). New York: Kluwer.

Extensive review of prevention with a framework for future conceptualization, application, and research.

Felner, R., Jason, L., Moritsugu, J., & Farber, S. (Eds.). (1983). *Preventive psychology: theory, research, and practice.* New York: Pergamon.

This compendium summarizes preventive psychology into six major areas: perspectives, competence-based, ecological and environmental, life stress, community practice, and future training. It provides an excellent status report of the field.

Gullotta, T., & Bloom, M. (Eds.). (2003). *Encyclopedia of primary prevention and health promotion.* New York: Kluwer.

Compendium including work on foundations of primary prevention and health promotion (13 contributions) and on primary prevention and health promotion topics (152 contributions).

Klein, D., & Goldston, S. (Eds.). (1977). *Primary prevention: An idea whose time has come.* Washington, DC: DHEW No. (ADM) 77–447.

The published proceedings of the Pilot Conference on Primary Prevention, this book was an early call to arms for primary prevention in mental health. It contains some important and useful articles.

Price, R., Ketterer, R., & Bader, B. (Eds.). (1980). *Prevention in mental health.* Beverly Hills, CA: Sage.

Part of the series on community mental health, this volume covers a wide spectrum of research, policy, and practice in mental health prevention.

Romano, J., & Hage, S. (2000). Prevention and counseling psychology: Revitalizing commitments for the 21st century. *The Counseling Psychologist, 28,* 733–763.

Important lead review article in a special issue on prevention and counseling psychology edited by the authors.

Rappaport, J. (1981). In praise of paradox: A social policy of empowerment over prevention. *American Journal of Community Psychology, 9,* 1–25.

This article is based on Rappaport's 1980 presidential address to the APA Division of Community Psychology. It called for new emphasis in community psychology, replacing primary prevention with the concept of empowerment. It is a bold and stimulating statement.

Rappaport, J., & Seidman, E. (Eds.). *Handbook of community psychology.* New York: Kluwer.

Compendium of community psychology containing work on concepts and frameworks, people in context, interventions, social systems, design methods, professional issues, and contemporary intersections.

Snyder, C., & Lopez, S. (Eds.). (2002). *Handbook of positive psychology.* New York: Oxford University Press.

Compendium on developing work in the broad area of positive psychology, including history, identifying strengths, emotion-focused approaches, cognitive-focused approaches, self-based approaches, interpersonal approaches, biological approaches, specific coping approaches, special populations and settings, and the future of the world.

U.S. Surgeon General (1999*). Mental health: A report of the surgeon general.* Washington, DC: U.S. Department of Health and Human Services.

Important report on the status of mental health in the United States. Provides a wealth of statistics on critical mental health matters.

U.S. Surgeon General (2001*). Culture, race, and ethnicity.* Washington, DC: U.S. Department of Health and Human Services.

This supplement to the mental health report of 1999 provides valuable information about mental health indices with regard to minority populations in the United States.

Web-Based References

The following Web sites provide a wealth of important data and reports about health and mental health care in the United States. Moreover, each can lead to related resources. These data can be useful in developing a generative base for prevention and for identifying targets for possible preventive programming and research.

www.cdc.gov/nch

www.FedStats.gov

www.surgeongeneral.gov

CHAPTER 2
Publications

Botvin, G., & Tortu, S. (1988). Preventing adolescent substance abuse through life skills training. In R. Price, E. Cowen, R. Lorion, & J. Ramos-McKay (Eds.), *14 ounces of prevention: A casebook for practitioners.* Washington, DC: American Psychological Association.

This chapter provides a detailed description of the fundamental processes involved with the life skills training approach of Botvin that has been elaborated and applied in subsequent studies.

Catalano, R., Berglund, M., Ryan, J., Lonczak, H., & Hawkins, D. (2002). Positive youth development in the United States: Research findings on evaluations of positive Youth Development Programs. *Prevention and Treatment, 5,* 1–112.

This extensive review article summarizes a wide array of research studies on the value of Positive Youth Development programs.

Csikszentmihalyi, M. (1990). *Flow: The psychology of optimal experience.* New York: Harper & Row.

"Flow" is examined and described as a route to optimal human experience.

Insel, P., & Moos, R. (1974). Psychological environments: Expanding the scope of human ecology. *American Psychologist, 29,* 179–188.

Provides a conceptual framework for understanding how environments can be conceived from a psychological perspective.

Keyes, C., & Lopez, S. (2002). Toward a science of mental health: Positive directions in diagnosis and interventions. In C. Snyder & S. Lopez (Eds.), *Handbook of positive psychology* (pp. 45–62.). New York: Oxford University Press.

The authors enumerate a science of mental health (opposed to mental dysfunction) with attention to psychological and to social well-being.

Maton, K. (2000). Making a difference: The social ecology of social transformation. *American Journal of Community Psychology, 28,* 25–57.

This article discusses the process of social transformation and makes excellent use of an adapted form of Bronfenbrenner's ecological levels in doing so.

Myers, J. (1992). Wellness throughout the life span. *Counseling and Human Development, 24,* 1–16.

This monograph examines health and wellness, focusing on the social, occupational, spiritual, physical, intellectual, and emotional aspects of wellness and their interactions.

Office of Disease Prevention and Health Promotion (2002). *Healthy people: 2010.* Washington, DC: U.S. Department of Health and Human Services.

Enumerates prevention and health promotion goals for the nation through 2010.

Seligman, M. (2002). *Authentic happiness: using the new positive psychology to realize your potential for lasting fulfillment.* New York: Free Press.

This book examines positive emotion, strength and virtue, and applications of positive psychology in such areas as work and personal satisfaction, love, and deriving meaning and purpose in life. The concept of "signature strengths" is elaborated, with assessment scales.

Seligman, M., & Csikszentmihalyi, M. (Eds.). (2000). Special Issue: Positive psychology: *American Psychologist, 55,* 5–183.

This special issue of the *American Psychologist* was devoted entirely to positive psychology, with a focus on happiness, excellence, and optimal human functioning.

Snyder, C., & Lopez, S. (Eds.). (2002). *Handbook of positive psychology.* New York: Oxford University Press.

Compendium on developing work in the broad area of positive psychology, including history, identifying strengths, emotion-focused approaches, cognitive-focused approaches, self-based approaches, interpersonal approaches, biological approaches, specific coping approaches, special populations and settings, and the future of the world.

Special Section on Positive Psychology (2001). *American Psychologist, 56,* 216–263.

Articles by Sheldon and King, Fredrickson, Masten Lyubomirsky, and Schneider discuss recent research in the area of positive psychology.

Walsh, B., Craik, K., & Price, R. (Eds.) (2000). *Person-environment psychology: New directions and perspectives* (2nd ed.). Mahwah, NJ: Erlbaum.

This book contains several chapters of value for everyday prevention, especially by Craik (on the lived day of an individual), Little (who discusses personal contexts and personal projects), and Wicker and August (who examine working lives in context).

Willi, J. (1999). *Ecological psychotherapy: Developing by shaping the personal niche.* Seattle, WA: Hogrefe & Huber.

This book focuses on ecological psychotherapy and examines the importance of interactive effectiveness, personal niches, and other factors as they relate to an effective life course.

Web Sites

http://www.authentichappiness.org

Provides access to a range of resources associated with positive psychology and authentic happiness.

http://nccam.nih.gov

Provides access to resources addressing complementary and alternative medicine.

CHAPTER 3
Publications

Conyne, R. *(1983)*. *Two* critical issues in primary prevention: What it is and how to do it. *Personnel and Guidance Journal, 61*, 331–334.

This article tackles the difficult matters of defining primary prevention and then of putting the major elements of the definition into action. It emphasizes working with at-risk-situations in a multifactoral approach.

Conyne, R. (1987). *Primary preventive counseling: empowering people and systems*. Muncie, IN: Accelerated Development.

This first edition of this book contained the original model for primary preventive counseling.

Conyne, R., & Horne, A. (Eds.). (2001). Special Issue: The use of groups for prevention. *Journal for Specialists in GroupWork, 26*, 205–292.

This special issue makes a case for the positive connection between prevention and group work and details several case examples.

Cowen, E. (1985). Person-centered approaches to primary prevention in mental health: Situation-focused and competency-enhancement. *American Journal of Community Psychology, 13*, 31–49.

The description of competency enhancement approaches to primary prevention contained in this article provides guidance for how professional counselors and counseling psychologists can undertake primary preventive counseling.

Cowen, E. (2000). Community psychology and routes to psychological wellness. In J. Rappaport & E. Seidman (Eds.), *Handbook of community psychology* (pp. 79–99). New York: Kluwer.

Cowen updated and elaborated his conception of psychological wellness.

Gullotta, T., & Bloom, M. (Eds.). (2003). *Encyclopedia of primary prevention and health promotion.* New York: Kluwer.

Compendium including work on foundations of primary prevention and health promotion (13 contributions) and on primary prevention and health promotion topics (152 contributions).

Maton, K. (2000). Making a difference: The social ecology of social transformation. *American Journal of Community Psych*ology, *28,* 25–57.

This article discusses the process of social transformation, making excellent use of an adapted form of Bronfenbrenner's ecological levels in doing so.

Morrill, W., Oetting, E., & Hurst, J. (1974). Dimensions of counselor functioning. *Personnel and Guidance Journal, 52,* 354–359.

This article, which provides the conceptual foundation for the special issue of which it is a part (C. Parker, Special Editor, "Thirty-Six Faces of Counseling"), develops a framework that greatly extends counseling into innovative areas. It gives rise to the subject of this book, primary preventive counseling.

Price, R., Ketterer, R., Bader, B., & Monahan, J. (Eds.). (1980). *Prevention in mental health: Research, policy, and practice.* Beverly Hills: Sage.

This edited book addresses, among other topics, the issue of targeting preventive interventions to at-risk settings, and it contains several chapters that provide examples of how this can be accomplished.

Remer, R., Niguette, G., Anderson, G., & Terrell, J. (1984). A meta-system for the delivery of primary preventive interventions. *Journal of Counseling and Development, 63,* 30–34.

These authors make a case for the delivery of primary preventive interventions through important cultural settings, namely, the family, the schools, and the church. They argue that such an approach would allow for the kind of delivery system so long lacking in primary prevention.

CHAPTER 4

Publications

Bloom, M. (1996). *Primary prevention practices.* Thousand Oaks, CA: Sage.

This book on primary prevention contains many important features, including a model of primary prevention from a social work perspective and a discussion on evaluation.

Cowen, E. (Ed.). (1982). Research in Primary Prevention in Mental Health. *American Journal of Community Psychology, 10,* 239–367. Whole Number.

This source presents primary prevention in mental health programs that have been carefully selected for their adherence to rigorous criteria of program evaluation.

Cowen, E. (1984). A general structural model for primary prevention program development in mental health. In M. Shaw & R. Goodyear (Eds.), Primary prevention in the schools. *Personnel and Guidance Journal, 62,* 485–490.

This article presents a five-step program developmental model for conducting primary prevention in mental health. Its attention to the concept of generative base is most useful.

Craig, D. (1978). *Hip pocket guide to planning & evaluation.* Austin, TX: Learning Concepts.

This manual and workbook presents a coherent and highly useful model for planning and evaluating that especially focuses on the planning process.

Durlak, J. (2003). Effective prevention and health promotion programming. In T. Gullotta & M. Bloom (Eds.), *Encyclopedia of primary prevention and health promotion* (pp. 61–69). New York: Kluwer.

This selection from the prevention encyclopedia enumerates and describes a set of very useful criteria for evaluating prevention programs.

National Institute on Alcohol Abuse and Alcoholism (1978). *Planning a prevention program.* Washington, DC: USDHEW Pub. No. (ADM) 78–647.

This handbook, specifically intended for the youth worker in an alcohol service agency, contains much practical guidance for any primary prevention worker.

Price, R., Cowen, E., Lorion, R., & Ramos-McKay, J. (Eds.). (1988). *14 ounces of prevention: A casebook for practitioners.* Washington, DC: American Psychological Association.

This book is based on an empirical study of prevention programs, selecting the best 14 to be included. They address programs across the life span. The selection evaluative criteria that were used are important for judging prevention excellence.

Weissberg, R., & Kumpfer, K. (Eds.). (2003). Prevention that works for children and youth. Special issue of the *American Psychologist, 58*, 425–490.

This source contains eight articles that address a broad range of topics related to prevention for children and youth. These topics include research and practice, community interventions, what works in prevention, family-strengthening approaches, school-based prevention, prevention in healthcare settings, and the policy considerations.

Web Sites

The two Web sites listed here were discussed in the text. They provide excellent access to prevention programs, especially to those that have undergone rigorous evaluation.

http://www.colorado.edu/cspv/blueprints

The Center for the Study and Prevention of Violence "Blueprints for Violence Prevention" Web site at the University of Colorado contains extensive information related to the evaluation of prevention programs.

http://modelprograms.samhsa

The Substance Abuse and Mental Health Administration (SAMHSA) produces a list of prevention programs, with brief descriptions, and follow-up information.

CHAPTER 9

Publications

Conyne, R. (1994). Preventive counseling. *Counseling and Human Development, 27*, Whole Issue.

A midrange exposition of preventive counseling (between the 1987 and the 2004 version) is presented.

Conyne, R. (1997). Educating students in preventive counseling. *Counselor Education and Supervision, 36*, 259–269.

A training agenda for preparing preventive counselors is detailed.

Conyne, R. (2000). Prevention in counseling psychology: At long last, has the time now come? *The Counseling Psychologist, 28*, 838–842.

This is a reaction article to the Romano and Hage lead article on the special section in *The Counseling Psychologist* on prevention in counseling psychology. It lauds the publication of the special section and the lead article and offers some additional perspective.

Matthews, C. (In review). Counseling and prevention: How are we doing? *Journal of Counseling and Development.*

This article, in preparation, reports on survey data collected to examine the present status of prevention training for counseling students.

Cowen, E. (1984). Training for primary prevention in mental health. *American Journal of Community Psychology, 12,* 253–259.

This article presents a definition of primary prevention in mental health, and then identifies the methodologies, content areas, and specific training needs that must be addressed.

Lewis, J., & Lewis, M. (1981). Educating counselors for primary prevention. *Counselor Education and Supervision, 29,* 172–181.

This article identifies the education needed by counselors who wish to engage in primary prevention. Educational program development and change agent skill clusters are highlighted.

Romano, J., & Hage, S. (2000). Prevention and Counseling Psychology: Revitalizing commitments for the 21st Century. *The Counseling Psychologist, 28,* 733–763.

The excellent lead article in the special section in TCP on prevention and counseling psychology contains, among other features, a set of recommendations for training.

Zolik, E. (1983). Training for preventive psychology in community and academic settings. In R. Felner, L. Jason, J. Moritsugu, & S. Farber (Eds.), *Preventive psychology: Theory, research, and practice* (273–289). New York: Pergamon.

This chapter comprehensively explores training needs and directions in both field and academic settings and at various levels of education, undergraduate through postdoctoral.

References

Albee, G. (1985). The argument for primary prevention. *Journal of Primary Prevention, 5,* 213–219.

Albee, G. (1986). Toward a just society: Lessons from observations on the primary prevention of psychopathology. *American Psychologist, 41,* 891–898.

Albee, G. (2000). Commentary on prevention and counseling psychology. *The Counseling Psychologist, 28,* 845–853.

Albee, G., & Gullotta, T. (Eds.). (1997). *Primary prevention works.* Thousand Oaks, CA: Sage.

Alexander, J., & Parsons, B. (1973). Short-term behavior interventions with delinquent families: Impact on family process and recidivism. *Journal of Abnormal Psychology, 81,* 219–225.

Alexander, J., Barton, C., Gordon, D., Grotpeter, J., Hansson, K., Harrison, R., Mears, S., Mihalic, S., Parsons, B., Pugh, C., Schulman, S., Waldron, H., & Sexton, T. (1998). *Blueprints for violence prevention, Book three: Functional family therapy.* Boulder, CO: Center for the Study and Prevention of Violence.

Alexander, J., Robbins, M., & Sexton, T. (2000). Family-based interventions with older, at-risk youth: From promise to proof to practice. *Journal of Primary Prevention, 42,* 185–205.

Annenberg/CPB Collection (1992). *An ounce of prevention.* Video #13 in The World of Abnormal Psychology series.

Antonovsky, A. (1979). *Health, stress, and coping.* San Francisco: Jossey-Bass.

Aos, S., & Barnoski, R. (1998). *Watching the bottom line: Cost-effective interventions for reducing crime in Washington.* Washington State Institute for Public Policy: RCW 13.40.500.

Baker, S., Swisher, J., Nadenichek, P., & Popowicz, R. (1984). Measured efforts of Primary prevention strategies. In M. Shaw & R. Goodyear (Guest eds.), Primary prevention in schools. *Personnel and Guidance Journal, 62,* 459–464.

Bales, J. (1987). Prevention at its best. *APA Monitor, 18,* 18–19.

Bandura, A. (1997). *Self-efficacy: The exercise of control.* New York: Freeman.

Bardon, J. (1985). On the verge of a breakthrough. In D. Brown & D. Kurpius (Guest eds.), Consultation. *The Counseling Psychologist, 13,* 355–362.

Beck, A. (1991). Cognitive therapy and the emotional disturbances. London: Penguin.

Becker, F., & Steele, F. (1995). *Workplace by design: Mapping the high-performance workscape.* San Francisco: Jossey-Bass.

Belkin, G. (1984). *Introduction to counseling* (2nd ed.). Dubuque, IA: Brown.

Bierman, K., Coie, J., Dodge, K., Greenberg, M., Lochman, J., & McMahon, R. (May 1996). Abstract: An initial evaluation of the FAST Track Program. In Proceedings of the Fifth National Prevention Conference, Tysons Corner, VA.

Bloom, M. (1996). *Primary prevention practices.* Thousand Oaks, CA: Sage.

Botvin, G., Griffin, K.W., Paul, E., & Macaulay, A. (2003). Preventing tobacco and alcohol use among elementary school students through life skills training.

Botvin, G., & Kantor, L. (2000). Preventing alcohol and tobacco use through life skills training. *Alcohol Research and Health, 24,* 250–257.

Botvin, G. J., Schinke, S. P., Epstein, J. A., Diaz, T., & Botvin, E. (1995). Effectiveness of culturally focused and generic skills training approaches to alcohol and drug abuse prevention among minority adolescents: Two-year follow up results. *Psychology of Addictive Behaviors, 9*(3), 183–194.

Botvin, G., & Tortu, S. (1988). Preventing adolescent substance abuse through life skills training. In R. Price, E. Cowen, R. Lorion, & J. Ramos-McKay (Eds.), *14 ounces of prevention: A casebook for practitioners.* Washington, DC: American Psychological Association.

Bower, E. (1963). Primary prevention of mental and emotional disorders: A conceptual framework and action possibilities. *American Journal of Orthopsychiatry, 33,* 837.

Branden-Muller, L., & Elias, M. (1991). Catalyzing the primary prevention revolution in schools: The role of school psychologists. *Journal of Educational and Psychological Consultation, 2,* 73–88.

Bronfenbrenner, U. (1979). *The ecology of human development: Experiments by nature and design.* Cambridge, MA: Harvard University Press.

Brown, B. (1997). Psychoeducation group work. *Counseling and Human Development, 29,* 1–14.

Brown, M., & Bolen, L. (2003). Introduction to the special issue: School-based health centers. *Psychology in the Schools, 40,* 245–251.

Burke, M.T., & Miranti, J. (Eds.). (1995). *Counseling: The spiritual dimension.* Alexandria, VA: American Counseling Association.

Campbell, D., & Stanley, J. (1963). *Experimental and quasi-experimental designs for research.* Chicago: Rand McNally.

Caplan, G. (1964). *Principles of preventive psychiatry.* New York: Basic Books.

Capra, F. (1996). *The web of life.* New York: Anchor Books.

Catalano, R. (1979). *Health, behavior, and the community.* New York: Pergamon.

Catalano, R., & Dooley, D. (1980). Economic change in primary prevention. In R. Price, B. Ketterer, & B. Bader (Ed.), *Prevention in mental health* (pp. 21–40). Beverly Hills, CA: Sage.

Catalano, R., & Hawkins, J.D. (1996). The social development model: A theory of antisocial behavior. In J.D. Hawkins (Ed.), *Delinquency and crime: Current theories* (pp. 149–197). New York: Cambridge University Press.

Catalano, R., Berglund, M, Ryan, J., Lonczak, H., & Hawkins, D. (2002). Positive youth development in the United States: Research findings on evaluations of positive youth development programs. *Prevention and Treatment, 5,* 1–112.

Center for Disease Control and Prevention (2002). *National Center for Health Statistics.*

Chronister, K., McWhirter, B., & Kerewsky, (2004). In R. Conyne & E. Cook (Eds.), *Ecological counseling: An innovative conceptualization for person-environment interaction.* Alexandria, VA: American Counseling Association.

Coie, J., Watt, N., West, S., Hawkins, J., Asarnow, J., Markman, H., Ramey, S., Shure, M., & Long, B. (1993). The science of prevention: A conceptual framework and some directions for a national research program. *American Psychologist, 48,* 1013—1022.

Conduct Problems Prevention Research Group (1992). A developmental and clinical model for the prevention of conduct disorder: The FAST Track Program. *Development and Psychopathology, 4,* 509–527.

Conduct Problems Prevention Research Group (2000). Merging universal and indicated prevention programs: The FAST Track Model. *Addictive Behaviors, 5,* 913–928.

Conoley, J., & Haynes, G. (1992). An ecological approach to intervention. In R. D'Amato & B. Rothlisberg (Eds.), *Psychological perspectives on interaction* (pp. 177–189). White Plains, NY: Longman.

Conyne, R. (1975). Environmental assessment: Mapping for counselor action. *Personnel and Guidance Journal, 54,* 150–155.

Conyne, R. (1983). Two critical issues in primary prevention: What it is and how to it. *Personnel and Guidance Journal, 61,* 331–334.

Conyne, R. (1987). *Primary preventive counseling: Empowering people and systems.* Muncie, IN: Accelerated Development.

Conyne, R. (1989). *How task and personal growth groups work.* Newbury Park, CA: Sage.

Conyne, R. (1994). Preventive counseling. *Counseling and Human Development, 27*(1), 1–10 (Whole Issue).

Conyne, R. (1997). Educating students in preventive counseling. *Counselor Education and Supervision, 36,* 259–269.

Conyne, R. (1999). *Failures in group work: How we can learn from our mistakes.* Thousand Oaks, CA: Sage.

Conyne, R. (2000). Prevention in counseling psychology: At long last, has the time now come? *The Counseling Psychologist, 28,* 838–844.

Conyne, R. (2004). Prevention groups. In J. DeLucia-Waack, D. Gerrity, C. Kalodner, & M. Riva (Eds.), *Handbook of group counseling and group psychotherapy.* Thousand Oaks, CA: Sage.

Conyne, R., & Clack, R. (1981). *Environmental assessment and design: A new tool for the applied behaviorial scientist.* New York: Praeger.

Conyne, R., & Cook, E. (Eds.) (2004). *Ecological counseling: An innovative conceptualization for person-environment interaction.* Alexandria, VA: American Counseling Association.

Conyne, R., & Horne, A. (Eds.). (2001). The use of groups for prevention (Special Issue). *Journal for Specialists in Group Work, 26*(3), 205–289.

Conyne, R., & O'Neil, J. (Eds.). (1992). *Organizational consultation: A casebook.* Thousand Oaks, CA: Sage

Conyne, R., Rapin, L., & Rand, J. (1997). A model for leading task groups. In H. Forester-Miller & J. Kottler (Eds.), *Issues and challenges for the group work practitioner* (pp. 117–132). Denver, CO: Love.

Conyne, R., & Wilson, F.R. (2001). Division 49 position paper: Recommendations of the task force for the use of groups for prevention. *The Group Psychologist, 11,* 10--11.

Conyne, R., Wilson, F.R., & Ward, D. (1997). *Comprehensive group work: What it means & how to teach it.* Alexandria, VA: American Counseling Association.

Conyne, R., Newmeyer, M., Goodman, J., Russ, K., Walker, L., Baker, P., Rosenthal, M., Rosen, C., Callery, P., & Rinon, M. (October 18, 2003). Counselor consultation with university faculty in problem-based learning group-based instruction: Results of a pilot project. Presentation at the annual meeting of the North Central Association for Counselor Education and Supervision, Cincinnati, Ohio.

Cook, R., Back, A., Trudeau, J., & McPherson, T. (2002). Integrating substance abuse prevention into health promotion programs in the workplace: A social-cognitive intervention targeting the mainstream user. In J. Bennett & W. Lehman (Eds.), *Preventing workplace substance abuse: Beyond drug testing to wellness* (pp. 97–133). Washington, DC: American Psychological Association.

Cook, R., & Schlenger, W. (2002). Prevention of substance abuse in the workplace: Review of research on the delivery of services. *Journal of Primary Prevention, 23,* 115–142.

Cormier, S., & Nurius, P. (5th ed.) (2003). *Interviewing and change strategies for helpers: Fundamental skills and cognitive-behavioral interventions.* Pacific Grove, CA: Brooks/Cole.

Covey, S., Merrill, A., & Merrill, R. (1994). *First things first: Coping with the ever-increasing demands of the workplace.* New York: Simon & Schuster.

Cowen, E. (1980). The wooing of primary prevention. *American Journal of Community Psychology, 8,* 258–284.

Cowen, E. (1983). Primary prevention in mental health: Past, present, and future. In R. Felner, L. Jason, J. Moritsugu, & S. Farber (Eds.), *Preventive psychology: Theory, research, and practice* (pp. 11–25). New York: Pergamon.

Cowen, E. (1984). A general structural model for program development in mental health. In M. Shaw & R. Goodyear (Guest eds.), Primary prevention in schools. *Personnel and Guidance Journal, 62,* 485–490.

Cowen, E. (1985). Person-centered approaches to primary prevention in mental health: Situation-focused and competence-enhancement. *American Journal of Community Psychology, 13,* 31–49.

Cowen, E. (2000). Community psychology and routes to psychological wellness. In J. Rappaport & E. Seidman (Eds.), *Handbook of community psychology* (pp. 79–99). New York: Kluwer.

Craig, D. (1978). *HIP pocket guide to planning & evaluation.* Austin, TX: Learning Concepts.

Craik, K. (1991). The lived day of an individual: A person-environment perspective. In W.B. Walsh, K. Craik, & R. Price (Eds.), *Person-environment psychology: New directions and perspectives.* Mahwah, NJ: Erlbaum.

Csikszentmihalyi, M. (1990). *Flow: The psychology of optimal experience.* New York: Harper & Row.

Curran, J., Wishart, P., & Gingrich, J. (1999). *JOBS: A manual for teaching people successful job search strategies.* Michigan Prevention Research Center, University of Michigan, Ann Arbor, MI.

Davis, L., & Tolan, P. (1993). Alternative and preventive interventions. In P. Tolan & B. Cohler (Eds.), *Handbook of clinical research and practice with adolescents* (pp. 427–451). New York: Wiley.

Diagnostic and statistical manual-IV (1994). Washington, D.C.: American Psychiatric Association.

D'Aunno,T., & Price, R. (1984). Methodologies in community research: Analytic and action approaches. In K. Heller, S. Reinharz, S. Riger, & A. Wandersman (Eds.), *Psychology and community change* (pp. 68–113). New York: Dorsey.

Diebold, C. (1998). Health promotion over prevention, standing up for empowering semantics and operations: Comment on Cowen. *The Community Psychologist, 31,* 6–9.

Dittmann, M. (2003). The social class factor. *Monitor on Psychology, 34,* 36.

Dougherty, A.M. (2000). Psychological consultation and collaboration in school and *community settings: A casebook.* Pacific Grove, CA: Brooks/Cole.

Dryfoos, J. (1990). *Adolescents at risk: Prevalence and prevention.* New York: Oxford University Press.

Durlak, J. (2003). Effective prevention and health promotion programming. In T. Gullotta & M. Bloom (Eds.), *Encyclopedia of primary prevention and health promotion* (pp. 61–69). New York: Kluwer.

Durlak, J., & Wells, A. (1997). Primary prevention programs for children and adolescents: A meta-analytic review. *American Journal of Community Psychology, 25,* 115–152.

Dusenbury, L., & Botvin, G. (1992). Applying the competency enhancement model to substance abuse prevention. In M. Keller, S. Goldston, & J. Joffe (Eds.), *The present and future of prevention.* Newbury Park, CA: Sage.

Eccles, J., & Gootman, J. (2001). (Eds.). *Community programs to promote youth development.* Washington, DC: National Academy Press. Education and Training Committee, Division 13, Society of Consulting Psychology, American Psychological Association. (2002). Principles of education and training at the doctoral and postdoctoral level in consulting psychology/organizational. *Consulting Psychology Journal: Practice and Research, 54,* 213–222.

Elias, M., & Branden, L. (1988). Primary prevention of behavioral and emotional problems in school-age populations. *School Psychology Review, 17,* 581–592.

Farquhar, J., Maccoby, N., Wood, P., Alexander, J., Breitrose, H., Brown, B., Haskell, W., McAlister, A., Meyer, A., Nash, J., & Stern, M. (1994). In A. Steptoe & J. Wardle (Eds.), *Psychosocial processes and Health: A reader* (pp. 316–324). New York: Cambridge University Press.

Felner, R., & Adan, A. (1988). The School Transitional Environment Project. In R. Price, E. Cowen, R. Lorion, & J. Ramos-McKay (Eds.), *14 ounces of prevention: A casebook for practitioners* (pp. 111–122). Washington, DC: American Psychological Association.

Felner, R.D., Brand, S., Adan, A.M., Mulhall, P.F., Flowers, N., Sartain, B, & DuBois, D.L. (1993). Restructuring the ecology of the school as an approach to prevention during school transitions: Longitudinal follow-ups and extensions of the school transitional environment project (STEP). *Prevention in Human Services, 10,* 103–136.

Felner, R., Felner, T., & Silverman, M. (2000). Prevention in mental health and social intervention. In J. Rappaport & E. Seidman (Eds.), *Handbook of community psychology* (pp. 9–42). New York: Kluwer.

Felner, R., Ginter, M., & Primavera, J. (1982). Primary prevention during school transitions: Social support and environmental structure. *American Journal of Community Psychology, 10,* 277–290.

Flynn, B., Worden, J., Secker-Walker, R., Pirie, P., Badger, G., Carpenter, J., & Geller, (1994). Mass media and school interventions for cigarette smoking prevention: Effects 2 years after completion. *American Journal of Public Health, 84,* 1148–1150.

Fogel, J. (2003). Media. In T. Gullotta & M. Bloom (Eds.), *Encyclopedia of prevention and health promotion* (pp. 683–689). New York: Kluwer.

Foote, A., & Erfut, J. (1980). Prevention in industrial settings: The employee assistance program. In R. Price, R. Ketterer, B. Bader, & J. Monahan (Eds.), *Prevention in mental health: Research, policy, and practice* (pp. 151–166). Beverly Hills, CA: Sage.

Frankl, V. (1962). *Man's search for meaning: An introduction to logotherapy.* New York: Washington Square Press.

Fredrickson, B. (2000). Cultivating positive emotions to optimize health and well-being. *Prevention & Treatment, 3,* 1–26.

Gallessich, J. (1985). Toward a meta-theory of consultation. In D. Brown & D. Kurpius (Guest eds.), Consulation. *The Counseling Psychologist, 13,* 336–354.

Geller, E.S. (2003). Achieving an ecologically sustainable future. In T. Gullotta & M. Bloom (Eds.), *Encyclopedia of primary prevention and health promotion* (pp. 85–92). New York: Kluwer.

Gibson, R. & Mitchell, M. (1995). *Introduction to counseling and guidance.* Englewood Cliffs, NJ: Prentice-hall.

Goldston, S. (1977). An overview of primary prevention programming. In D. Klein &

S. Goldston (Eds.), *Primary prevention: An idea whose time has come* (pp. 23–40). Washington, DC: DHEW No. (ADM).

Goodyear, R. (1976). Counselors as community psychologists. *Personnel and Guidance Journal, 54,* 512–516.

Gordon, R. (1983). An operational classification of disease prevention. *Public Health Reports, 98,* 107–109.

Gottlieb, B., & Hall, A. (1980). Social networks and the utilization of preventive mental health service. In R. Price, R. Ketterer, B. Bader, & J. Monahan (Eds.), *Prevention in mental health: Research, policy, and practice* (pp. 167–194). Beverly Hills, CA: Sage.

Greenberg, J. (1985). Health and wellness: A conceptual differentiation. *Journal of School Health, 55,* 403–406.

Greenberg, M., Weissberg, R., O'Brien, U., Zins, J., Fredericks, L., Resnik, H., & Elias, M. (2003). Enhancing school-based prevention and youth development through coordinated social, emotional, and academic learning. In R. Weissberg & K. Kumpfer (Guest eds.), Special issue, Prevention that works for children and youth. *American Psychologist, 58,* 466–474.

Gross, R. (2002). *Socrates' way: Seven master keys to using your mind to the utmost.* New York: Tarcher/Putnam.

Gullota, T. (1987). Prevention technology. *Journal of primary prevention, 7,* 176–196.

Gullotta, T., & Bloom, M. (Eds.). (2003). *Encyclopedia of primary prevention and health promotion.* New York: Kluwer.

Hahn, A., Leavitt, T., & Aaron, P. (1994). Evaluation of the Quantum Opportunities Program, Heller Graduate School, Center for Human Resources, Brandeis University, Waltham, MA.

Hawkins, J.D., Catalano, R., & Kosterman, R. (1999). Preventing adolescent health-risk behaviors by strengthening protection during childhood. *Archives of Pediatric Medicine, 153,* 226–234.

Hawkins, J.D., Catalano, R., & Miller, J. (1992). Risk and protective factors for alcohol and other drug problems in adolescence and early adulthood: Implications for substance abuse prevention. *Psychological Bulletin, 112,* 64–105.

Hawkins, J.D., Catalano, R., Morrison D., O'Donnell, J., Abbott, R., & Day L. (1992). The Seattle Social Development Project: Effects of the first four years on protective factors and problem behaviors. In J. McCord & R.Tremblay (Eds.), *The prevention of antisocial behavior in children* (pp. 130–161). New York: Guilford.

Heller, K., Price, R., & Sher, K. (1980). Research and evaluation in primary prevention: Issues and guidelines. In R. Price, R. Ketterer, B. Bader, & J. Monahan (Eds.), *Prevention in mental health* (pp. 285–313). Beverly Hills, CA: Sage.

Hershenson, D., & Power, P. (1987) *Mental health counseling: Theory and practice.* New York: Pergamon.

Hettler, B. (1991). Keynote speech: Wellness. Paper presented at the American Association of Counseling and Development, Reno, NV.

Hogan, R., & Roberts, B. (2000). In W.B. Walsh, K. Craik, & R. Price (Eds.), *Person-environment psychology: New directions and perspectives.* Mahwah, NJ: Erlbaum.

Howd, A. (1999). Smart plan to save marriages. *Insight.*

Insel, P., & Moos, R. (1974). Psychological environments: Expanding the scope of human ecology. *American Psychologist, 29,* 179–188.

IOM. (1994). *Reducing risks for mental disorders: Frontiers for preventive intervention and research.* Washington, DC: National Academy Press.

Ivey, A., & Ivey, M. (2003) (5th ed.). *Intentional interviewing and counseling: Facilitating client development in a multicultural society.* Pacific Grove, CA: Brooks/Cole.

Jason, L. (1980). Prevention in the schools: Behavioral approaches. In R. Price, R. Ketterer, B. Bader, & J. Monahon (Eds.), *Prevention in mental health: Research, policy, and practice* (pp. 167–194). Beverly Hills, CA: Sage.

Jessor, R. (1984). Adolescent development and behavioral health. In J. Matarazzo, S. Weiss, J. Herd, & N. Miller (Eds.), *Behavioral health: A handbook of health enhancement and disease prevention.* New York: Wiley.

Jessor, R., & Jessor, S. (1977). *Problem-behavior and psychosocial development: A longitudinal study of youth.* New York: Academic Press.

Johnson, D. (1988). Primary prevention of behavior problems in young children: The Houston Parent-Child Development Center. In R. Price, E. Cowen, R. Lorion, & J. Ramos-McKay (Eds.), *14 ounces of prevention: A casebook for practitioners* (pp. 44–52). Washington, DC: American Psychological Association.

Johnson, D., (1990). Developing family environments with families. In F. Kaslow (Ed.), *Voices in family psychology.* Beverly Hills, CA: Sage.

Johnson, D., & Walker, T. (1987). Primary prevention of behavior problems in Mexican American children. *American Journal of Community Psychology, 15,* 375–385.

Johnson, D. & Walker, T. (1991). A follow-up evaluation of the Houston Parent-Child Development Center: School performance. *Journal of Early Interventions, 15,* 226–236.

Jordaan, J., Myers, R., Layton, W., & Morgan, H. (Eds.). A definition in 1968. *The Counseling Psychologist.* Washington, DC: American Psychological Association.

Kasambira, K.P., & Edwards, L. (June 2000). Counseling and human ecology: A Conceptual framework for counselor educators. Paper presented at the 8th International Counseling Conference, San José, Costa Rica.

Ketterer, R. (1981). *Consultation and education in mental health.* Beverly Hills, CA: Sage.

Ketterer, R., Bader, B., & Levy, M. (1980). Strategies and skills for promoting mental health. In R. Price, R. Ketterer, B. Bader, & J. Monahan (Eds.), *Prevention in mental health: Research, policy, and practice.* Beverly Hills, CA: Sage.

Keyes, C. (1998). Social well-being. *Social Psychology Quarterly, 61,* 121–140.

Keyes, C., & Lopez, S. (2002). Toward a science of mental health: Positive directions in diagnosis and interventions. In C. Snyder & S. Lopez (Eds.), *Handbook of positive psychology* (pp. 45–62). New York: Oxford University Press.

Kiselica, M., & Look, C. (1993). Mental health counseling and prevention: Disparity between philosophy and practice? *Journal of Mental Health Counseling, 15,* 3–14.

Klein, D., & Goldston, S. (Eds.), Primary prevention: An idea whose time has come (DHEW Pub. No. (ADM) 77–447), 49–60. Washington, DC: U.S. Government Printing Office.

Kline, M., & Snow, D. (1994). Effects of a worksite coping skills intervention on the stress, social support, and health outcomes of working mothers. *Journal of Primary Prevention, 15,* 105–121.

Klonoff, E. (1983). A star is born: Psychologists and the media. *Professional Psychology: Research and practice, 14,* 847–854.

Kolbe, L., Collins, J., & Cortese, P. (1997). Building the capacity of schools to improve the health of the nation: A call for assistance from psychologists. *American Psychologist, 52,* 256–265.

Koop, C.E. (1995). A personal role in health care reform. *Health, 85,* 759–760.

Kraus, K. (2003). *Exercises in group work.* Columbus, OH: Merrill Prentice Hall.

Kumpfer, K., & Alvarado, R. (2003). Family-strengthening approaches for the prevention of youth problem behaviors. In R. Weissberg & K. Kumpfer (Guest eds.), Special issue, Prevention that works for children and youth, *American Psychologist, 58,* 457–465.

Kurpius, D., & Brubaker, J. (1976). *Psychoeducational consultation: Definition, functions, preparation.* Bloomington: Indiana University Press.

Larimore, W. (2003). *10 essentials of highly healthy people.* Grand Rapids, MI: Zondervan.

Lattimore, C., Mihalic, S., Grotpeter, J., & Taggart, R. (1998). *Blueprints for violence prevention, Book Four: The Quantum Opportunities Program.* Boulder, CO: Center for the Study and Prevention of Violence.

Lazarus, R., & Folkman, S. (1984). *Stress, appraisal, and coping.* New York: Springer.

Leavell, H., & Clark, E. (Eds.). (1953). *Textboook of preventive medicine.* New York: McGraw-Hill.

Lee, C., & Walz, G. (Eds.). (1998). Social advocacy: A mandate for counselors. Alexandria, VA: American Counseling Association.

Leff, S., Power, T., Manz, P., Costigan, T., & Nabors, L. (2001). School-based aggression prevention programs for young children: Current status and implications for violence prevention. *School Psychology Review, 30,* 344–362.

Lewin, K. (1951). *Field theory in social science: Selected theoretical papers.* New York: Harper.

Lewis, J., Lewis, M., Daniels, J., & D'Andrea, M. (2003). *Community counseling.* Pacific Grove, CA: Brooks/Cole.

Lewis, J., Arnold, M., House, R., & Toporek, R. (2002). Advocacy competencies: Task force on advocacy competency. Approved by the American Counseling Association Governing Council at the annual meeting of the American Counseling Association, Anaheim, CA, March, 2003.

Lewis, J., Lewis, M., Daniels, J., & D'Andrea, M. (2003). *Community counseling.* Pacific Grove, CA: Brooks/Cole.

Libassi, M. (1983). An integrative approach to primary prevention in the field. In J. Bowker (Ed.), *Education for primary prevention in social work* (pp. 75–92). New York: Council on Social Work Education.

Little, B. (2000). Free traits and personal contexts: Expanding a social ecological model of well being. In W.B. Walsh, K. Craik, & R. Price (Eds.), *Person-environment psychology: New directions and perspectives* (2nd ed., pp. 87–116). Mahwah, NJ: Erlbaum.

Lonczak, H. (2002). Effects of the Seattle Social Development Project on sexual behavior, pregnancy, and sexually transmitted disease outcomes by age 21 years. *Archives of Pediatric & Adolescent Medicine,* May Issue.

Lopez, S. & McKnight, C. (2002). Moving in a positive direction: Toward increasing the utility of positive youth development efforts. *Prevention & Treatment,* 5, Article 19. Available at http://www.journals.apa.org/prevention/volume5/pre0050019C.html.

Luks, A. (2001). *The healing power of doing good: The healthy and spiritual benefits of helping others.*

Maddux, J. (2000). Stopping the "madness": Positive psychology and the deconstruction of the illness ideology and the DSM. In C. Snyder & S. Lopez (Eds.), *Handbook of positive psychology* (pp. 13–25.). New York: Oxford University Press.

Maddux, J., Snyder, C.R., & Feldman, D. (2003). Mental health, adulthood. In T. Gullotta & M. Bloom (Eds.), *Encyclopedia of primary prevention and health promotion* (pp. 696–704). New York: Kluwer.

Mager, R. (1962). *Preparing instructional objectives.* Palo Alto, CA: Fearon.

Mancini, J., Martin, J., & Bowen, G. (2003). Community capacity. In T. Gullotta & M. Bloom (Eds.), *Encyclopedia of primary prevention and health promotion* (pp. 319–330). New York: Kluwer.

Masten, A. (2001). Ordinary magic: Resilience processes in development. *American Psychologist, 56,* 227–238.

Masten, A., & Reed, M-G. (2002). Resilience in development. In C. Snyder & S. Lopez (Eds.), *Handbook of positive psychology* (pp. 74–88). New York: Oxford University Press.

Maton, K. (2000). Making a difference: The social ecology of social transformation. *American Journal of Community Psychology, 28,* 25–57.

Matthews, C. (In preparation). Counseling and prevention: How are we doing?

Matthews, C., Conyne, R., Kenney, M., & O'Neil, J. (August 2003). Teaching prevention. Continuing Education Workshop presented at the annual meeting of the American Psychological Association, Toronto, Canada.

McCafferty, D. (2003). The Happiest Guy. *USA Weekend.*

McGill, D., Mihalic, S., & Grotpeter, J. (1998). *Blueprints for violence prevention, Book Two: Big Brothers Big Sisters of America.* Boulder, CO: Center for the Study and Prevention of Violence.

McMahon, T., Ward, N., Pruett, M., Davidson, L., & Griffith, E. (2000). Building full-service schools: Lessons learned in the development of interagency collaboratives. *Journal of Educational and Psychological Consultation, 11*, 65–92.

McWhirter, E. H. (1994). *Counseling for empowerment.* Alexandria, VA: American Counseling Association.

McWhirter, J., McWhirter, B., McWhirter, A., & E.H. McWhirter. (1995). Youth at risk: Another point of view. *Journal of Counseling & Development, 73*, 567–569.

Meyers, A., & Swerdlik, M. (2003). School-based health centers: Opportunities and challenges for school psychologists. *Psychology in the Schools, 40*, 253–264.

Michigan Prevention Research Center (2003). The JOBS project for the unemployed: Update. Ann Arbor, MI: Institute for Social Research.

Miller, D., Lipsedge, M., & Litchfield, P. (Eds.). (2002). *Work and mental health: An employers' guide.* London: Gaskell.

Mirowski, J., & Ross, C. (1989). *Social causes of psychological distress.* Hawthorne, NY: Aldine.

Mitchell, M., & Gibson, R. (2002). *Introduction to counseling and guidance.* Columbus, OH: Prentice Hall.

Moffitt, P. (1986). Cooling out: Deciding what to do with the second half of your life. *Esquire, 106*, 47–48.

Morrill, W., Oetting, E., & Hurst, J. (1974). Dimensions of counselor functioning. *Personnel and Guidance Journal, 52*, 354–359.

Mrazek, P., & Haggerty, R. (Eds.). (1994). *Reducing risks for mental disorders: Frontiers for preventive intervention.* Washington, DC: National Academy Press.

Murray, B. (October, 2003). Rebounding from losses. *Monitor on psychology: A publication of The American Psychological Association, 34*, pp. 42–43.

Myers, J. (1992). *Wellness throughout the lifespan* (Vol. 24, Whole issue.). Denver, CO: Love.

Myers, J. (2003). Coping with caregiving stress: A wellness-oriented, strengths-based approach for family counselors. *The Family Journal: Counseling and Therapy for Couples and Families, 11*, 153–161.

Myers, D., & Diener, E. (1995). Who is happy? *Psychological Science, 6*, 10–19.

Nation, M., Crusto, C., Wandersman, A., Kumpfer, K., Seybolt, D., Morrisey-Kane, E., & Davino, K. (2003). What works in prevention: Principles of effective prevention programs. In special issue, Prevention that works for children and youth (R. Weissberg & K. Kumpfer, Guest eds.), *American Psychologist, 58*, 449–456.

National Vital Statistics Report (2001). Divorce. Volume 50, No. 14.

Neimeyer, R. (1993). An appraisal of constructivist psychotherapy. *Journal of Consulting and Clinical Psychology, 61*, 221–234.

NIH Publication (April 2003). No. 03–4594. Printed January 2001.

NIMH (1998). *Mental health matters.* Washington, DC.

O'Donnell, J., Hawkins, J.D., Catalano, R., Abbott, R., & Day, L. (1995). Preventing school failure, drug use, and delinquency among low-income children: Effects of a long-term prevention project in elementary schools. *American Journal of Orthopsychiatry, 65*, 87–100.

Office of Disease Prevention and Health Promotion (2002). *Healthy People: 2010.* Washington, DC: U.S. Department of Health and Human Services.

Ornish, D. (1990). *Dr. Dean Ornish's program for reversing heart disease.* New York: Ballantine.

Owens, Scott, R. (2003). Truly magical thinking. *Spirituality and Health: The Soul/Body Connection, 6,* 4.

Oxley, D. (2000). The school reform movement: Opportunities for community psychology. In J. Rappaport & E. Seidman (Eds.), *Handbook of community psychology* (pp. 565–590). New York: Kluwer.

Oxley, D. (2001). Organizing Schools into Small Learning Communities. *NASSP Bulletin, 85,* 5–6.

Patterson, G., Chamberlain, P., & Reid, J. (1982). A comparative evaluation of a parent education training program. *Behavior Therapy, 13,* 638–650.

Patton, M.Q. (1997). *Utilization-focused evaluation.* Thousand Oaks, CA: Sage.

Pearlin, L., & Schooler, C. (1978). The structure of coping. *Journal of Health and Social Behavior, 19,* 2–21.

Pearson, R. (1985). Primary prevention-oriented groups. In R. Conyne (Ed.), *The group workers' handbook: Varieties of group experience* (pp. 277–292). Springfield, MA: Thomas.

Pearson, R. (1990). *Counseling and social support.* Newbury Park, CA: Sage.

Pietrofesa, J., Hoffman, A., & Splete, H. (1984). *Counseling: An introduction* (2nd ed.). Boston: Houghton Mifflin.

Pittman, K., & Fleming, W. (September 1991). *A new vision: Promoting youth development.* Written transcript of live testimony by Karen J. Pitmann given before the House Select Committee on Children, Youth, and Families. Washington, DC: Center for Youth Development and Policy Research.

Price, R. (1974). Etiology, the social environment, and the prevention of psychological dysfunction. In P. Insel & R. Moos (Eds.), *Health and the social environment.* Lexington, MA: Heath.

Price, R. (June 1978). Evaluation research in primary prevention: Lifting ourselves by our bootstraps. Paper presented at the Primary Prevention Conference, Denver, CO.

Price, R. (1983). The education of a prevention psychologist. In R. Felner, L. Jason, J. Moritsugu, & S. Farber (Eds.), *Preventive psychology: Theory, research, and practice* (pp. 290–296). New York: Pergamon.

Price, R. (1992). Psychosocial impact of job loss on individuals and families. *Current Directions in Psychological Science, 1,* 9–11.

Price, R. (May 1, 2003). Personal communication.

Price, R., Cowen, E., Lorion, R., & Ramos-McKay, J. (Eds.). (1988). *14 ounces of prevention: A casebook for practitioners.* Washington, DC: American Psychological Association.

Price, R., Ketterer, R., Bader, B., & Monahan, J. (Eds.). (1980). *Prevention in mental health: Research, policy, and practice.* Beverly Hills, CA: Sage.

Price, R., van Ryn, M., & Vinokur, A. (1992). Impact of a preventive job search intervention on the likelihood of depression among the unemployed. *Journal of Health and Social Behavior, 33,* 158–167.

Prochaska, T., & Norcross, J. (2003). *Systems of psychotherapy: A theoretical analysis* (5th ed.). Pacific Grove, CA: Brooks/Cole.

Prochaska, T., Norcross, J., & DiClemente, C. (1994). *Changing for good.* New York: Avon.

Quick, J.C., Quick, J.D., Nelson, D., Hurrell, J., Jr. (1997). *Preventive stress management in organizations.* Washington, DC: American Psychological Association.

Rapin, L. (2004). Ecological applications to organizational development. In R. Conyne & E. Cook (Eds.), *Ecological counseling: An innovative conceptualizing for person-environment interaction.* Alexandria, VA: American Counseling Association.

Rappaport, J. (1972). From an address delivered for Psy Chi, University of Illinois.

Rappaport, J. (1977). *Community psychology: Values, research, and action.* New York: Holt, Rinehart & Winston.

Rappaport, J. (1981). In praise of paradox: A social policy of empowerment over prevention. *American Journal of Community Psychology, 9,* 1–25.

Rappaport, J., & Seidman, E. (Eds.) (2000). *Handbook of community psychology.* New York: Kluwer/Plenum.

Rappaport, J., Swift, C., & Hess, P. (1984). Studies in empowerment: Steps toward understanding and action. *Prevention and Human Services, 3,* 1–230.

Reker, G., & Chamberlain, K. (Eds.). (2000). *Exploring existential meaning: Optimizing human development across the life span.* Thousand Oaks, CA: Sage.

Remer, R., Niguette, G., Anderson, G., & Terrell, J. (1984). A meta-system for the delivery of primary preventive interventions. *Journal of Counseling and Development, 63,* 30–34.

Reyes, O., & Jason, L. (1991). An evaluation of a high school dropout prevention program. *Journal of Community Psychology, 19,* 221–230.

Romano, J., & Hage, S. (2000). Prevention and Counseling Psychology: revitalizing commitments for the 21st Century. *The Counseling Psychologist, 28,* 733–763.

Rosenstock, I., Strecher, V., & Becker, M. (Summer 1988). Social learning theory and the health belief mode. *Health Education Quarterly, 15*(2).

Ross, M., Powell, S., & Elias, M. (2002). New roles for school psychologists: Addressing the social and emotional learning needs of students. *School Psychology Review, 31,* 43–52.

Ryan, R., & Deci, E. (2001). On happiness and human potential: A review of research on hedonic and eudaimonic well-being. *Annual Review of Psychology, 52,* 141–166.

Ryff, C. (1989). Happiness is everything, or is it? Explorations on the meaning of psychological well-being. *Journal of Personality and Social Psychology, 7,* 1069–1081.

Ryff, C., & Keyes, C. (1995). The structure of psychological well-being revisited. *Journal of Personality and Social Psychology, 69,* 719–727.

SAMHSA (2002). National Survey on Drug Use and Health. U.S. Department of Health and Human Services, Washington, DC.

Sauter, S.L., Murphy, L.R., & Hurrell, J.J., Jr. (1990). Prevention of work-related psychological disorders: A national strategy proposed by the National Institute for Occupational Safety and Health. *American Psychologist, 45,* 1146–1158.

Sauter, S.L., Lim, S.Y., & Murphy, L.R. (1996). Organizational health: A new paradigm for occupational stress research at the National Institute for Occupational Safety and Health. *Japanese Journal of Occupational Mental Health, 4,* 248–254.

Seligman, M. (1999). *The good life.*

Seligman, M. (2002a). *Authentic happiness: Using the new positive psychology to realize your potential for lasting fulfillment.* New York: Free Press.

Seligman, M. (2002b). Positive psychology, positive prevention, and positive therapy. In C. Snyder & S. Lopez (Eds.), *Handbook of positive psychology* (pp. 3–9). New York: Oxford University Press.

Seligman, M., & Csikszentmihalyi, M. (2000). Positive psychology: An introduction. *American Psychologist, 55,* 5–14.

Seligman, M., & Csikszentmihalyi, M. (Eds.). (2000). Special Issue: Positive psychology: *American Psychologist, 55,* 5–183.

Sexton, T., & Alexander, J. (1999). *Functional family therapy: Principles of clinical intervention, assessment, and implementation.* Henderson, NV: RCH Enterprises.

Sexton, T., & Alexander, J. (2002). Functional Family Therapy for at-risk adolescents and their families. In F. Kaslow (Ed.), *Comprehensive handbook of psychotherapy: Volume 2, Cognitive-Behavioral approaches* (pp. 117–140). New York: Wiley.

Shaw, M. (1986). The prevention of learning and interpersonal problems. *Journal of Counseling & Development, 64*, 624–627.

Sheldon, K., & King, L. (2001). Why positive psychology is necessary. *American Psychologist, 56*, 216–217.

Shure, M., & Spivack, G. (1988). Interpersonal cognitive problem solving. In R. Price, E. Cowen, R. Lorion, & J. Ramos-McKay (Eds.), *14 ounces of prevention: A casebook for practitioners* (pp. 69–82). Washington, DC: American Psychological Association.

Snow, D., & Kline, M. (1995). Preventive interventions in the workplace to reduce the negative psychiatric consequences of work and family stress. In C. Mazure (Ed.), *Does stress cause psychiatric illness?* (pp. 221–270). Washington, DC: American Psychological Association.

Snow, D., Swan, S., Raghavan, C., Connell, C., & Klein, I. (Ms. under review). The effects of work stressors, coping, and social support on psychological symptoms among female secretarial employees.

Snyder, C., & Lopez, S. (Eds.). (2002). *Handbook of positive psychology.* New York: Oxford University Press.

Special Section on Positive Psychology (2001). *American Psychologist, 56*, 216–263.

Stanley, S. (2001). Making the case for premarital training. *Family Relations, 50*, 272–280.

Steele, F. (1973). Physical settings and organization development. Reading, MA: Addison-Wesley.

Steenbarger, B., Conyne, R., Baird, M., & O'Brian, J. (1995). Prevention in college health: Counseling perspectives. *Journal of American College Health, 43*, 157–162.

Stephenson, M., Palmgreen, P., Hoyle, R., Donohew, L., Pugzles Lorch, E., & Colon, S. (1999). Short-term effects of an anti-marijuana media campaign targeting high sensation seeking adolescents. *Journal of Applied Communication Research, 27*, 175–195.

Super, D., & Sverko, B. (Eds.). (1995). *Life roles, values, and careers: International findings of the work impact study.* San Francisco: Jossey-Bass.

Terry, R. (1993). *Authentic leadership.* San Francisco: Jossey-Bass.

Thoits, P. (1986). Social support as coping assistance. *Journal of Consulting and Clinical Psychology 54*, 416–423.

UNESCO (1995). Illiteracy.

UNICEF (1997). Life Skills.

U.S. Department of Labor (2003). *Poverty in the U.S.: 2002.* Washington, DC.

U.S. Surgeon General (1999). Mental Health: A report of the Surgeon General. Washington, DC: U.S. Department of Health and Human Services.

U.S. Surgeon General (2001). *Mental health: Culture, race, and ethnicity.* Washington, DC: U.S. Department of Health and Human Services.

van Ryn, M., & Vinokur, A. (1992). How did it work? An examination of the mechanisms through which an intervention for the unemployed promoted job-search behavior. *American Journal of Community Psychology, 20*, 577–597.

Vandenbos, G., & Miller, M. (1980). Delinquency prevention programs: Mental health and the law. In R. Price, R. Ketterer, B. Bader, & J. Monahan (Eds.), *Prevention in mental health: Research, policy, and practice* (pp. 135–150). Beverly Hills, CA: Sage.

Vincent, J., & Trickett, E. (1983). Preventive interventions and the human context: Ecological approaches to environmental assessment and change. In R. Felner, L. Jason, J. Moritsugu, & S. Farber (Eds.), *Preventive psychology: Theory, research, and practice* (pp. 67–86). New York: Pergamon.

Vinokur, A., Price, R., & Schul, Y. (1995). Impact of the JOBS intervention on unemployed workers varying in risk for depression. *American Journal of Community Psychology, 23*, 39–74.

Vinokur, A., Schul, Y., Vuori, J., & Price, R. (2000). Two years after a job loss: Long term impact of the JOBS program on reemployment and mental health. *Journal of Occupational Health Psychology, 5,* 32–47.

Wagenaar, A., Gehan, J., Jones-Webb, R., Wolfson, M., Toomey, T., Forster, J., & Murray, D. (1999). Communities mobilizing for change on alcohol: Lessons and results from a 15-community randomized trial. *Journal of Community Psychology, 27,* 315–326.

Wagenaar, A., Murray, D., Gehan, J., Wolfson, M., Forster, J., Toomey, T., Perry, C., & Jones-Webb, R. (1998). Communities mobilizing for change on alcohol: Outcomes from a randomized community trial. *Journal of Studies on Alcohol, 61,* 85–94.

Wagenaar, A., Murray, D., & Toomey, T. (2000). Communities mobilizing for change on alcohol (CMCA): Effects of a randomized trial on arrests and traffic crashes. *Addiction, 95,* 209–217.

Walsh, B., Craik, K., & Price, R. (Eds) (2000). *Person-environment psychology: New directions and perspectives* (2nd ed.). Mahwah, NJ: Erlbaum.

Wandersman, A., & Florin, P. (2003). Community interventions and effective prevention. In R. Weissberg & K. Kumpfer (Guest eds.), Special issue, Prevention that works for children and youth. *American Psychologist, 58,* 441–448.

Weissberg, R., Hampton, R., Ryan, B., & Adams, G. (Eds.). (1997). *Establishing preventive services.* Thousand Oaks, CA: Sage.

Weissberg, R. & Kumpfer, K. (Eds.). Special issue: Prevention that works for children and youth. *American Psychologist, 58,* 425–490.

Werner, E. (1996). Vulnerable but invincible—High-risk children from birth to adulthood. *European Child & Adolescent Psychiatry, 5,* 47–51.

Werner, E. (1997). Risk, resilience and recovery—Perspectives from the Kauai longitudinal study. *Development and psychopathology, 5,* 503–515.

WHO (1993). Life skills.

Willi, J. (1999). Ecological psychotherapy: Developing by shaping the personal niche. Seattle, WA: Hogrefe & Huber.

Wilson, F.R., & Yager, G. (1981). A process model for prevention program research. In R. Remer (Guest ed.), The counselor and research: Part I. *Personnel and Guidance Journal, 59,* 590–595.

Witmer, J., & Sweeney, T. (1992). Wellness and prevention as a model for counseling and human development throughout the life-span. *Journal of Counseling and Development, 71,* 140–148.

Wyche, K. (2003). In M. Dittmann, The social class factor. *Monitor on Psychology, 34,* 36.

Yalom, I. (1995). *The theory and practice of group psychotherapy.* New York: Basic Books.

Zolik, E. (1983). Training for preventive psychology in community and academic settings. In R. Felner, L. Jason, J. Moritsugu, & S. Farber (Eds.), *Preventive Psychology: Theory, research, and practice* (pp. 273–289). New York: Pergamon.

WEB SOURCES

Health/Mental Health Statistics

www.cdc.gov/nchs[National Center for Health Statistics of the Center for Disease Control and Prevention]

http://www.juvjus.state.nc.us/cpsv/schoolcounselor.htm [Center for the Prevention of School Violence]

www.FedStats.gov [FedStats: The gateway to statistics from over 100 U.S. federal agencies]

http://www.healthfinder.gov/ [Healthfinder]

http://www.healthypeople.gov [Healthy People 2010]
http://www.health.gov/nhic/ [National Health Information Center]
http://nccam.nih.gov [National Center for Complementary and Alternative Medicine]
www.nimh.nih.gov [National Institute of Mental Health]
www.nmha.org/ [National Mental Health Association]
http://odphp.osophs.dhhs.gov/ [Office of Disease Prevention and Health Promotion]
www.surgeongeneral.gov [Office of the Surgeon General of the United States]
http://portal.unesco.org [UNESCO Institute of Statistics]
http://www.worldbank.org/data/datafaq.htm [World Bank Group data and statistics]

Directories of Effective Prevention Programs

http://modelprograms.samhsa.gov/matrix_all.cfm [SAMHSA Model Programs
 Comparisons]
http://www.colorado.edu/cspv/blueprints/ [Center for the Study and Prevention of
 Violence: Blueprints for Violence Prevention, University of Colorado]

Professional Prevention Newsletters

www.berkeleywellness.com [University of California at Berkeley Wellness Letter
www.health.harvard/edu [Harvard University Health Newsletter]
www.hopkinsafter50.com [Johns Hopkins Health After 50]
www.PrevConn.com [Prevention Connection: Integrating Substance Abuse Prevention
 and Health Promotion]

Centers and Professional Associations Focusing
on Issues, Populations, and Settings

http://www.authentichappiness.org [Authentic happiness, a positive psychology
 source]
www.CASEL.org [Collaborative for Academic, Social, and Emotional Learning]
www.centerforworkforcehealth.com [Center for Workforce Health: Improving the
 Health and Productivity of Today's Workforce]
www.epi.umn.edu/alcohol [Alcohol Epidemiology Program]
www.schoolcounselor.org [American School Counselor Association: see National
 Model]
www.SpiritualityHealth.com) [Spirituality & Health: Spiritual Practices for Human
 Being]

Popular Magazine Sites Focused on Wellness and Prevention

www.prevention.com [*Prevention Magazine* Web site]
www.psychologytoday.com [*Psychology Today* magazine Web site]

Index